Leonhard Stejneger

The Russian Fur-Seal Islands

Leonhard Stejneger

The Russian Fur-Seal Islands

ISBN/EAN: 9783337297602

Printed in Europe, USA, Canada, Australia, Japan

Cover: Foto ©ninafisch / pixelio.de

More available books at **www.hansebooks.com**

U. S. COMMISSION OF FISH AND FISHERIES,
JOHN J. BRICE, Commissioner.

THE RUSSIAN FUR-SEAL ISLANDS.

BY

LEONHARD STEJNEGER,
Of the United States National Museum.

Extracted from U. S. Fish Commission Bulletin for 1896. Article 1, Pages 1 to 148, Plates 1 to 66.

WASHINGTON:
GOVERNMENT PRINTING OFFICE.
1896.

THE RUSSIAN FUR-SEAL ISLANDS.

BY

LEONHARD STEJNEGER,
Of the United States National Museum.

TABLE OF CONTENTS.

	Page.
I. Introduction	3
Scope of the Work	3
Itinerary	4
Acknowledgments	5
II. The Russian Seal Islands	7
1. The Commander Islands	7
Hydrographic Notes	8
Meteorology	12
Fauna and Flora of the Commander Islands	19
Native Population	26
a. Bering Island	36
General Description	36
Seal Rookeries	39
North Rookery	40
South Rookery	42
b. Copper Island	43
General Description	43
Seal Rookeries	45
Karabelni	45
Glinka	48
2. Robben Island	52
Description	52
History	54
3. Other Islands	58
III. Seal Life on Commander Islands	60
Historical and General	60
Latitude in the Phenomena of Seal Life	62
Proportionate Number of Sexes and Ages on Rookeries	63
Virility of Bulls	66
Do all Bachelors haul out?	67
Food of Seals at the Islands, and Excrements on the Rookeries	69

	Page.
III. Seal Life on Commander Islands—Continued.	
Effect of Driving	71
Description of a Drive on Pribylof Islands	71
Description of Drives on Commander Islands	72
Does the Female Seal nurse her own Pup only?	77
Mortality of Pups	78
Alleged Changes of Habits	82
Feeding-grounds	87
IV. The Russian Sealing Industry	88
Historical	88
Eighteenth Century	88
Russian-American Company	89
Interregnum	90
Hutchinson, Kohl, Philippeus & Co.	91
Russian Seal Skin Company	93
Statistics	95
Administration	102
Condition of the Commander Islands Rookeries	104
Preliminary remarks	104
Comparison between the Condition of the Rookeries in 1882-83 and 1895	106
Bering Island	106
Copper Island	112
Comparative Condition of the Bering Island and Copper Island Rookeries, in 1895	117
Raiding of Commander Islands Rookeries	118
Pelagic Sealing at Commander Islands	122
V. Conclusions	134
Summary	134
Cause of the Decline	134
Future Prospects on Commander Islands	136
Recommendations	136
List of Maps and Illustrations	138-140
Index	141-148

U. S. COMMISSION OF FISH AND FISHERIES,
JOHN J. BRICE, Commissioner.

RUSSIAN FUR-SEAL ISLANDS.

BY

LEONHARD STEJNEGER,
Of the United States National Museum.

Extracted from U. S. Fish Commission Bulletin for 1896. Article 1, Pages 1 to 148, Plates 1 to 66.

WASHINGTON:
GOVERNMENT PRINTING OFFICE
1896

1.—THE RUSSIAN FUR-SEAL ISLANDS.

By LEONHARD STEJNEGER,
Of the United States National Museum.

I.—INTRODUCTION.

The following treatise is based upon observations gathered during two different visits to the Commander Islands, off the coast of Kamchatka, the first undertaken in 1882–83, during the palmiest days of the fur-seal industry, the latter being last year (1895), as a special attaché of the United States Fish Commission, to study the recent decline and to compare the conditions as I knew them thirteen years ago with those of the present day.

I undertook the trip with a full understanding of the difficulties awaiting me, both in the studies in the field and in the working up of the report. I was fully aware that, alone in an almost untrodden field, my work would of necessity be fragmentary and for that reason unsatisfactory. Nevertheless, I felt that I ought to do it for several reasons. In the first place I was in possession of a great amount of interesting information about the Russian seal islands never published, or else very inaccessible to those concerned in the fate of the fur-seal, which it might be useful to bring together. In the second place, I felt convinced that but few men were in the same fortunate position as myself of having had the opportunity to study the Russian fur-seal industry at close quarters while it was still flourishing, and that, consequently, I was in an exceptionally good position for instituting the desired comparison.

Finally, I reflected, having kept aloof from all the strife and controversy of recent years concerning seal matters, because I had no pet theories of my own to ventilate nor any personal interest of myself or friends to advance, I would be less liable to suspicion of being prejudiced or biased by any outside motive. I have earnestly endeavored to preserve this independence, personal and scientific, in the investigations which I have undertaken, and I claim that the conclusions I have reached are based upon the facts as I have been able to discern them. It is my hope that the logic of my deductions will not be found lacking.

SCOPE OF THE WORK.

At the suggestion of Mr. Richard Rathbun, in charge of the scientific inquiry of the Fish Commission, and with the approval of the Acting Commissioner of Fisheries, Mr. Herbert A. Gill, the scope of the report was extended so as to include all other obtainable information concerning the Russian seal islands, and it has thus assumed somewhat the character of a monograph. But I wish it distinctly understood that it does not pretend to exhaust the subject in any direction. Some of the chapters are only brief résumés, thus causing great inequality in the treatment of the various questions. This could not well be otherwise, for it would have been manifestly impossible to prepare a work of that scope, with all the labor and research it involves, in the short time of $3\frac{1}{2}$ months which I have had at my disposal for writing this treatise. Moreover, such an exhaustive work could not be done here in Washington or even in this country. It would have been necessary to consult records and archives in San Francisco and in St. Petersburg, as well as the libraries in the latter city.

In preparing this work I have had the hearty cooperation of the authorities of the United States Fish Commission, and I wish particularly to express my grateful appreciation of the truly scientific spirit and liberality shown by Mr. Rathbun in giving me every possible latitude for working out the problems in my own fashion without attempting to influence my opinion in any direction. His only injunction to me has been a desire for the facts as I have seen them. It has been my endeavor to supply them to the best of my ability.

ITINERARY.

My first visit to the Commander Islands was undertaken in March, 1882, under the joint auspices of the Smithsonian Institution and the United States Signal Service. With a notice of only two days, I left Washington on March 22, 1882, and sailed from San Francisco in the *Aleksander II* the following April 5, landing on Bering Island a month later—on May 7. During the summer I studied the fur-seals and rookeries on this island. In the fall of 1882 I undertook a circumnavigation of Bering Island in open boat, returning to the village after a successful trip of two weeks. The winter was passed on Bering Island, but part of the following summer, particularly the sealing season, I spent on the various rookeries of Copper Island. In October, 1883, I took passage in the *St. Paul* from Petropaulski, Kamchatka, to San Francisco, arriving in Washington the following November 26. The results of this trip have been published in numerous memoirs and papers, mostly issued by the United States National Museum.

The itinerary of my trip in 1895 is as follows: After receiving my appointment on May 21, I left Washington on May 28 with letters from the Russian legation, authorized telegraphically by the authorities in St. Petersburg, and arrived in San Francisco on Sunday, June 2. Various preparations for the journey occupied me until June 6, when I sailed in the steamship *Bertha* for Unalaska. In this port I was to join the Fish Commission steamer *Albatross*, which, it was calculated, would have returned to Unalaska from its first trip to the Pribylof Islands at the time I was due there. In such an event Captain Drake had orders to bring me to Bering Island via the Pribylofs, in order to afford me an opportunity to witness and compare the mode of driving the seals on both groups. Upon my arrival at Unalaska on June 17 I found, however, that the *Albatross* had only arrived there the day before, without having as yet been to the Pribylofs. The following week was consumed in Unalaska taking in coal. The *Albatross* left Unalaska on June 23, and on June 25 we were landed at the village, St. Paul Island. The rookeries near the village were inspected the same afternoon.

Thanks to the zeal and courtesy of the Treasury agent, Mr. J. B. Crowley, and the company's general agent, Mr. J. Stanley-Brown, a small drive of seals was at once arranged for the following morning. Mr. F. W. True, of the United States National

Museum, and I partook in the drive, which lasted from 2 o'clock in the morning to 10 a. m. At 1 p. m. I embarked again on the *Albatross* and steamed at once away for Bering Island; anchored off the main village on July 3, and on the 4th, with Captain Drake and Mr. C. H. Townsend, went per dog-sledge to the great North Rookery. After having landed my effects, the *Albatross* left on the following day.

My next trip to the North Rookery was per boat, in company with Governor Grebnitski, on July 7. On July 15 I again proceeded to the same rookery in dog-sledge, returning to the main village by the same means July 20. Bad weather prevented the carrying out of my intentions of visiting the South Rookery at this time. On July 27 I took passage on the Russian Seal Skin Company's steamer *Kotik*, Capt. C. E. Lindquist, for Copper Island, and on July 30, in company with the governor, Mr. Grebnitski, who bore the expense of the trip, started from the main village on an openboat expedition around the island. Spent the evening and the next morning at the sea-otter rookery. July 31 and August 1 were devoted to inspecting and photographing the Karabelni rookeries and August 2 to 11 to the Glinka rookeries, the latter being the more important ones, finishing the circumnavigation August 12. On the steamer *Kotik* I then returned to Bering Island, anchoring off the North Rookery August 13. Visited the South Rookery August 17, securing photographs and a map of the rookery. On August 18 I called on board the British cruiser of the third class *Porpoise*, Commander Francis R. Pelly (doing patrol service on the 30-mile limit), then at anchor off Nikolski. On August 21 I went in dog-sledge to the North Rookery, returning two days later. The captain of the *Porpoise* having kindly offered to take me to Petropaulski, I gladly accepted his offer, as it was somewhat doubtful whether the *Kotik*, in which I intended to return to San Francisco, would be able to call at the islands before going home, and I did not dare to risk the possibility of wintering on Bering Island. I arrived in Petropaulski August 25. The company's agent having decided to make another trip to the islands, I returned in the *Kotik* and was thus enabled to again inspect the Bering Island South Rookery on September 9 and the North Rookery September 16, being back in Petropaulski September 18, which port I left on September 24 in the *Kotik*, bound for San Francisco, where I arrived on October 11.

The weather was unprecedentedly stormy and rainy during my entire stay at the islands and interfered greatly with my work. The great distances between the habitations and the rookeries and the primitive means of transportation also added to the difficulties, while much valuable time was lost owing to the uncertainty of the movements of the steamer.

Under such adverse circumstances I should have been unable to accomplish even what I did had it not been for the kind assistance I received on all sides.

ACKNOWLEDGMENTS.

In the first place, it gives me great pleasure to acknowledge the aid and courtesies received at the hands of Governor N. Grebnitski, the administrator of the islands, without which I should have been seriously embarrassed in my work. The following report would undoubtedly have been more replete with official data and statistics relating to the sealing industry on the islands had not the documents relating thereto been either sent away already or packed ready for shipment in anticipation of Mr. Grebnitski's prospective departure for St. Petersburg.

I am also under great obligations to the firm and officers of the Russian Seal Skin Company, the present lessees of the islands, especially Mr. C. A. Williams, New London, Conn., and Mr. Thomas F. Morgan, Groton, Conn., as well as Mr. Constantine M. Grunwaldt, of St. Petersburg, at present the representative of the firm on the Pacific Coast; Mr. John Malovanski, of San Francisco, the general agent of the company; Capt. C. E. Lindquist, of the *Kotik*; Capt. D. Grœnberg, of the *Bobrik*; Mr. Kluge, the resident agent on Bering Island, and Mr. Cantor, on Copper Island.

It would be ungrateful not to mention the hospitality received from the Alaska Commercial Company and its functionaries, especially during my first visit to the islands. The liberality with which the members of this firm have been ever ready to assist scientific endeavors has contributed greatly to the success of my undertakings.

To Lieut. Commander F. J. Drake, U. S. N., commanding the United States Fish Commission steamer *Albatross*, and his officers, and to the scientific staff of the vessel, and more particularly to Mr. C. H. Townsend, special thanks are due for courtesies during my stay on board, and to the latter for valuable information received during the preparation of this report, due credit for which is given in each instance.

It is with great pleasure that I acknowledge my obligations to the captain of H. M. S. *Porpoise*, Commander Francis R. Pelly, R. N., and his officers, for hospitalities and for aid in transportation.

Finally, I wish to express my appreciation of the willingness and promptness with which my desire to witness a seal-drive on St. Paul Island was gratified by the Treasury agent, Mr. J. B. Crowley, and by Mr. J. Stanley-Brown, the general agent of the North American Commercial Company, the present lessees of the Pribylof Islands.

II.—THE RUSSIAN SEAL ISLANDS.

Until the purchase of the Territory of Alaska by the United States, in 1867, all the resorts of the northern fur-seal north of California belonged to the Russian Empire, and the fur-seal industry of the North Pacific was entirely monopolized by the Russian American Company.

These resorts were in all instances uninhabited islands, and at the time of their discovery by the Russian fur-hunters, in the middle and latter part of the last century, even unknown to the native races. The seals when first found on the rookeries, about one hundred and fifty years ago, had never been interfered with by man while on their breeding-grounds. The islands alluded to were the Commander group, certain small islands in the Okhotsk Sea, certain small islands in the Kuril chain, and the Pribylof group.

In 1867 the Pribylof Islands were sold to the United States, and in 1870 Russia ceded the Kurils to Japan in exchange for the southern half of the island of Sakhalin. There remain thus, in the possession of the Russian Crown at the present date, only the Commander Islands and the islands in the Okhotsk Sea.

1.—THE COMMANDER ISLANDS.

The Commander Islands (also occasionally called the Commodore Islands; Russian, *Komandorski Ostrova*), so named in memory of the great commander, Bering, who discovered the group, comprise two main islands, Bering and Copper, situated off the east coast of Kamchatka, between $54°$ $33'$ and $55°$ $22'$ north latitude, and $165°$ $40'$ and $168°$ $9'$ east longitude, approximately 97 miles from Cape Kamchatka, the nearest point on the mainland. The southeast point of Copper Island is distant from Attu, the nearest American island, about 180 miles, and is less than 75 miles from the imaginary boundary line across Bering Sea between Russia and the United States. The distance between Bering Island and the port of Petropaulski is somewhat more than 280 miles, while a straight line between the nearest points of the Commander group and the Pribylof group is 750 miles. The steamer's track between the former and San Francisco is something like 3,100 miles.

Geographically the Commander Islands are the westernmost group of the Aleutian chain. Politically, however, they form a separate administrative district of the so-called Coast Province (*Primorskaya Oblast*). This enormous territory extends from Korea to the Arctic Ocean, and, including the peninsula of Kamchatka, is ruled by the governor-general of the Amur Province, residing at Khabarovka, on the Amur River, more than 1,200 miles, as the crow flies, from the Commander Islands. The administrative position of these islands, however, is somewhat complicated, inasmuch as they also depend directly under the Minister of the Imperial Domain in St. Petersburg, 4,600 miles away. In other words, their position corresponds very much to that of our Pribylof Islands, which are subject both to the governor of Alaska and to the Secretary of the Treasury.

The Commander Islands were discovered on November 4, 1741 (old style). On that day the vessel *St. Peter*, with the commander, Vitus Bering, and nearly the entire crew, sick to death with the scurvy, slowly approached the southern extremity of Copper Island from the east, on their return voyage, after having discovered the mainland of America. Owing to the universal sickness, the ship's reckoning was entirely out, and the officers believed themselves off the coast of Kamchatka. The next day the vessel, over which the exhausted crew had hardly any control, drifted toward the east shore of Bering Island, and in the night following, a beautiful, still November night, of which this coast knows but few, the unfortunate craft came pretty near being left by the receding tide and wrecked on the projecting reefs at the southern entrance to the little bay called Komandor on the map (plate 4). By an exceptional piece of good luck, the breakers carried it safely over the rocks into the basin beyond, and a landing was effected.

To such extremity were the discoverers reduced that it was decided to winter on this inhospitable shore. Hollows were dug in the ground for shelter and covered with skins of wild animals and sails. Many of the crew died of the scurvy, and on the 8th of December (old style) Bering himself. He was buried near the place marked on the map "Bering's grave." The others, 46 only out of 77, recovered slowly under the care of G. W. Steller, who accompanied the expedition as a naturalist. The vessel was thrown up on the beach during a heavy gale in the night between November 28 and 29 (old style), and all attempts to float it were in vain. The next spring, after a winter full of suffering and privations, the crew broke up the old vessel and of the materials built a smaller one, in which they landed at Petropaulski, Kamchatka, August 27, 1742.

The present writer visited the place of the shipwreck and the wintering August 30, 1882, and has given an account of it, with a ground-plan of the hut and a sketch map of the locality, in Deutsche Geogr. Blätter, 1885, pp. 265-266. A partial rendering of this is found in Prof. Julius Olsen's translation of Lauridsen's "Vitus Bering" (Chicago, S. C. Griggs & Co., 1889), p. 184, and additional notes, pp. 214, 215. The relics of the expedition found by me are deposited in the United States National Museum.

HYDROGRAPHIC NOTES.

It is astonishing how very little is definitely known about the hydrography of the western side of Bering Sea. But few vessels fitted for such work have visited that part of the world of late years, and those few have only made hurried passages through. In that way a small amount of material has been accumulated, which has been utilized by the Russian admiral, S. O. Makarof, in his interesting work "Vitiaz i Tikhi Okean" (2 volumes, St. Petersburg, 1894), in which, so far as the investigations relating to temperature and specific gravity of the waters of the western Bering Sea are concerned, his own observations on board the corvette *Vitiaz* form the most valuable part. This being the case, I have no hesitation in presenting, in a brief abstract, the substance of those paragraphs in his book which refer to the matter in hand, especially since a full understanding of the phenomena in question is a necessary basis for an equally full understanding of the distribution of the food animals of the seals and of the seals themselves.

On July 29, 1888, the *Vitiaz* left Petropaulski on a short trip to the Commander Islands. The bathymetric observations in Bering Sea have shown that the bed of warm water of a temperature of $+9°$ C. is very thin near the coasts of Kamchatka. At a depth of 10 meters a temperature of $+2.3°$ C. is found and at 25 meters only

$+0.6°$. Near the Commander Islands, with the same surface temperature of $+9°$ C., $+7.1$ was found at 25 meters and $+4.3°$ at 50 meters. We have here absolutely the same phenomenon as in the Japan Sea, viz, that the cold water predominates in the lower beds of the western portion of the sea. The identical phenomenon has been observed in the Okhotsk Sea and the Straits of Tartary.

The bathymetric observations in Bering Sea, at stations Nos. 108, 109, 110, and 113, have established another peculiarity of this sea, viz, the presence in the deeper portions of warm water of high salinity. Near the coast of Kamchatka the increase in temperature is shown as follows: At station No. 108, from $0°$ C. at 200 meters to $+3.5°$ C. at 400 meters; at station 109, from $+0.6°$ C. at 150 meters to $+2.6°$ C. at 175 meters and $+3.7°$ C. at 200 meters; at station 110, in longitude 165° 56′ E., at a depth of 100 meters a temperature of $+2°$ C. was found, and at 150 meters and below, $+3.9°$ C. The details are shown in the accompanying diagram (pl. 3).

These temperatures prove to us that the bed of warm water of great specific gravity is found nearer the surface at the Commander Islands than along the coast of Kamchatka. A similar phenomenon has also been observed in the Okhotsk Sea. In other words, the cold and less saline water in descending from north to south approaches the coast toward the western side of the sea and forces the warm water of high salinity to a greater depth.

Plate 3 shows a section of Bering Sea from the coasts of Kamchatka to the Commander Islands. The cold water here occupies an intermediate bed between the surface and a depth of 250 meters. As in the Okhotsk Sea, the bed thickens toward the mainland coast and tapers off as it recedes from it. It will also be seen that this cold water, with a temperature lower than $0°$ C., has a specific gravity of 1.0252 to 1.0254. Where does this water come from? Makarof concludes that as it can not come from the Pacific Ocean, which has no such temperature, it must descend from the surface. Since the surface water has a specific gravity of only about 1.0250, he suggests that the great salinity of this surface water is due to freezing in winter. As to the route this water follows, he believes that, as indicated by the temperatures observed by the *Tuscarora*, it advances from the southwest along the coast of Kamchatka and consequently also along the Kuril Islands.

The surface temperatures of the western portion of Bering Sea are indicated on pl. 2, showing the existence of two cold zones, viz, one near Capes Tchaplin and Tchukotski, the other between Capes Navarin and St. Thaddaeus. Everywhere else the cold water occupies the western part of Bering Sea and the warm water its eastern portion. In the other places the distribution of the temperature is pretty regular; it decreases gradually toward the north. The temperature near Petropaulski is $11°$ C., and near the island of St. Lawrence about $8°$ C., i. e., the mean temperature of August.

Fragmentary as is our knowledge of the waters themselves in the western portion of Bering Sea, the bottom of the sea over which they flow is hardly better known. In fact, until the U. S. Fish Commission steamer *Albatross* ran the three lines of deep-sea soundings in 1892 and 1895, the shape and nature of the bottom were even less known. Even to-day we do not know the depth of the passage between Kamchatka and the Commander Islands. The Russian and English men-of-war patrolling the seas around the islands have of late years added a number of soundings at 100 fathoms and under, so that it has been possible on the appended map (pl. 1) to trace the 100-fathom line with some degree of accuracy, but not even Makarof in the *Vitiaz* seems to have been provided with an apparatus fit to take soundings deeper than 400 fathoms. The soundings which he made in the passage alluded to, therefore, only prove that it is deeper than 400 fathoms, but how much we are unable to say. True, we find on the Russian Hydrographic Department chart No. 1454 (Vost. Okean, Bering. Mor.) two definite soundings, viz, 390 fathoms in 53° 41' north latitude and 163° 29' east longitude, but this being station No. 109 of the *Vitiaz*, and therefore in all probability taken from its records, we find upon turning to the latter that bottom was not found at 713 meters, or 390 fathoms. The other sounding on the same chart is 400 fathoms in 54° 45' north latitude and 162° 50' east longitude. By examining the records of the *Vitiaz* we find no soundings taken by that vessel in that latitude, but we find on the other hand that station No. 113 was in 53° 45' north latitude and 162° 50' east longitude, and that a sounding was there taken with the result that bottom was not touched in 732 meters, or 400 fathoms. The above figures are too close not to make it almost absolutely certain that by a clerical error the sounding in question was plotted a whole degree too far north and the dash with the dot over left out.

In the chart of the western portion of Bering Sea which I have prepared and appended herewith (pl. 1), the 100-fathom curve around the Commander Islands is drawn for the first time with some pretensions to accuracy. Even in some recent publications it is asserted that the Commander Islands "belong to the Kamchatka system, Copper Island resting just within the 100-fathom curve from the Asiatic coast." On the contrary, we know now that the sea between the mainland and the islands is over 400 fathoms deep. On my map they are connected with the peninsula of Kamchatka by the 500-fathom curve, but even that is only conjectural, though probable. The deep-sea soundings of the *Albatross* are here first shown on any map of the region, as well as the curves connecting them with the *Tuscarora* soundings of 1874. It will thus be seen that nearly all our knowledge of the bottom in this part of the sea is due to ships belonging to the United States.[1]

The curves of the various depths from 100 fathoms down to 2,000 fathoms and over are, as a matter of necessity, highly conjectural. In the northeastern section of the map they appear even somewhat problematical, in view of the fact that a series of shallow soundings running southwest from Cape Olintorski, on the charts of the United States Hydrographic Office, have been left out of consideration altogether. The reason is that the series is crossed by the deep soundings of the *Albatross* on her return passage from the Commander Islands in 1895 in such a manner that it is impossible to reconcile them. They may possibly belong farther west—a not unreasonable supposition, since the determination of the longitude of the various coasts and promontories in that part of the world is in such utter confusion[2] that a resurvey of the whole coast from Petropaulski to Providence, or Plover, Bay is imperatively demanded.

---

[1] I find on Berghaus's "Chart of the World on Mercator's Projection" a sounding of 2,700 fathoms indicated in (approx.) latitude 56° 40' north and longitude 168° 20' east, the authority for which I am ignorant of. It is situated almost in a line between the 1895 *Albatross* soundings of 2,137 and 1,806 fathoms, and if correct would indicate a depression below the general level of about 2,100 fathoms in that part of Bering Sea.

[2] Witness the fact that the various charts of the region for more than ten years have borne the following inscription: "The coast of Kamchatka north of Cape Koslof is reported to be charted 15 miles too far east." Yet nothing has been done to clear up the doubt.

Nevertheless, in all this uncertainty, the following points may now be regarded as fairly well established:

(1) The Commander Islands are situated on the extreme eastern point of a plateau-like ridge having a probable average depth of about 500 fathoms and extending eastward from the coast of Kamchatka.

(2) This plateau, upon which the Commander Islands are located, rises very abruptly from an ocean floor of a little more than 2,000 fathoms, so that the islands themselves on their northern and eastern sides rise nearly perpendicular out of this depth.

(3) Between the Commander Islands and Attu, the nearest of the American Aleutian Islands, there is a gap certainly more than 1,900 fathoms deep. Whether the *Albatross* maximum sounding of 1,996 fathoms, only a short distance from the south end of Copper Island, is really the maximum depth, thus indicating a slightly elevated ridge between the floor of the Bering Sea and the so-called *Tuscarora* deep, or whether there may not be a channel of 2,100 fathoms, or thereabouts, on one side of the sounding in question, remains to be seen.

(4) The bottom of Bering Sea to the east of the Commander Islands forms a nearly level floor of an almost uniform depth of 2,100 fathoms, sending off an arm, or bay, of equal depth to the north of the islands toward the neck of the Kamchatkan peninsula. The walls of this basin are excessively steep at the islands, but are believed to slope off gradually toward the curve of the coast between Capes Oserni and Olintorski.

To complete the account I append the records of the soundings taken by the *Albatross* and the *Vitiaz* in the waters covered by the map (plate 1).

Records of recent soundings in the western portion of Bering Sea.

Hydro. station.	Date.	Time.	N. lat.	E. long.	Depth.	Bottom.	Vessel.
	1888.		° ′ ″	° ′ ″	*Fth'ms.*		
107	July 29	1 p.m.	52 58 0	160 02 0	49		Vitiaz.
108	July 29	6.10 p.m.	53 02 0	160 16 0	458		Do.
109	July 30	9 a.m.	53 41 0	163 20 0	390		Do.
110	July 30	8.15 p.m.	54 15 0	165 56 0	300		Do.
111	July 31	8.37 p.m.	54 39 0	166 35 0	55		Do.
112	Aug. 1	2.30 p.m.	55 02 0	165 15 0	109		Do.
113	Aug. 2	4.30 a.m.	53 45 0	162 50 0	400		Do.
	Aug. 2	4 p.m.	52 55 0	160 14 0	175		Do.
	1892.						
3231	May 29	10.40 p.m.	53 13 0	172 38 0	1,447	yl. M. fne. S.	Albatross.
3232	May 30	5.43 a.m.	53 38 0	171 28 0	1,818		Do.
3233	May 30	11.35 a.m.	54 02 0	170 17 0	1,853	fne. bk. S.	Do.
3234	May 30	6.12 p.m.	54 19 0	169 03 0	1,996	yl. M. S.	Do.
3235	May 31	12.03 a.m.	54 30 0	168 07 0	47	fne. gy. S.	Do.
3236	May 31	1.34 p.m.	55 39 0	165 51 0	25	rky.	Do.
3237	May 31	3.10 p.m.	55 10 0	165 47 0	33	rky. M.	Do.
3238	May 31	4.33 p.m.	55 08 0	165 48 0	36	gy. S.	Do.
3239	May 31	5.34 p.m.	55 19 30	165 45 0	32	do	Do.
	1895.						
3546	June 30	3.04 p.m.	55 59 0	178 43 0	2,105	br. M. oz.	Do.
3547	June 30	10.25 p.m.	55 55 0	177 12 0	2,113	do	Do.
3548	July 1	7.05 a.m.	55 52 0	175 25 0	2,120	do	Do.
3549	July 1	4.35 p.m.	55 53 0	173 53 0	2,111	do	Do.
3550	July 2	2.37 a.m.	55 59 0	171 57 0	2,086	do	Do.
3551	July 2	10.29 a.m.	56 00 0	169 46 0	2,154	do	Do.
3552	July 2	4.58 p.m.	56 00 0	168 16 0	2,153	do	Do.
3553	July 2	11.07 p.m.	55 58 0	166 43 0	2,119	gy. S. M.	Do.
3554	July 3	2.21 a.m.	55 43 0	166 15 0	2,090	do	Do.

Records of recent soundings in the western portion of Bering Sea—Continued.

Hydro. station.	Date.	Time.	N. lat.	E. long.	Depth.	Bottom.	Vessel.
	1895.		° ′ ″	° ′ ″	Fth'ms.		
3555	July 5	5.14 a. m.	55 25 0	165 46 0	70	gy. S. M.	Albatross.
3556	July 5	6.24 a. m.	55 16 0	165 32 30	20	crs. S. rky.	Do.
3557	July 5	7.10 a. m.	55 12 0	165 34 0	35	gy. S.	Do.
3558	July 5	7.34 a. m.	55 11 0	165 40 0	37	....do	Do.
3559	July 5	8.04 a. m.	55 11 30	165 46 20	15	rky.	Do.
3560	July 5	12.22 p. m.	55 25 30	165 48 0	144	fne. gy. S.	Do.
3561	July 5	12.49 p. m.	55 27 0	165 49 0	66	rky.	Do.
3562	July 5	1.17 p. m.	55 28 30	165 51 30	341	gy. S. M.	Do.
3563	July 5	2.20 p. m.	55 32 0	165 56 30	1,087	S.	Do.
3564	July 6	1.17 a. m.	56 25 0	167 52 0	2,137	gr. oz.	Do.
3565	July 6	7.15 a. m.	56 50 0	169 06 0	1,866	bl. M. oz	Do.
3566	July 6	12.01 p. m.	57 16 0	169 41 0	972	....do	Do.
3567	July 6	2.29 p. m.	57 29 0	170 09 0	410	gs. S. M.	Do.
3568	July 6	4.15 p. m.	57 35 0	170 24 0	537	br. oz. G	Do.
3569	July 6	6 p. m.	57 41 0	170 39 0	609	br. oz. S.	Do.
3570	July 6	7.32 p. m.	57 47 0	170 54 0	540	gn. oz. G	Do.
3571	July 6	8.44 p. m.	57 53 0	171 09 0	696	gn. M. oz.	Do.
3572	July 11	12.37 a. m.	58 13 0	171 51 0	1,469	....do	Do.
3573	July 11	3.05 a. m.	58 36 0	172 17 0	1,896	hard	Do.
3574	July 11	10.55 a. m.	58 23 0	174 17 0	1,978	bl. M. oz	Do.
3575	July 11	5.04 p. m.	58 12 0	175 49 0	2,041	br. M. oz	Do.
3576	July 11	11.07 p. m.	58 01 0	177 21 0	2,068	....do	Do.

METEOROLOGY.

The climate of the Commander Islands, in spite of their vicinity to Kamchatka, is not particularly severe, but the excessive moisture and the low summer temperature make it rather disagreeable, though by no means unhealthy. The chief interest centers in the temperature, the moisture, precipitation, and cloudiness for the months of May to November, inclusive, during which time the fur-seals stay on the islands. But as the meteorological observations made on the islands have never been published in full, or collectively, I have appended a set of tables of the monthly means for the four years during which the United States Signal Service maintained a station at Nikolski, Bering Island.

One of the objects of my trip to the Commander Islands, in 1882, was to establish meteorological stations there and in Petropaulski. The village at Copper Island was found unsuitable for the purpose and no regular observations were taken there. At Nikolski, however, I established and maintained during my entire stay a three-daily station, beginning May 22, 1882. During my sojourn there I trained the late Mr. George Chernick, agent of Hutchinson, Kohl, Philippens & Co., in the use of the instruments, so that whenever I was absent from the station exploring, collecting, or investigating the rookeries, he took the observations. At my departure he was appointed a United States Signal Service observer, whose duties he conscientiously fulfilled until his resignation in April, 1886, at which time the station was abandoned.

The observations were taken simultaneously with those in Washington, D. C., viz, at 7 a. m., 3 p. m., and 11 p. m., Washington time, or, respectively, 11.12 p. m., 7.12 a. m., and 3.12 p. m., local time.

The instruments used were as follows:

A mercurial barometer, United States Signal Service, No. 1837.
An exposed thermometer, No. 939.
A minimum thermometer, No. 618.
A maximum thermometer, after June, 1883.
A wet-bulb thermometer, for determining the relative humidity, after June, 1883.
A Robinson's anemometer.
A wind vane, belonging on the island.
A Signal Service standard rain-gauge.

THE RUSSIAN FUR-SEAL ISLANDS.

The barometer cistern was 20 feet above sea level.

The thermometers were hung in a large lattice box on the north side of my house, the box covering the window; and the instruments were read through the latter from the inside.

The rain-gauge[1] had to be located very high (9 feet) and in an exposed place to keep it from the marauding sledge-dogs. This instrument was not satisfactory in a high wind. The wind in blowing across the mouth of the funnel would actually suck the air out of the latter, thus preventing the rain or snow from entering. Many a time after a considerable rain I have found the rain-gauge dry inside. The actual amount of precipitation is therefore greater than shown in the table given below, though the figures in the latter may serve for comparison with those from similar localities in the United States, particularly on the Pribylof Islands and in Alaska, where the same kind of rain-gauge was in use.

The following tables I have transcribed directly from the original records. The monthly means are those of the means of the three daily observations. The method of observing, correcting, and tabulating is that in vogue in the Signal Service, and the figures are strictly comparable with those of the other stations of the same Service.

Monthly means of Meteorologic Observations made by Leonhard Stejneger and George Chernick at Nikolski, Bering Island, from May, 1882, to April, 1886, inclusive.

MEAN MONTHLY BAROMETER.

[Corrected for temperature and instrumental error only. Elevation of barometer, 26 feet above sea level. Centr. gravity, + 0.030.]

Year.	Jan.	Feb.	Mar.	Apr.	May.	June	July.	Aug.	Sept.	Oct.	Nov.	Dec.
1882					*29.805	29.738	29.720	29.827	29.842	29.807	29.669	29.524
1883	29.392	30.053	29.784	29.846	29.783	29.752	29.637	29.816	29.775	29.683	29.817	29.512
1884	29.565	29.540	29.579	29.744	29.811	29.938	29.721	29.785	29.947	29.747	29.355	29.560
1885	29.397	29.848	29.805	29.710	29.705	29.693	29.840	29.766	29.882	29.765	29.750	29.612
1886	29.517	29.794	29.781	29.600								

*Means of 10 observations.

MEAN TEMPERATURE.

[The mean temperature was obtained by adding together the observations made at 7.12 a. m., 3.12 p. m., and 11.12 p. m., local time, and dividing by 3.]

Year.	Jan.	Feb.	Mar.	Apr.	May.	June	July.	Aug.	Sept.	Oct.	Nov.	Dec.
	°F.	°F.	°F.	°F.	°F.	°F.	°F.	°F.	°F.	°F.	°F.	°F.
1882					*39.7	42.7	48.2	51.1	50.5	36.8	28.7	27.0
1883	25.5	26.7	25.2	28.6	35.3	41.7	45.0	51.9	45.2	36.0	31.4	28.8
1884	25.9	28.9	28.3	30.7	36.6	42.2	48.1	49.5	45.9	37.4	31.1	26.4
1885	26.9	25.7	27.4	27.7	33.1	41.9	46.2	44.3	45.6	34.8	29.9	26.0
1886	27.4	27.0	27.2	30.7								
Means	26.4	27.0	27.0	29.4	35.7	42.1	47.1	51.0	46.8	37.2	30.3	27.3

Annual means: 1883, 35.5; 1884, 35.9; 1885, 34.7.
*Mean of 10 observations, May 22 to 31, not included in the means.

[1] Report Chief Sig. Off., 1887, II, p. 382, pl. XXXVI, fig. 97.

14   BULLETIN OF THE UNITED STATES FISH COMMISSION.

Monthly means of Meteorologic Observations at Bering Island—Continued.

MAXIMUM TEMPERATURE.

Year.	Jan.	Feb.	Mar.	Apr.	May.	June.	July.	Aug.	Sept.	Oct.	Nov.	Dec.
	°F.	°F.	°F.	°F.	°F.	°F.	°F.	°F.	°F.	°F.	°F.	°F.
1882										*48.0	*40.3	*39.1
1883	*33.0	*33.9	*38.0	*56.0	59.5	57.5	63.0	57.0	49.1	42.9	40.7
1884	36.6	36.8	38.9	39.5	45.4	53.5	62.7	55.7	50.0	49.9	38.2	37.0
1885	36.1	43.4	36.0	39.8	48.5	56.6	62.9	57.1	53.6	51.0	44.0	38.0
1886	37.0	38.6	37.0	39.0								

Highest: 1883, August 23d, 63.0; 1884, July 19th, 62.7; 1885, July 24th, 62.9.
* Highest exposed.

MEAN MAXIMUM TEMPERATURE.

Year.	Jan.	Feb.	Mar.	Apr.	May.	June.	July.	Aug.	Sept.	Oct.	Nov.	Dec.
	°F.	°F.	°F.	°F.	°F.	°F.	°F.	°F.	°F.	°F.	°F.	°F.
1882												
1883					*46.1	51.0	56.9	49.6	43.1	35.8	33.1
1884	29.8	32.4	32.6	35.3	41.5	47.3	52.8	53.5	51.0	41.6	34.8	30.3
1885	30.8	30.7	30.7	31.5	39.1	46.8	51.6	52.4	49.4	39.2	34.4	30.5
1886	30.7	30.2	31.3	38.1								

* Mean of 28 observations.

NUMBER OF DAYS OF MAXIMUM THERMOMETER BELOW 32°.

Year.	Jan.	Feb.	Mar.	Apr.	May.	June.	July.	Aug.	Sept.	Oct.	Nov.	Dec.
1882												
1883						0	0	0	0	0		12
1884	17	11	14	4	0	0	0	0	0	0	4	17
1885	17	15	18	16	1	0	0	0	0	0	10	20
1886	17	17	13	5								
Means.	17.0	14.3	15.0	8.3	0.5	0.0	0.0	0.0	0.0	0.0	7.3	16.3

Total: 1884, 67 days; 1885, 97 days.

MINIMUM TEMPERATURE.

Year.	Jan.	Feb.	Mar.	Apr.	May.	June.	July.	Aug.	Sept.	Oct.	Nov.	Dec.
	°F.	°F.	°F.	°F.	°F.	°F.	°F.	°F.	°F.	°F.	°F.	°F.
1882						31.3	36.4	41.6	35.3	17.6	8.8	-1.4
1883	3.3	10.8	11.2	5.3	25.8	32.4	34.6	39.5	31.3	24.5	15.5	9.8
1884	6.3	9.5	12.2	0.6	27.4	31.5	37.3	38.2	30.4	22.4	13.4	6.2
1885	3.4	3.0	0.9	4.5	22.5	31.2	36.2	37.2	34.2	17.9	6.9	12.4
1886	5.0	15.0	13.0	13.0								

Lowest: 1882, -1.4 December 21; 1883, 3.3 Jaunary 6; 1884, 0.6 April 1; 1885, 0.9 March 17.

MEAN MINIMUM TEMPERATURE.

Year.	Jan.	Feb.	Mar.	Apr.	May.	June.	July.	Aug.	Sept.	Oct.	Nov.	Dec.
	°F.	°F.	°F.	°F.	°F.	°F.	°F.	°F.	°F.	°F.	°F.	°F.
1882						38.6	45.0	50.7	44.5	33.7	23.5	21.7
1883	29.9	24.8	23.1	24.0	*29.4	37.6	36.1	48.3	41.3	33.0	27.8	22.8
1884	21.2	24.0	24.1	26.2	32.5	38.0	43.8	46.0	40.2	32.6	20.5	20.9
1885	21.7	20.1	23.1	21.9	32.0	38.2	42.9	44.9	42.1	29.6	24.4	22.2
1886	23.8	24.6	23.8	27.9								

* Mean of 20 observations.

THE RUSSIAN FUR SEAL ISLANDS.

Monthly means of Meteorologic Observations at Bering Island—Continued.

NUMBER OF DAYS OF MINIMUM THERMOMETER BELOW 32°.

Year.	Jan.	Feb.	Mar.	Apr.	May.	June.	July.	Aug.	Sept.	Oct.	Nov.	Dec.
1882....						1	0	0	0	11	26	28
1883....	31	26	30	27	11	0	0	0	1	15	23	30
1884....	31	26	31	26	13	1	0	0	1	10	24	31
1885....	30	26	30	26	11	1	0	0	0	21	25	29
1886....	30	25	29	27								
Means.	30.5	25.8	30.0	26.5	11.7	0.8	0.0	0.0	0.5	14.2	24.5	29.5

Total: 1883, 194 days; 1884, 194 days; 1885, 199 days.

NUMBER OF CLEAR DAYS.

[A "clear" day has no clouds, or less than 0.3 clouds.]

Year.	Jan.	Feb.	Mar.	Apr.	May.	June.	July.	Aug.	Sept.	Oct.	Nov.	Dec.
1882....						0	0	3	4	0	1	0
1883....	0	5	0	0	0	0	0	0	3	0	0	0
1884....	0	0	0	0	0	0	1	0	3	0	1	0
1885....	0	0	0	0	0	4	2	3	0	0	0	0
1886....	0	0	0	0								
Means	0	1.2	0	0	0	1	0.8	1.5	2.5	0	0.5	0

Total number of clear days: 8 in 1883; 5 in 1884; 9 in 1885; annual mean, 7.

NUMBER OF FAIR DAYS.

[A "fair" day has from 0.3 to 0.7 clouds.]

Year.	Jan.	Feb.	Mar.	Apr.	May.	June.	July.	Aug.	Sept.	Oct.	Nov.	Dec.
1882....							5	5	19	11	17	12
1883....	8	6	8	7	4	4	7	10	12	13	5	14
1884....	2	5	6	8	16	6	5	1	16	12	8	10
1885....	4	4	4	6		7	18	11	6	13	12	9
1886....	8	5	7	7								
Means.	5.5	5.0	6.2	7.0	8.0	5.7	8.8	6.8	13.2	12.2	10.5	11.2

Total number of fair days: 98 in 1883; 83 in 1884; 110 in 1885; annual mean, 97.

NUMBER OF CLOUDY DAYS.

[A "cloudy" day has from 0.8 to 1.0 clouds.]

Year.	Jan.	Feb.	Mar.	Apr.	May.	June.	July.	Aug.	Sept.	Oct.	Nov.	Dec.
1882....							26	23	7	20	12	19
1883....	23	17	23	23	27	26	24	21	15	18	25	17
1884....	29	24	25	22	27	24	25	30	11	19	21	21
1885....	27	24	27	24	15	19	11	17	24	18	18	22
1886....	23	23	24	23								
Means.	25.5	22.0	24.8	23.0	23.0	23.0	21.5	22.8	14.2	18.8	19.0	19.8

Total number of cloudy days: 259 in 1883; 276 in 1884; 246 in 1885; annual mean, 261.

Monthly means of Meteorologic Observations at Bering Island—Continued.

NUMBER OF FOGGY DAYS.

Year.	Jan.	Feb.	Mar.	Apr.	May.	June.	July.	Aug.	Sept.	Oct.	Nov.	Dec.
1882							9	10	0	0	0	0
1883	0	0	0	0	2	3	9	10	2	0	1	0
1884	0	0	0	0	0	0	2	0	0	0	0	0
1885	0	0	0	0	0	1	2	1	0	0	0	0
1886	0	0	0	0								
Means.	0	0	0	0	0.7	1.3	5.5	5.2	0.7	0	0.2	0

CLOUDINESS, EXPRESSED IN PERCENTAGES.

[The percentage of cloudiness was obtained from the eye estimates of the observer, recorded on a scale of 0 to 10 at each observation. The mean of the three daily observations was used as the mean for the day; 100 per cent represents sky completely overcast.]

Year.	Jan.	Feb.	Mar.	Apr.	May.	June.	July.	Aug.	Sept.	Oct.	Nov.	Dec.
1882							93	83	60	79	73	78
1883	85	72	86	84	90	92	89	85	73	74	77	78
1884	81	89	88	79	87	81	66	87	65	79	83	81
1885	84	88	90	86	75	75	63	73	86	76	77	80
1886	84	86	86	81								

Annual means: 82 in 1883, 81 in 1884, 80 in 1885.

PERCENTAGE OF RELATIVE HUMIDITY.

Year.	Jan.	Feb.	Mar.	Apr.	May.	June.	July.	Aug.	Sept.	Oct.	Nov.	Dec.
1882												
1883						89.9	91.1	92.5	87.9	84.0	85.2	82.6
1884	83.3	84.5	87.4	90.1	88.5	85.1	92.2	91.8	82.4	86.3	90.8	90.2
1885	89.9	93.2	89.3	89.0	89.4	90.3	92.7	92.3	91.5	84.7	90.2	87.0
1886	95.1	92.1	90.0	90.3								
Means.	89.4	89.9	88.9	89.8	89.0	88.4	92.0	92.5	87.3	85.0	88.7	86.6

Annual means: 87.7 for 1884, 90 for 1885.

RAINFALL AND MELTED SNOW—AMOUNT OF PRECIPITATION.

Year.	Jan.	Feb.	Mar.	Apr.	May.	June.	July.	Aug.	Sept.	Oct.	Nov.	Dec.
	Inches.	Inches.	Inches.	Inches.	Inches.	Inches.	Inches.	Inches.	Inches.	Inches.	Inches.	Inches.
1882						2.97	1.45	1.07	1.92	3.29	2.23	2.21
1883	0.61	2.94	0.64	1.63	0.38	2.38	1.77	2.25	2.50	2.90	2.20	1.96
1884	0.94	1.49	1.44	1.36	1.31	0.26	2.27	1.74	1.70	3.26	3.30	0.06
1885	0.58	0.99	0.25	0.86	1.19	1.63	4.95	3.15	3.33	1.34	4.08	1.61
1886	0.66	1.50	1.33	1.25								

Total: 21.57 inches in 1883; 20.11 inches in 1884; 21.45 inches in 1885.

NUMBER OF DAYS ON WHICH 0.1 INCH OR MORE RAIN OR SNOW FELL.

Year.	Jan.	Feb.	Mar.	Apr.	May.	June.	July.	Aug.	Sept.	Oct.	Nov.	Dec.
1882						13	18	16	5	13	7	8
1883	20	19	14	18	10	20	20	19	16	16	18	19
1884	12	14	15	12	11	5	13	15	14	20	13	16
1885	18	8	10	7	12	12	12	14	14	12	18	8
1886	13	12	11	9								

Total: 209 days in 1883; 160 days in 1884; 145 days in 1885.

Monthly means of Meteorologic Observations at Bering Island—Continued.

PREVAILING WINDS.

Year.	Jan.	Feb.	Mar.	Apr.	May.	June.	July.	Aug.	Sept.	Oct.	Nov.	Dec.
1882						N.	S.	S.	S. & SW.	N	NW.	S.
1883	NE.	S.		E.	N.	S.	S.	S.	S.	SW. & NW.	SW.	E.
1884	NE.	NE.	N.	N.	N.	S.	S.	E.	NW.	N.	NE.	E.
1885	E.	NE.	NE.	N.	N.	S.	S.	N.	S.	NW.	N.	NE.
1886	NE.	E.	N.	SW.								

MAXIMUM HOURLY VELOCITY (IN MILES).

[Taken from current velocities.]

Year.	Jan.	Feb.	Mar.	Apr.	May.	June.	July.	Aug.	Sept.	Oct.	Nov.	Dec.
1882							29		37	42	15	54
1883	54	41	39	36	34	36	29	47	30	43	44	42
1884	40	48	40	43	26	18	22	40	39	46	37	34
1885	35	43	35	35	38	32	27		25	18	37	18
1886	37	26	41	42								

A considerable amount of *snow* falls during the winter. The fierce winter gales usually blow it off the plateaus, forming immense drifts in the valleys and on the lee side of the mountains. In deep shadowy gullies it often remains all summer, and in cold seasons, as for instance 1895, large drifts still remain unmelted as late as September, even at the level of the sea.

Drift ice seems to be of rare occurrence in recent times. I do not know how much reliance can be placed in old Pitr Burdukovski's story to me that formerly, say about 1850, "drift ice was yearly observed coming from the north in large masses." Certain it is that Steller expressly states that during the winter no ice collected in the sea (Ber. Ins., p. 270).

To complete the meteorologic account I may mention that *thunderstorms* are of rare occurrence on the Commander Islands. In 1879, on November 19, Mr. Krebs, after a residence of eight years in the main village on Copper Island, experienced the first thunderstorm. In 1881, on February 8, he records "a stroke of lightning and a short, but strong thunderclap about 7 p. m." Mr. Chernick, in Nikolski, Bering Island, reports "thunder and lightning" on September 12, 1878. I myself observed a thunderstorm passing over Nikolski, September 18, 1882. The first lightning was observed at 9ʰ 58ᵐ p. m., local time; wind, SW., 13 miles an hour; barometer, 29.552 inches; temperature of air, 52.2° F.; clouds, cumulo-stratus, 8, direction SW.; intervals between first lightning and thunder, 96 seconds; sixth thunderclap (10ʰ 25ᵐ p. m.), 12 seconds after lightning; tenth, 40 seconds; eleventh lightning before thunder of tenth. This was the last distinct thunder heard, 10ʰ 35ᵐ p. m. After that continued distant lightning lit up a narrow strip along the northern horizon. No lightning seen after 11ʰ 10ᵐ p. m.

Aurora borealis is equally scarce. At Nikolski, on November 15, 1882, I observed a faint northern light at 12ʰ 30ᵐ a. m., local time, extending to about η *Urs. majoris*. On November 17, 1882, I observed another at 10ʰ 40ᵐ p. m., local time, consisting of a uniform greenish white light below, above which most of the time a large rosy space was seen filling the arch between γ and η *Urs. majoris*; a similarly colored but often broken arch extended through the constellations of *Cygnus, Cassiopeia, Gemini,* and *Auriga,* sometimes fainter, sometimes more fiery, especially in *Cygnus.* Very seldom the red color filled the space between the rosy spot below *Ursa major* and the upper arch, and then only for a few seconds. At 11 p. m. the sky became so overcast as to cut off further observation.

Corresponding observations made at St. Paul Island, Pribylof group, from 1872 to 1883, and published by the United States Weather Bureau (Fur Seal Arb., II, App. pp. 591-593), afford means of exact comparison between the Russian and the American seal islands, except as regards mean temperature, the latter being obtained on St. Paul from observations made at 7 a. m., 2 p. m., and 9 p. m.

But even a comparison of the *mean temperature* affords several very interesting results. Thus, while the annual means apparently differ but slightly, there is also the same relative proportion between the various months from December to September. But while the figures representing the mean temperatures for these months are higher on Bering Island than on St. Paul, those of October and November are higher on the latter. The chief exception from the relative proportion between the months is shown by the mean temperatures of August, which is about 4 degrees higher than July and September in Bering Island, but only about 2 degrees in St. Paul.

Turning now to the *maximum temperature,* it will be seen to be 63° F. in Bering Island as against 62° on St. Paul. But on the other hand, while the *minimum temperature* in Bering Island was hardly ever below zero during the four years of observation, it often drops below that point in St. Paul. Thus, the difference between the summer and winter extremes is less on Bering Island than on St. Paul.

Coming now to the question of *cloudiness,* it will be seen that while the annual percentage is almost identical, the monthly distribution is radically different. Thus, while in St. Paul Island there are five times as many clear days during November to April as during May to October, on Bering Island the proportion is reversed, there being four times as many clear days during the latter period as during the former. Of fair days, St. Paul enjoys nearly twice as many during the above six winter months as during the six summer months, while Bering Island has a good many more fair days in summer than in winter. Consequently, the entirely overcast days preponderate on St. Paul in summer, while on Bering Island their number is greater in winter. The latter island, moreover, has about 10 per cent more overcast days during the whole year, but on the contrary also about 10 per cent less overcast during the summer months, or during the time the seals remain on the islands.

Unfortunately the percentage of *relative humidity* is not given for St. Paul Island. A glance at the table for Bering Island will show how excessively humid the climate of the latter is, the annual means reaching 90 per cent, the monthly means occasionally exceeding 95 per cent, and never lower than 82 per cent. The months showing the greatest percentage of relative humidity are July and August.

The Weather Bureau tables alluded to do not contain any data relating to *precipitation* on St. Paul Island, and all the published information I have been able to find relates only to the months May to November.[1] Compared with the corresponding tables for Bering Island, they show that the precipitation on the latter island is considerably smaller during that period than on St. Paul Island.

---

[1] Fur Seal Arb., VIII, pp. 518-519.

FAUNA AND FLORA OF THE COMMANDER ISLANDS.

The animals and plants of the Commander Islands have been studied since Steller set foot on the virgin ground of Bering Island in 1741. He collected and described all the new things he saw, and if he had lived to elaborate his collections and finish his work, but little would have been left for his successors. Since then Vosnessenski has been on the island; Dr. Dybowski collected during various visits between 1879 and 1883; Nordenskiold's *Vega* expedition, with his admirable staff of scientists, Nordquist, Kjellman, Stuxberg, and Almquist, used their five days' stay in 1879 exceedingly well; and, above all, Mr. Grebnitski has devoted work, time, and money during nearly twenty years to enrich the Russian museums, particularly that of the Imperial Academy of Sciences in St. Petersburg, with extensive and costly collections of natural history. The United States National Museum is also indebted to him for valuable material. Finally, during my stay in 1882-83, and to a less extent in 1895, I myself have been able to add my mite to our knowledge of the flora and fauna of these islands, nearly all my collections being now in the United States National Museum. Yet the subject is not exhausted; many animals and plants occurring there remain uncollected, while many of the collections in the museums await the arrival of the specialist to work them up.

Lack of time and space prevents more than the briefest possible résumé of the subject in the present connection; a more exhaustive treatise would make a book in itself. There is abundant evidence in the material at hand to show that the islands during the period previous to which they received their present fauna and flora were totally covered by the sea, and that since that time they have not been connected with the mainland on either side. From this it follows that the animals and plants are not truly indigenous, though I have no doubt that many of the numerous species described as new from these islands are really peculiar, and not found elsewhere; but in that case their origin on the islands is undoubtedly due to comparatively recent isolation. The sporadic character of the fauna and flora as shown in the great number of genera in proportion to the species, as well as the absence of many forms which, from their general distribution, would be expected to occur, is clearly indicative of the accidental immigration of the component species. They evidently immigrated, especially and more regularly from the west, from Asia, by means of prevailing winds—currents and driftwood carried by these—and more seldom from the east, from America. That such inhabitants as are more independent of the above agencies likewise show nearer relationship to the Asiatic fauna is partly due to the shorter distance and partly to the well-known effort of the Asiatic fauna to extend beyond its own limits.

As might be expected from their location, the islands are chiefly palaearctic in their bio-geographical relations, with a fair sprinkling of circumpolar, American, and North Pacific forms. The marine fauna and flora partake more particularly of this latter character, and it is probable that Dr. W. H. Dall's conclusions, derived from a study of the mollusks, applies to most of the other marine animals, viz:

> The fauna of Commander Islands, as far as known, is intimately related to the general Arctic fauna and especially to the Aleutian fauna, somewhat less so to the Kamchatka fauna, but presents in itself nothing distinctive. While the faunal aspect of the mollusca is boreal, there is a number greater than might be expected of species common to Japan and California.

To this statement he afterwards added the note:

> The connection with Japan is rather that the northern forms extend southward into Japan than that any characteristic Japanese forms extend north. (Proc. U. S. Nat. Mus., IX, 1886, p. 219.)

MAMMALS.

The chief zoological interest centers in the four marine mammals revealed to the scientific world in Steller's famous treatise "De Bestiis Marinis" (Novi Comm. Ac. Sc. Imp. Petrop., II, 1751, pp. 289-398, pls. XIV-XVI), which must always remain a monument to the learning and industry of its author. In this he described for the first time the sea-cow, the sea-lion, the fur-seal, and the sea-otter.

Of these, the sea-cow (*Hydrodamalis gigas*, also known as *Rytina gigas* or *stelleri*) possesses greatest interest, on account of its early extermination by man, which took place in 1768, twenty-seven years after its discovery. The sea-cow was an herbivorous animal, anteriorly shaped somewhat like a seal, but with a large caudal fin like that of a whale or fish, but no hind legs, and belonging to the mammalian order of *Sirenia*, the few living relations of which, the manati and dugong, now only inhabit the tropical waters of both hemispheres. There is no indisputable evidence of its having ever inhabited other coasts than those of the Commander Islands, as the find of a rib on Attu Island does not necessarily prove that the animal once lived there, though that is not improbable. The history of this animal, imperfectly known as it is, fills volumes, and all we can do in the present connection is to refer to some of the more recent literature (Büchner, Die Abbildungen der nordischen Seekuh, Mém. Ac. Imp. Sc. St. Petersb., 7 ser., XXXVIII, 1891, No. 7.—Stejneger, Proc. U. S. Nat. Mus., 1883, pp. 78-86; 1884, pp. 181-189.—Stejneger, On the Extermination of the Great Northern Sea Cow, Am. Geogr. Soc. Bull., No. 4, 1886, pp. 317-328.—Stejneger, How the Great Northern Sea Cow (*Rytina*) Became Exterminated, Amer. Natural., XXI, Dec., 1887, pp. 1047-1054).

The sea lion (*Eumetopias stelleri*) was formerly quite abundant, but has now become nearly extinct on both islands, though still numerous in certain localities on the Kamchatkan coast. In 1895 I saw only one individual on Sivutchi Kamen at the North Rookery, Bering Island.

The fur-seal (*Callotaria ursina*) being the chief subject of this report, needs no further mention in this connection.

The fate of the sea-otter (*Latax lutris*) in the Commander Islands is highly instructive and interesting. When Bering and his unfortunate followers landed on Bering Island they found the sea-otters so numerous that these animals furnished food for the entire crew during the whole winter. On their return to Kamchatka the following year (1742) they brought with them more than 700 skins of this costly fur. Then followed a period of reckless slaughter of these animals by the rapacious promyshleniks. Thus, in 1745, Bassof and Trapeznikof secured 1,600 skins; in 1748 about 1,350 were killed. The result was that within a very few years the sea-otter almost disappeared from Bering Island, for Tolstykh's expedition obtained only 47 during the winter of 1749-50; Drushinin's men, in 1754-55, took only 5; while in the account of Tolstykh's second expedition, winter 1756-57, it is expressly said that "no sea-otters showed themselves that year." It is interesting to note that even in those days Copper Island offered a safer retreat for the sea-otter, since Yugof, who also visited that island, returned home in 1754 with 790 skins.

While not actually and literally exterminated on Bering Island—Trapeznikof's expedition of 1762-63 secured 20 otters there—it did not become common there again, except possibly during an alleged sudden reappearance in 1772, until after the abandonment of the island, when the Russian-American Company was organized. Upon the recolonization of the island the otters were found common in places; thus it is said that in 1827 no less than 200 otters were killed in one week at the Reef near the present Nikolski village (Slunin, Promysl. Kamch. Sakh. Komand. Ostr., 1895, p. 103). But the reckless slaughter of former days was resumed and the sea-otter long ago ceased to be a regular inhabitant of that island. Occasionally a solitary individual strays over from Copper Island, where the same careful management which resulted in the increase of the fur-seal has succeeded in preserving and increasing the sea-otter to such an extent that I believe there is no other place in the world where so many sea-otters can be seen at the present day. The condition of the herd is now such that 200 animals can be killed off yearly without detriment. The places where the sea-otter have their rookeries are constantly guarded, to keep intruders off. Shooting, making fire, or smoking is strictly prohibited near these places. Only nets are now used to capture the otters; and if any females or yearlings are caught alive they must be set free. The number to be taken is determined in advance by the administration, and the hunting expeditions of the natives are undertaken in common, under the leadership of the chief, though each hunter keeps the otter he secures. They are taken off their hands by the Russian Government at a certain fixed price.

Of other marine mammals occurring at the Commander Islands, we may further mention four species of hair-seals, viz, *Phoca larglna*, *fœtida*, *grœnlandica*, and *fasciata*; three species of ziphioid whales, viz, *Ziphius grebnitzkii*, *Berardius bairdii*, and *Mesoplodon stejnegeri*; a sperm whale (*Physeter macrocephalus*); several delphinoid whales, among which the terrible enemy of the fur-seal, the killer (*Orca gladiator*), as well as several species of fin-back whales.

The land mammals are few, the most important being the Arctic fox (*Vulpes lagopus*). These animals, which are now fairly common, yielding a handsome income to the natives, belong almost exclusively to the dark-bluish phase. Their economic importance will be treated of elsewhere in this report.

There are two rodents on Bering Island, but both have been introduced by the agency of man during late years. *Mus musculus*, the common house-mouse, was brought to Bering Island in 1870 by the schooner *Justus*, in a cargo of flour. The short-tailed red field-mouse (*Microtus rutilus*), which now overruns the islands in vast numbers, was introduced from Kamchatka at a much later date, probably with the firewood. This is probably also the origin of the bats (*Vespertilio?*) which are said to have been seen at Nikolski during the last couple of years.

The introduction of the reindeer (*Rangifer tarandus*) will be mentioned elsewhere (p. 33).

BIRDS.

I have reported upon the birds in a separate volume (Results of Ornithological Explorations in the Commander Islands and in Kamtschatka. By Leonhard Stejneger. Bull. No. 29, U. S. Nat. Mus. 1885; 382 pp. + 8 plates) and in a later supplementary paper (Revised and Annotated Catalogue of the Birds Inhabiting the Commander Islands; Proc. U. S. Nat. Mus. 1887, pp. 117-145 + 3 plates), to which I would refer the reader for detailed information. In the last-mentioned paper I enumerated 143 species of birds as having been collected in the Commander Islands. To these I can now add three species, viz: (1) *Garia alba*, the ivory gull, a specimen of which Mr. Grebnitski presented to me (U. S. Nat. Mus., No. 151983); (2) *Eurynorhyuchus pygmæus*, the spoon-bill sandpiper, two specimens of which were shot during the latter part of

September, 1894, and sent by Grebnitski to the museum in St. Petersburg; and (3) *Milvus melanotis*, the black-eared kite, a mere straggler, taken once on Bering Island. The specimen was presented to the *Vega* expedition by Mr. Grebnitski (Palmén, Vega Exp. Vetensk. Iaktt., V, 1887, p. 294).

One of the Commander Island birds (*Phalacrocorax perspicillatus*) deserves at least a passing notice, not only because we know of no other locality in which it has with certainty occurred, but because it has become extinct within recent years through the agency of man. The history of this rare bird (only 4 specimens exist in museums) is traced and full description given by me in a separate paper (Contribution to the History of Pallas's Cormorant; Proc. U. S. Nat. Mus., XII, 1890, pp. 83-88). In 1882 I fortunately disinterred a number of bones of this bird, which have been described and figured by Mr. F. A. Lucas (*tom. cit.*, pp. 88-94, pls. II-IV). An additional collection made by me in 1895 will also shortly be elaborately described and figured by him. A preliminary note may be found in *Science*, November 15, 1895, p. 661.

FISHES.

A collection of littoral and river fishes occurring at the Commander Islands, brought together by Mr. Grebnitski and myself, is now being reported upon by Dr. Tarleton H. Bean. The report will be published in the Proceedings of the United States National Museum, as No. 11 of the "Contributions to the Natural History of the Commander Islands."

TUNICATES.

Styela arctica has been described by Swederus (Vega Exp. Vet. Iakt., IV, 1887, p. 108) as a new species from Bering Island.

INSECTS.

Mosquitos are numerous on Bering Island and very annoying on the few otherwise pleasant days of which the summers of that region can boast. *Geometridæ* and *Microlepidoptera* are rather numerous, *Noctuidæ* less so. I have only seen one specimen of diurnal Lepidoptera, viz, a butterfly very much like *Vanessa urticæ*. Of the Coleoptera, the large staphylinid, *Creophilus villosus*, is very numerous on the seal-killing grounds. Mr. John Sahlberg has reported upon a few (9) Coleoptera and (1) Hemiptera collected by the *Vega* expedition (Vega Exp. Vet. Iakt., IV, 1885, pp. 61-68), one of which is described as new, viz, *Anisotoma abbreviata*, one of the *Siphidæ*. My own collections are considerably larger and contain (besides the Microlepidoptera), according to a preliminary census by Mr. M. Linell, 46 species, of which 33 are Coleoptera. These include all of Sahlberg's species except *Oxypoda opaca* and *Anisotoma abbreviata*, so that the Coleoptera from the Commander Islands now number 35 species. Of these, no less than 12 species belong to the *Staphylinidæ*. The other orders are represented by 2 species of *Hemiptera*, 5 *Diptera*, 3 *Hymenoptera*, 1 *Siphonaptera*, and 1 Lepidopter, viz, *Agrotiphila alaskæ* Grote.

It should be remarked that the insects collected of late years in the neighborhood of the main villages must not be given too great weight in determining the zoological relationship of the islands, for many have undoubtedly been introduced recently from Petropaulski, Kamchatka, in the large quantity of firewood shipped to the islands every year. In fact, some of the species collected by me in 1895 were taken on or near the wood-pile.

MYRIAPODS.

The three species brought home by me have been determined by Bollman. *Linotænia chionophila* and *Lithobius sulcipes*, both from Bering Island, are known from other localities, but the species described by him as new, under the name of *Lithobius stejnegeri*, is the only one thus far found only on the Commander Islands (Bull. U. S. Nat. Mus. No. 46, 1893, p. 199).

ACARIDS.

The acarids collected by the *Vega* expedition have been described by Kramer and Neuman (Vega Exp. Vet. Iakt., III, 1883, pp. 519-532, pls. XLI-XLIV). No less than 5 new species were described from Bering Island, 4 of which were found only on the latter, as follows: *Nesaea arctica, Bdella villosa, Leodes borealis, I. fimbriatus,* and *Gamasus arcticus*. Of these I obtained only *I. borealis*.

SPIDERS.

It was my intention to get as nearly complete a collection of spiders as possible, and I succeeded in obtaining quite a number of species, which were turned over to the United States National Museum. They were lent to the late Dr. Marx to be determined, but the report was not finished before his death.

CRUSTACEANS.

The crustaceans collected have not been worked up as yet, except the entomostraca, which have been described by Prof. W. Lilljeborg, of Upsala, Sweden (On the Entomostraca collected by Mr. Leonhard Stejneger, on Bering Island, 1882-83. Proc. U. S. Nat. Mus., X, 1887, pp. 154-156). Five species were collected, of which I found *Branchipus paludosus, Daphnia longispina,* and the new species *Diaptomus ambiguus*, in small fresh-water ponds at Ladiginsk, Bering Island. The other new species is *Eurycercus glacialis*, which, however, has also been found in Greenland and Vaigatch Island, at the entrance to the Kara Sea.

The crabs have been identified by Mr. J. E. Benedict, as follows: *Oregonia gracilis* Dana; *Teimessus cheiragonus* (Tilesius); *Eupagurus gilli* Benedict; *Eupagurus hirsutiusculus* (Dana); *Eupagurus middendorfii* Brandt; *Eupagurus nudosus* Benedict; and *Hapalogaster grebnitskii* Schalfeef, recently described from Bering Island (Bull. Acad. Sc. St. Petersb., XXXV, No. 2, 1892, p. 335, fig. 3). Schalfeef identifies another species of *Hapalogaster*, also collected by Mr. Grebnitski on Bering Island, as *H. mandtii*.

MOLLUSKS.

Among the invertebrates, the mollusks have been most extensively collected and most thoroughly reported upon. The *Vega* expedition obtained 26 species. Mr. Grebnitski sent the National Museum 23 species, and I myself 45 species, out of a total of 75 species thus far collected. Of these, 10 are land or fresh-water species. Dr. W. H. Dall has published two reports upon the Commander Islands collections (Proc. U. S. Nat. Mus., VII, 1884, pp. 340-349; and IX, 1886, pp. 209-219). In the last paper he gives a full list of the species, including those of the *Vega* expedition which have been reported upon by Westerlund and Aurivillius. The species of land and freshwater mollusks thus far collected on the islands are: *Limax* (*Agriolimax*) *hyperboreus; Vitrina exilis; Hyalina radiatula; Conulus fulvus,* var.; *Patula ruderata,* var. *pauper;*

Pupilla decora and *arctica*; *Acanthinula harpa*; *Limnæa ovata*; *L. humilis*; *Pisidium equilaterale*. The new species described from Bering Island by Aurivillius is *Pleurotoma beringi*; and by Dall, in his first paper, *Lacunella reflexa* (p. 344, pl. II, figs. 1–3), *Cerithiopsis stejnegeri* (p. 345, pl. II, fig. 4), and *Strombella callorhina* var. *stejnegeri* (p. 346, pl. II, figs. 5, 6).

WORMS.

At least one species of earthworm occurs, and several leeches, but, like the rest of the lower invertebrates collected, they have not been reported upon as yet. Wirén has described a new species of chætopod from Bering Island, viz, *Potamilla neglecta* (Vega Exp. Vet. Iakt., II, 1883, p. 422).

SPONGES.

A new variety (*arctica*) of *Esperia lingua* has been described from Bering Island (5–10 fathoms) by Fristedt (Vega Exp. Vet. Iakt., IV, p. 449, pl. XXV, figs. 20–24; pl. XXIX, fig. 18).

PLANTS.

It was quite to be expected that Steller, as an expert botanist, should have made extensive botanical collections on Bering Island, and as he seems to have collected 211 species of plants there (see Pennant. Arct. Zool., Suppl., 1787, p. 38), he gathered more species than any of the various collectors who visited the island afterwards. Thus the combined collections of Dybowski, Wiemuth, and Kjellman include 144 phanerogams, while I have brought home nearly exactly the same number of species. The combined number of species, however, is much greater. Dr. Kjellman has published an interesting account of the flora as revealed in the first-mentioned collections (Vega Exp. Vet. Iakt., IV, 1887, pp. 281–309), while the late Prof. Asa Gray, in 1885, reported upon my collections in the Proceedings of the United States National Museum, VII, pp. 527–529, to which paper I added a few remarks (*ibid.*, pp. 529–538). During my trip in 1895 I had but scant time and facilities for collecting plants, and I confined myself chiefly to an unsuccessful search for *Cassiope oxycoccoides* in the exact locality and about the same season as I had collected it in 1882. Nevertheless, I was able to add a few species to the flora, which Dr. J. N. Rose, of the National Herbarium, has kindly determined for me as *Carex rariflora*, *Kœnigia islandica*, and *Ranunculus hyperboreus*. From the lists published it should now be possible to compile a tolerably complete flora of Commander Islands phanerogams.

Dr. Asa Gray described one of my ericaceous plants as new, viz, *Cassiope oxycoccoides*, and the late Dr. George Vasey afterwards determined one of the grasses to be new and named it *Alopecurus stejnegeri* (Proc. U. S. Nat. Mus., X, 1887, p. 153; figured as fig. 2, pl. XXIV, Grasses Pacif. Slope, by Vasey, pt. 1, 1892). As these species have not as yet been recorded from other localities they must be regarded, provisionally at least, as peculiar to the Commander Islands, and Dr. Kjellman's statement to the contrary effect (*tom. cit.*, p. 286) must be modified accordingly.

Dr. Kjellman's concluding remarks (*tom. cit.*, p. 289) are so interesting and important that I venture to translate them here, as follows:

> The flora of the Commander Islands is chiefly composed of two elements. One of these consists of species not entering the present Arctic region, or at any rate not to be regarded as belonging to the characteristic plants of this region. Most of these have their chief range of the present day extending over the islands and coasts of the Northern Pacific Ocean. These form the bulk of the vegetation

and determine its character. I regard them as arcto-tertiary species, of which many, at least, have formerly had a wider distribution than at present.

The other element consists of species which by their present distribution are indicated as arctic-alpine. Several of these are to be regarded as among the characteristic plants of the present Arctic regions.

The Commander Islands, with the other Aleutian Islands, compose a floral district which forms a transition chiefly between three other districts, viz, the Manchu-Japanese, the Americo-Pacific, and the Arctic district, although less closely related to the latter than to the other two, the northern outpost of which it may be regarded to represent.

Dr. Ernst Almquist has investigated the lichens of Bering Island and has published a very interesting account of his studies (Vega Exp. Vet. Iakt., IV, 1887, pp. 518-519, 521, 524-531), in which he gives an ingenious explanation of the curiously sculptured surface of the heath like plant covering of the lower plateaus as due to a natural rotation of the plants composing it.

The general character of the flora is very much like that of the treeless regions of Northern Europe, the most discrepant features being the splendid rhododendrons (*R. kamtschaticum* and *chrysanthum*) and the beautiful dark-maroon-colored Saranna-lily (*Fritillaria camtschatcensis*), the bulbs of which the natives gather for food in late summer. These plants indicate the close relationships to the flora of Kamchatka and the other Aleutian Islands. The plants of both islands are in most cases identical, but the manner of their immigration very likely has caused the occurrence of some species in one island which are absent in the other. Thus I have from Copper Island the conspicuous yellow flowering *Viola biflora* (also found by me at Petropaulski), which I failed entirely to find on Bering Island, and which I could scarcely have overlooked.

The islands are completely destitute of trees, the few species of *Salix*, *Pyrus*, and *Betula* hardly ever rising above 6 to 8 feet, though I have a section of *Betula ererzmanni* from Bering Island, with a diameter of 2 inches at the root. The *Pyrus*, in many places, forms extensive, nearly impenetrable thickets.

There are two tolerably well-defined belts of vegetation on the island, one a very luxuriant growth of higher plants in the lower valleys and plains, the other a heath-like formation above the former.

The luxuriance of the vegetation in the lower belt, due to a rich soil and extreme moisture, is marvelous. Some species familiar to me from boyhood I could hardly recognize in the enormous specimens before me. Such plants as *Anemone narcissiflora* and *Geranium erianthum* sometimes reach a height of 3 feet, while in some particularly favored localities many acres of ground may be found covered with an almost impenetrable jungle of *Archangelica*, *Heracleum lanatum*, *Artemisia tilesii*, *Pieris japonica*, *Spiræa kamtschatica*, *Aconitum*, *Veratrum album*, etc., often reaching a height of 5 to 6 feet. The exuberance of the umbellifers, particularly near the coast, is very striking, as shown in the accompanying photograph of *Heracleum lanatum* (pl. 15a). Near the beach this belt shows the usual influence of the neighborhood of salt water in the presence of such plants as *Lathyrus maritimus*, *Mertensia maritima* and *Ligusticum scoticum*.

The heath commences often quite abruptly above this belt, covering the surface of the beach terraces and the lower plateaus. Its presence does not depend so much upon the altitude as the character of the ground, for where the coast escarpment is low the heath formation commences even at an altitude of 20 to 30 feet. The fundamental plant of this formation is *Empetrum nigrum*, richly interspersed with *Loiseleuria procumbens*, *Cassiope lycopodoides* and other ericaceous plants, chiefly *Bryanthus*, and in the lower portions *Rhododendron chrysanthum*. Where the ground is marshy the salmon berry. *Rubus chamæmorus*, is rather common. Higher up on the mountain sides the vegetation grows more and more scanty and alpine in character.

The *pelagic flora* around Bering Island has been studied by Dr. F. R. Kjellman (Kgl. Svenska Vetensk. Akad. Handling., (n. s.), XXIII, 1889, No. 8, 58 pp., 7 pls), who observes that at Bering Island all conditions are found favorable to the development of a rich flora of *algæ* of the pelagic type. "It may even be said with safety that there are but few parts of the ocean the flora of which exceeds or even approaches that around Bering Island, in so far as multitude of individuals or number of magnificent forms are concerned."

NATIVE POPULATION OF THE COMMANDER ISLANDS.

The Commander Islands, when discovered in 1741, were uninhabited, and no trace of any former population has been found. For over 80 years the islands remained without a regular population, although they were visited almost yearly up to the end of the eighteenth century by numerous parties of Russian fur-hunters, or promyshleniks, as they are called. In the early days it was the custom of these hardy frontiersmen to pass the first winter on Bering Island in order to secure provisions of sea-cow meat for their further expeditions. Sometimes the crews of several vessels wintered there at the same time, in one year at least (1754-55) numbering over 100 men. Those were gay days on Bering Island, when the sea cow, the sea-otter, the blue fox, and the fur-seal were still plentiful. But these precious animals were soon exterminated, literally, as the sea-cow, or commercially, as the three other species, and the inhospitable and dangerous shores of the Commander Islands were but seldom visited by sailors or hunters.

When the colonial district of Atkha was established by the Russian-American Company, in 1826, it was decided to locate a number of natives from the other Aleutian Islands, and consequently two colonies of Aleuts and half-breeds, the offspring of Russian promyshleniks and Aleut women, were planted on Bering and Copper islands. A similar colony, located on the Kuril Islands, was made up mostly from natives of the Kadiak district. The colony of Bering Island consisted chiefly of natives of Atkha Island, or the Andreanovski group, in general, while the Copper islanders were made up mostly of men and women from Attu. Although the inhabitants of the two islands by transfer and intermarriage have become considerably mixed of late, yet the difference in origin is still traceable in the dialects spoken, the Atkha people still preponderating on Bering Island, the Attu islanders on Copper Island.

Of late years two other elements have been added to the native population. As noted above, the Russian-American Company had located a colony of natives, mostly from the Kadiak district, on the Kuril Islands. When the latter islands were ceded to Japan these natives and their offspring declared their intention of remaining Russian subjects and were transferred to Kamchatka. After a miserable existence for several years in a small village outside of Petropaulski, they were located on the east coast near Cape Lopatka, in order to hunt sea-otters. Their village was situated in a small bay just back of Cape Zholti.[1] They did not do well there, and during the last few years (1888) were transferred to Bering Island, their number helping to swell the total of the Commander Islands population. This was not a very desirable addition, however, and has not resulted in elevating the morals of the former inhabitants.

The other addition consists in a number of girls from Petropaulski. It was found that the inbreeding of the natives on the two islands was not only having a deleterious effect upon the health and vitality of the community, but intermarriage had made the inhabitants so interrelated that it was difficult to find people who could be married at all without violating the intricate laws of the Russian Church governing marriage between relatives. Under these circumstances a number of unmarried young men from both islands were encouraged to go to Petropaulski and provide themselves with brides.

The following tables of the population on the islands are derived from various official returns, published and unpublished. The figures for 1860 are from Tikhmenief's book. The figures for 1895 have been mislaid, but the total for both islands is believed to be about 650(?). The tables are meant to show only the native population, and not to include those temporarily living there, as the administrator, his assistant, the doctor, the midwife, the priests, the deacon, the kossaks and soldiers, the company's agents, or their families. They would increase the total about 20; and the entire population of the Commander Islands in 1895 may therefore be set down as about 670 of both sexes.

Native population of Commander Islands, 1860 to 1892.

Year.	Bering Island.			Copper Island.			Total, both islands.
	Male.	Female.	Total.	Male.	Female.	Total.	
1860			300			90	390
1870	126	111	237	80	73	153	390
1875	139	132	271	90	81	171	442
1880	164	145	309	91	101	192	501
1881			310			203	513
1883	164	155	319	93	114	207	526
1892			336			300	636

Apart from the sudden increase, due to the importation of the Zholti Mys natives, a pretty steady, though slow, increase of the population is noticeable since 1870. This is rather interesting in a mixed population of but indifferent vitality and, moreover, afflicted by a tendency to scrofulous and pulmonary diseases, the more so since a couple of rather severe epidemics of influenza and scarlet fever have swept over the islands of late years.[2] The question of the movement of this population during the years 1868 to 1881 has been studied by Dr. B. Dybowski,[3] whose tables relating to births and deaths are interesting enough to deserve a place in this connection.

---
[1] I have partly traced the history of these natives in an article in *Science* (n. s. II, July 19, 1895, pp. 62–63). When that was written, I little thought that on the very day of its publication I should be living among these same natives on Bering Island.

[2] As a result, the native population of Bering Island, according to Dr. Slunin (Prom. Bog. Kamch., etc., p. 57), between 1886 and 1891 suffered a decrease of 16, there being 111 births only against 127 deaths. His statement, however, that the population of Copper Island has not increased during the 20 years from 1872 to 1892 is not in conformity with the facts as shown in the above table.

[3] Wyspy Komandorskie, pp. 78–87.

Number of births and deaths on Commander Islands, 1868 to 1881.

Year	Bering Island						Copper Island						Total, both islands	
	Births			Deaths			Births			Deaths				
	Male	Fem.	Total	Male	Fem.	Total	Male	Fem.	Total	Male	Fem.	Total	Births	Deaths
1868	2	4	6	6	0	15	0	0	3	1	4	6	19	
1869	4	2	6	4	13	17	2	3	5	0	0	0	11	17
1870	5	4	13	3	7	10	3	5	8	0	2	2	21	12
1871	5	3	8	3	1	4	2	2	4	0	0	0	12	4
1872	7	9	16	6	4	10	3	2	5	1	0	1	21	11
1873	7	7	14	3	0	3	2	2	4	3	1	4	18	7
1874	8	10	18	3	3	6	6	6	12	0	5	5	30	11
1875	5	6	11	4	6	10	2	6	8	3	2	5	19	15
1876	8	6	14	2	2	4	5	6	11	4	2	6	25	10
1877	10	5	15	3	8	11	4	6	10	6	1	7	25	18
1878	6	9	15	2	5	7	5	7	12	4	0	4	27	11
1879	11	12	23	2	5	7	3	6	9	6	4	10	32	17
1880	6	8	14	7	7	14	7	4	11	3	2	5	25	19
1881	7	7	14	9	3	12	6	5	11	5	5	10	25	22
Total	95	92	187	57	73	130	50	60	110	36	27	63	297	193

Births and deaths on Commander Islands, according to months, from 1868 to 1881.

Months	Births									Deaths								
	Bering Island			Copper Island			Both islands			Bering Island			Copper Island			Both islands		
	Male	Female	Total	Male	Female	Total	Male	Female	Total	Male	Female	Total	Male	Female	Total	Male	Female	Total
January	3	12	15	3	5	8	6	17	23	4	3	7	2	0	2	6	3	9
February	5	4	9	3	6	8	7	10	17	2	3	5	2	3	3	5	5	8
March	6	3	9	6	4	10	12	7	19	2	5	7	2	3	5	5	4	9
April	3	4	7	2	8	10	5	12	17	3	1	4	2	3	5	5	4	9
May	7	5	12	8	3	11	15	8	23	6	4	10	0	1	1	6	5	11
June	7	9	16	4	8	11	13	9	24	1	17	18	1	5	6	2	22	24
July	4	7	11	3	4	7	7	11	18	2	4	6	1	3	3	3	4	9
August	6	8	14	2	0	2	8	8	16	5	9	14	2	10	13	11	24	
September	10	9	19	5	3	8	15	12	27	5	5	12	6	2	8	13	7	20
October	17	8	25	5	7	12	22	15	37	4	2	6	3	6	6	7	5	12
November	7	9	16	5	6	8	14	23	6	4	10	3	0	3	9	4	13	
December	8	3	11	3	6	9	11	9	20	4	5	9	0	2	2	6	5	11
Month unknown	5	4	9	0	0	0	5	4	9	2	10	12	0	2	2	2	12	14
Total	88	85	173	44	55	99	132	140	272	48	70	118	31	22	53	79	92	171

The Commander Islanders, being derived from the other Aleutian Islands, do not differ from their relatives now under American authority in any essential point, and they naturally possess the characteristics, both good and bad, of the latter. By nature gentle, intelligent, and honest, the worst of their present vices have been acquired by contact with white men. I have spent twenty months among them, and I have only the most pleasant recollections of these simple-hearted people.

Notwithstanding their common origin, there is a marked difference between the natives on Bering Island and those on Copper Island. The former are more reticent, less ambitious, and, therefore, to most people, less attractive than the latter, whose gaiety and whim make a very favorable impression on the visitor. This difference seemed more marked during my visit to the islands last year than on the former occasion, and, on the whole, it seemed as if the Bering Islanders had deteriorated. Even theft was not uncommon among the younger generation on Bering Island—though an almost unknown thing fourteen years ago. But even now real criminal offenses are not frequent. Occasionally a serious offender has to be sent to Vladivostok for punishment, but ordinarily deportation from one island to the other, extra service at the South Rookery, or fines, are resorted to. The kossaks have often to arrest disturbers of the peace, resulting from the general spree on the great holidays, or *prasniks*; but a night's lodging in the lock up sobers them up, and neither island has thus far needed a jail. As an illustration of the patriarchal ways of justice in vogue not many years ago the following literal abstract from the station log of Bering Island is both instructive and amusing:

DECEMBER 3, 1877.—A married woman was on trial for stealing a petticoat from a clothes-line. As she would not confess, the judges (natives) took two pieces of paper, on one of which was written "I have stolen," and on the other "I did not"; and it happened that she drew the one with the inscription "I have stolen." She was sentenced to wash the floor in the church.

The moral decline of the people I attribute largely to the recent introduction of intoxicating liquors. In 1882 it was forbidden the natives both to import spirits and to brew "beer" of sugar. As a result they were tractable and contented, except as to this particular point. I was then told a story, the literal truth of which I can not guarantee, however, but it is to the point: A "revisor" arrived at the island to inquire if the natives were treated well, and he called a meeting to receive any complaints that they might have to make. The chief, after consulting with the other men, finally declared that they had absolutely nothing to complain of except the discrimination made against them, among all the children of the tsar, that they were not allowed to get drunk on the great church and state holidays, and that they were not conscious of any conduct which would merit such an unusual and severe punishment.

Whether this petition had any weight, or whether the American Company, which had been instrumental in establishing the prohibition, was losing its influence, I don't know; certain it is that at my second visit to the islands the natives were allowed to import and consume many hundred dollars' worth of alcohol, the result being the usual one.

Until within the last few years the condition of these natives has been the enviable one of being the richest and most prosperous community in Bering Sea, or along any of its shores. Not only the increase in the number of seal skins taken, and later on the increased payment for the skins when the number began to fall off, contributed to this end, but also the flourishing condition of the sea-otter and blue-fox hunt, due to the enforcement of wise regulations for the protection and chase of these animals.

The sea-otter long ago became extinct on Bering Island, but on Copper Island it is still common. The "rookeries" or breeding-places of this valuable animal, which furnishes the costliest of all furs,[1] are guarded and protected with jealous care. The animal, which is now nearing its extermination on all the American islands and shores, where it is not protected at all, is actually increasing on Copper Island, and yields, besides a handsome return to the Government, sufficient income to keep the natives in comparative affluence, as this island can easily produce 200 skins a year. The sea-otter is there hunted by the natives in common, but the individual hunter secures the price for the animal he catches. Only nets are allowed in their capture. The Government buys all the skins from the natives at a certain fixed rate, 140 rubles for the first quality, 75 rubles for the second, and disposes of them to the company as per contract.

[1] A single first-class sea-otter skin brought at auction in London, spring of 1895, $1,100.

The following table, based upon official returns, shows the gradual increase until the present capacity of the island, about 200, was reached:

Number of sea-otters killed on Copper island, 1872–1882.

Year.	Sea-otters.	Year.	Sea-otters.
1872	9	1879	*2
1873	14	1880	128
1874	54	1881	190
1875	48	1882	200
1876	35		
1877	68	Total	840
1878	94		

*Thrown out by the sea. There was evidently no hunt that year. Dybowski (Wysp Komand., p. 61), upon the "authority of the overseer at Copper Island," gives 20 for 1879.

The arctic blue fox is common on both islands, most of the animals now found there being of the costlier dark phase, only a few white ones occurring occasionally on Bering Island. These are killed regardless of place or season, to keep the strain as pure as possible. The Copper Island fox skins are of a better quality, being larger and darker. The capture of the foxes is subject to as stringent and efficient regulations as that of the sea-otter. The island is divided into a number of well-defined districts (19 in Bering Island) for fox-hunting purposes, in each of which there is a hut (*yurt*, or *odinotska*) for the hunters. All the males between 18 and 60 years take part in the hunt, which ordinarily begins on November 10 (old style) on Bering Island, and November 20 (old style) on Copper Island, closing December 31. In each district a certain number of men, forming a gang, are detailed. Each gang hunts in common, and the proceeds of the hunt are divided according to shares, or each man to take his own foxes, as each gang may decide. As the various districts are more or less productive, a certain rotation is established so that each man has his chance at the best places as his turn arrives. Care, however, is taken that the old men are located in the more comfortable places.

The following table shows that the number of foxes decreases greatly when they are hunted for several successive years. The hunt is therefore suspended for one or two seasons, with intervals according to circumstances, in order to give the animals time to recuperate. The importance of the hunt is also shown, and the relative scarcity of the white phase.

Number of foxes killed on Bering and Copper islands, 1871–1883.

Bering Island.			Copper Island.	
Season.	Blue foxes.	White foxes.	Season.	Foxes.
1871–72	836	4	1872	100
1872–73	580	28	1873	457
1873–74	514	21	1874	447
1874–75			1875	
1875–76	1,087	50	1876	696
1876–77	573	19	1877	
1877–78			1878	
1878–79	789		1879	691
1879–80			1880	503
1880–81			1881	
1881–82	1,447	20	1882	1,033
1882–83	872	13		
Total	6,698	158	Total	3,927

The blue foxes must now be taken in traps exclusively. Shooting them is entirely forbidden, and as the foxes mostly live near the coast it is also forbidden to travel with dog sledges and to fire any shot near the coast after September 1 (old style). It was found that by digging them out of their holes females were mostly obtained, and this method has consequently been prohibited. The dried skins are sold to the company at a fixed price. As the natives are now paid 14 rubles for each first-class fox skin and 7 rubles for each second-class skin, it will be seen that the foxes are a valuable source of income to them.

Owing to the ease with which the natives could procure seal meat for food, they have paid but little attention to other means of subsistence, particularly as the ready money obtained from the company for skins and work secured sufficient variation from the company's stores, whence they also obtain their flour, hard bread, tea, sugar, etc., not to forget canned provisions. As a result, the sea fishery does not yield what it otherwise might. On Copper Island, however, the natives catch some cod and halibut. They have a tolerably good boat harbor and many boats. On Bering Island however, the lack of a sheltered harbor and landing-place is a great drawback. On the other hand, the rivers and creeks of Bering Island are filled with salmon during the summer months, thus yielding the natives an abundant supply of fish for themselves and their dogs. The Saranna River is particularly important in this respect, The salmon are here caught in a substantial weir built across the river at the village of Saranna. During each summer nearly all the women are kept busy cleaning and drying from 60,000 to 100,000 salmon (pls. 60, 61). The weir is kept open from Saturday night to Monday morning to allow fish to ascend the river and lake to spawn. The bulk of the salmon put up belongs to the two species "Krasnaya riba," or redfish (*Oncorhynchus nerka*), and kisutch, or silver salmon (*O. kisutch*).

There is very little game now to hunt on the islands. The natives are very fond of the meat of the various sea birds, especially early in spring, and being provided with modern breech-loading guns and an unlimited supply of ammunition,[1] the result is that birds have become comparatively scarce—very much so, in fact—near the villages. Ptarmigans (*Lagopus ridgwayi*) are, I believe, still numerous on Bering Island.

During their lease Hutchinson, Kohl, Philippeus & Co. introduced a herd of Kamchatka cattle on Bering Island and kept it at an expense entirely disproportionate to the benefits derived. The company has given up keeping cows, but the cattle have passed into the hands of the natives, while the white families on the island also have a few head to keep them supplied with milk. It has been supposed that cattle-raising might have a future on Bering Island, but past experience disproves the prediction, at least with the present breed of cattle. It has even been suggested "that these sturdy cattle might be advantageously introduced into the Aleutian Archipelago," but aside from the fact that it requires a good deal of care and fodder to bring them successfully through the winter, even on Bering Island, the breed is highly objectionable from the fact that the cows refuse milk the moment their calves are taken away from them.

On the other hand, I firmly believe that with a suitable breed sheep-raising could be made a success, not only on the Commander Islands, but on the American Aleutian Islands as well. The climate is not more severe nor more moist than on some of the

---

[1] Mr. Kluge says the natives on Copper Island annually use 800 to 900 pounds of gunpowder.

Scotch islands, or the Faeroes, where sheep raising and fishing are the main industries. But, of course, if an experiment is to be made, it must not be undertaken with sheep from California or some other country with a climate differing widely from that of the islands. It is imperatively necessary that a race like the Scotch black-face be employed; otherwise, the experiment would be sure to be a failure; but with proper precautions, and under the guidance of experienced men, I feel convinced that sheep-raising would be the proper solution of the food question in the Aleutian Islands.

On Bering Island the sledge dogs would be an insurmountable obstacle to the introduction of sheep. As a matter of fact, however, the dogs are now of but little use, and should be exterminated—the sooner the better. The increasing number of boats have made the dogs superfluous along the coasts and for inland transportation, particularly from the main village, Nikolski, to the North Rookery. The introduction of a few Kamchatkan ponies would do the work much more satisfactorily, as proven by the success of the mules on the Pribylof Islands. In the fall of 1882 a couple of horses were brought over from Petropaulski, let loose, and allowed to take care of themselves during the entire winter, which was a rather severe one. The winter gales swept the level places nearly bare of snow and the horses found more than plentiful food in the dry grass thus exposed. So far from suffering hunger, the horses in spring were found to be slick and well fed; in fact, in better condition than when they arrived on the island. They were afterwards sold to a native, but died later, a circumstance undoubtedly due to the ignorance or lack of care of the owner.

The sledge-dogs are still one of the most interesting features of Bering Island. There must be at least 600 dogs in Nikolski, but while formerly they were allowed to run loose, and afterwards kept chained outside of the owner's house, Mr. Grebnitski has of late years banished all the dog-pens to the sand-hills back of the village, much to the improvement of good order and comfort in the village. Each dog has a hole in the ground large enough for him to lie down in while chained to a stout pole near by. Here they pass their days howling or sleeping, when not out traveling. For traveling a number of them, mostly 11 or 13, are hitched in pairs to a low sledge. A trained leader is tied on in front. This is an intelligent and valuable animal, and is guided entirely by the driver's voice. In winter, on the snow, such a team will haul a load weighing 400 pounds, and I have traveled 40 miles in a day, though without any baggage worth mentioning. But they are also used in summer on the bare ground. Of course, the rocky places are avoided as much as possible, and the summer tracks are preferably located over the marshes and in the low places. On frequented routes, as between Nikolski and North Rookery, or Saranna, the constant travel has worn deep ruts in the ground—in some places 2 to 3 feet deep. These ruts being veritable ditches, drain the surroundings, and are, therefore, usually in a very slippery condition, to which the droppings of the dogs add materially, making it fast if not pleasant traveling. Some of these routes are shown by dotted lines on the map of Bering Island (plate 4).

Most of the dogs differ greatly from the Kamchatkan dogs, belonging, in fact, to an entirely different race. They have large, hanging ears, and were originally brought to the island from Okhotsk. Of late years teams of Kamchatkan dogs, which have erect, pointed ears, and are very much like the ordinary Eskimo dogs, have been imported, as the original hang-eared dogs were degenerating from inbreeding, and now mongrels of all possible shades and with ears of all possible shapes are common enough. The hang-ear dogs are furthermore distinguished by having the regular dog bark, while the Kamchatkan dogs can only howl.

The recent introduction of reindeer into Bering Island seems to have been a success. Hutchinson, Kohl, Philippens & Co., in 1882, by the efforts of Dr. B. Dybowski, secured 4 male and 11 female reindeer in Kamchatka, which were safely landed on Bering Island July 15. During the following winter 2 females were killed by natives, but the herd increased by the birth of 6 or 7 calves. The reindeer took up pastures in the southern, mountainous part of the island, and are said to have multiplied rapidly. I did not see them in 1895, but I heard estimates of their number varying between 600 and 1,000 deer. A careful selection of bucks for killing would add to the fresh-meat supply, and at the same time promote the rapid increase of the herd.

It is not improbable that the reindeer might do well on Copper Island, in spite of the smaller size of the island, but I am inclined to the belief that the introduction of a *suitable, hardy race of goats* would be a better investment.

A few hens and tame ducks are kept in the villages on both islands.

A glance at the meteorological tables, pages 13–17, will show that any agriculture, in the proper sense of the word, is out of the question. On Bering Island there is a half-hearted, half-successful attempt at raising a few vegetables. Formerly most of the native families had "gardens" at Staraya Gavan, where turnips and potatoes were raised with varying success. The place was entirely too far from the main village, however, and new gardens have been started at Fedoskia, on the west coast, a few miles south of Nikolski. In 1895 there was only one man who still had a vegetable patch at Staraya Gavan. I believe that this industry could be made more successful if the natives were taught proper methods. One common error now committed is that all the vegetables are planted entirely too close together. It would also be necessary to look out for hardy plant seeds and seed potatoes raised in a northern climate.

The *fuel* used by the natives consists of coal and birch wood, the latter brought from Kamchatka and sold by the company, and of driftwood collected by the natives along the beaches. The latter article is very uncertain and is now often very scarce, though formerly abundant enough. Coal, on account of the long transportation, is expensive, and, like the birch wood, requires cash to purchase it. A couple of ship-loads of the latter are required every year, and while the supply in Kamchatka is almost limitless at the present time, yet it is not so accessible now at places where there are people to cut it and where it can be loaded into a vessel. With the decreasing number of seals affecting the revenues both of the natives and of the company, the day does not seem distant when the former will be unable to buy, while the latter may find it unprofitable to have a steamer constantly plying between the islands and Kamchatka. Knowing, moreover, that the fuel question was a grave one on the other Aleutian Islands and that peat bogs may be expected to be found on many of the latter, as they occur on Bering Island, I undertook, in 1883, to investigate them and to bring samples of peat home for analysis. East of Nikolski, behind the sheltering hills and sand-dunes, a large swamp extends back to the foot of the three Savanna Baidar Mountains, covering several square miles. In suitable localities large beds of peat of excellent quality are found. On June 15, 1883, I had a couple of men cut about 350 pieces of peat from near the surface. The pieces, averaging about 2 by 16 by 8 inches, were spread out on a hillside to drain, and ten days later they were stacked in pyramids in such a manner that the intervals between the pieces gave the air uninterrupted circulation between them.

When leaving the island in the autumn I found the pieces of good consistency and took a fair quantity with me to have the properties of the peat tested. They were turned over to Dr. Fred. P. Dewey, then curator of metallurgy at the United States National Museum, who kindly furnished me with a report of his analysis of the peat, which he found of good quality. It should be observed that the peat was from the surface, and therefore not nearly so good as it would have been if it had been taken deeper down. Dr. Dewey's report has never been printed, and, in view of the great importance of this question, both for Bering Island and the other Aleutian Islands, I think it well to submit it in full:

REPORT ON PEAT FROM BERING ISLAND.

As received, the sample consisted of about 30 slabs of the peat, most of them of considerable size, so that it can be considered as a fairly average sample; since, however, it had been collected several years, it was unusually dry. It was first tested by building a fire under a small boiler. It ignited with great ease and gave off its volatile matter at a low temperature, forming a good, solid flame without much smoke and giving off a good amount of heat. It required only a small amount of kindling wood to thoroughly start the fire, and after it was once started and had been thoroughly observed it was left to itself, and at the end of five hours it still had vitality enough to ignite fresh material, showing that it had good staying power. If there had been sufficient material on hand to build a large fire, it would probably have held its fire for 15 to 20 hours, but only a small fire could be built, and the result is very satisfactory. A small piece was cut off from each large piece and the small pieces properly ground and sampled for a chemical analysis, which yielded the following results:

Water	7.60
Volatile matter	51.97
Fixed carbon	22.06
Ash	18.37
	100.00

As might be expected from the time since the sample was collected, the analysis shows an unusually small amount of water, and while the ash is rather high, the whole analysis shows the peat to be above the average in its contents of actual combustible material, and that, therefore, it would undoubtedly form a very valuable fuel in the country where it is found.

As prepared for use by simply air-drying, peat frequently contains from 15 to 25 per cent of water, and unless artificial heat is used in drying it is not probable that this one could be dried to less than 20 to 25 per cent of water; and on this basis its composition would be—

Water	20.00	25.00
Volatile matter	45.00	42.19
Fixed carbon	19.10	17.90
Ash	15.90	14.91
	100.00	100.00

These results compare favorably with the following analysis of a peat from Devonshire, England, which has been used extensively for fuel:

Water	25.56
Volatile matter	35.41
Fixed carbon	29.30
Ash	9.73
	100.00

Should it be necessary to use artificial heat, it could, of course, readily be obtained by the combustion of a portion of the peat itself in a suitably designed furnace.

I am satisfied that this peat will make an excellent fuel, and that the proper steps should be taken to introduce its use among the natives of the region.

Most of the natives on both islands live in neat frame *houses*, built and presented to them by Hutchinson, Kohl, Philippeus & Co., instead of the damp and filthy sod huts (here called *yurt*) which they formerly lived in. If properly located and built, however, the sod-house is well suited to the climate and the needs of the people, and the munificence of the above company ceasing with the expiration of the lease, the Zholti Mys natives, as well as many a new-wed young couple, have erected new sod huts. These are built over a wooden frame, lined inside with boards, and the site properly drained (plates 15*b* and 16*a*).

Nowadays the males *dress* almost exclusively in imported ready-made clothes, and the women make themselves dresses of calico or woolen goods, though for heavy overcoats and capes they wear also imported ready-made articles. Even the latest fashions penetrate rapidly to these distant shores. My surprise may well be imagined at seeing girls there last year wearing gay-colored waists with enormous "leg-o'-mutton" sleeves! Ready-made shoes are also used in great quantities, for although a few men have been taught shoemaking, comparatively little repairing is done. The old home-made garments are going out of use. The old rain-coat, made of dried seal-guts, is being laid aside for the oil coat, and the native *torbassi*—moccasins made of seal skin or the inside throat-lining of the old bull seals—are giving way to rubber boots. Even the baidarka, the graceful skin canoe, is a thing of the past, as the sea lion has become nearly exterminated on the islands, and the same fate has befallen the large skin baidaras, great lighters made of a framework of wood over which was stretched sea-lion skins sewed together. The framework is taken apart and used for other purposes, and the steamers' boats do the work of the baidara.

The *municipal institutions* of the two Commander Island communities are particularly interesting, not only because they are peculiar, but because they differ so radically on the two islands. The system on Bering Island is one of nearly pure communism, while on Copper Island it may be termed individualistic by comparison. The local administration has of course a great power and influence, but the natives have also a great deal to say in regard to their own affairs. They elect for a certain term a chief and an assistant chief, subject to the approval of the administrator or local governor. The chief, in a measure, represents the community, and through him all communications to the natives have to go. This is particularly the case with reference to the company and its agents, who have absolutely no authority whatsoever over the natives, much less over the chief. The men attend to their internal affairs, receive the Government's communications, and hold their elections in their assembly house. The chief's business, among other things, is to see that the governor's orders are executed, that work to be undertaken is properly done, and that the moneys coming to the natives are properly distributed, etc. If I wanted a team of dogs and sledge I could not arrange with any native I pleased, but had to notify the chief, who would then send me the one whose turn, as duty or privilege, it would be to furnish the dogs.

A specified tariff for all work is provided. On Bering Island the total proceeds from the seal killing, 1.50 rubles per skin, is paid into the community fund and then distributed according to shares, each family, according to the individual rating of the members, receiving a certain number of shares and fraction of shares. For this the able-bodied men have to do the community work, including the sealing, without further compensation. On Copper Island an entirely different system prevails. There each family is paid for each skin which a member of the family brings to the salt-house. Hence men, women, and children are engaged in the work, each family trying to bring in as many skins as possible. This system has been found necessary there, as the population would have been entirely inadequate to handle the catch if the Bering Island scheme had been adopted. It has resulted in overworking the Copper Islanders, especially the females; but I am not certain that their more cheerful and independently open character, as contrasted with the more sulky and indifferent aspect of the Bering Island natives, is not due to the competition, on one hand, and the paralyzing communism on the other.

The *religion* of the natives is, of course, the orthodox Russian Greek-Catholic faith. They have built a fine and expensive church on each island. They also support a priest on each island, and on Bering Island an assistant priest or "diakon." The moral plane of the church—its methods, men, and members—is similar to that of the same institution in Alaska.

Schools are provided for both islands and housed in roomy and well-lighted buildings, very creditable in every respect. The children are provided with all the modern improvements in school furniture, as well as apparatus for object lessons, maps, and colored charts of animals and plants decorating the walls, on which, over the teacher's rostrum, also hang the portraits of the tsar and the tsarina. Whether the knowledge received by the boys and girls is up to the fine apparatus, I am not able to say. Anyway, the boys used to write a good hand, at least when the late Mr. Volokitin taught them. I also saw the apparatus of a modern school gymnasium, but as it was outside the schoolhouse and being painted dead-black, I surmise that the authorities had come to the conclusion that it was carrying coal to Newcastle to give the outdoor children of Aleut extraction the additional physical exercise of indoor gymnastics.

A *doctor*, appointed and paid by the Government, is now stationed on Bering Island, with a good drug store on each island. He has for an assistant a "feltcher" or barber, a native boy who has undergone a training at Vladivostok. The midwife, sent out from St. Petersburg by the authorities there, must also be regarded as the doctor's assistant.

A.—BERING ISLAND.

GENERAL DESCRIPTION.

Bering Island, the northwestern island of the Commander group, is situated between (approximately) $55°\ 22'$ and $54°\ 42'$ north latitude and $165°\ 40'$ and $166°\ 41'$ east longitude (pl. 4). Its greatest length from northwest to southeast is a little less than 50 miles, the average width being about 10 miles.

Two outlying islets, both not far from the northwestern extremity, properly belong here—*Toporkof Island*, a flat-topped, low island, about 2 miles west of the main village, and *Ari Kamen*, on older charts usually called Sivutchi Kamen, a higher basaltic rock, with a two-peaked top, $4\frac{1}{2}$ miles farther west.

The southern two-thirds of Bering Island are exceedingly mountainous, with peaks rising to about 2,200 feet. The maximum elevation is nearer the western side than the eastern, and the rise from the sea consequently more abrupt along the former coast, the mountains sloping more gently toward the east. The valleys, as a rule, are shorter, narrower, and V-shaped on the west side, longer and more open on the other. The passes are usually high, 600 to 1,000 feet, but at one place, viz, between *Gladkorskaya* on the west coast and *Polarino* on the east, the two valleys are continuous, with a very low watershed, thus dividing the mountains into two separate masses. In these the peaks, ridges, and intervening valleys are distributed without any apparent regular system. In the northern mountain mass, however, it is easy to recognize a dominating central stock between *Polutosnaya* and *Bayan*, from which several of the largest streams of the island radiate west, north, and east, as, for instance, *Polutiosnaya*, *Fedoskia*, *Kamennaya*, the *Staraya Garan* River, and the *Bayan* River. The most conspicuous mountain of the southern mass, and in fact the highest on the island, is the one which I have named Mount Steller.[1] It is located just south of the low valley between Gladkovskaya and Polavino, mentioned above, and is particularly impressive and beautiful viewed from the latter place. The mountains grow more forbidding and precipitous as the southern extremity of the island is approached, the last cape, a bold and knife-sharp promontory, the Stolehnoi Mys, better known as *Cape Manati*, being particularly picturesque.

The northern third of the island has an entirely different aspect from the remainder. In a general way it may be described as being low, the highest elevation being but slightly more than 600 feet. In reality it consists of a series of usually well-marked terraces. First comes the present beach followed by a steep coast escarpment averaging about 30 feet. In the deep bays this escarpment recedes inland so as to inclose the lakes formed by the rise of the land, and the heaping up by the sea of gravel and sand in front of them. Then follows a strip of varying width of nearly level or gently sloping land to the base of an intermediate, often abrupt, terrace, which brings us to an elevation of from 200 to 300 feet. The level following leads to the next and last rise, which is the highest, but also usually the most gentle, though in some places still quite precipitous. The level above this rise forms either large plateaus with a somewhat undulating surface, or the tops of singularly regular, flat-topped table mountains, which the natives, from their appearance suggesting overturned boats, have given the graphic name of *Lotka*, or Baidara, mountains. There are two groups of these table mountains, both very conspicuous when one approaches at sea the main village, viz the *Sereruic Lotki*, two very regular and round tables, between 3 and 4 miles (nautical) north of Nikolski, and the *Saranskie Lotki*, three equally well marked, though less regular mountains, about 5 miles distant to the northeast, on the west side of the great Saranna Lake. The highest altitude of the former group I have measured to be 577 feet; of the latter, 617 feet. The two main plateaus, which are situated north of the great lakes, are the *Northern Plateau* between Cape Zapadnie and Saranna, and *Tonkoi Plateau* from the latter place, where a deep cut, in which flows the Saranna River, separates the two plateaus, to East Tonkoi Mys, the *Cape Waxell* of many charts.

Between the terraced plateaus, which form the foothills and northern extension of the mountainous southern portion of the island, and the two detached table-lands named above, there is a depression extending across the island, which is filled by one very large and a number of smaller lakes, as well as by extensive swamps.

The large lake alluded to, *Saranna Lake*,[2] is quite an imposing sheet of water for so small an island, covering, as it does, an area of about 20 square miles. It connects with the sea at the Saranna village, on the north shore of the island, by means of a short river less than a mile long. The level of the lake is about 40 feet above that of the sea. From the western end of this lake there is almost continuous communi-

---

[1] Deutsche Geograph. Blaetter, VIII, 1885, p. 210.
[2] On some maps called Fedoskia Lake, a name unknown on the island.

cation through a small swamp with two smaller lakes, which empty into the sea at the western side, through the *Ladiginskaya* River. A somewhat larger lake, the *Gavanskoye Ozero*, occupies the center of a large swamp immediately east of the main village. The stream by which it discharges its water passes the latter, and is Steller's Osernaya Reshka. The low land between the lake and sea is protected near the latter by several rows of high sand-dunes from the village to Ladiginsk.

It is a curious fact that Steller (Neuste Nord. Beytr., II, 1793, pp. 266–267) describes this lake as the largest on the island, and that he has entirely overlooked the existence of Saranna Lake. It is pretty good evidence that Steller did not visit that part of the island personally (unless possibly when it was covered with ice and snow) and explains also his omission of mentioning the great North seal rookery. There are a few small lakes, or rather ponds, in the southern mountainous portion, which need no special mention, except the one in *Lissonkovaya* Bay, as the natural conditions there are a miniature reproduction of the Gavanskoye Ozero. It may be added that Lissonkovaya is Steller's Yushin's Valley.

Bering Island has no sheltered harbors, and the few anchorages are indifferent or even dangerous under anything but the most favorable circumstances. The principal anchorage is in the corner off Nikolski, but with southerly or westerly winds it is not safe. It can be approached from the west by keeping close to the south shore of Toporkof Island, in order to avoid an outlying rock off the so-called Vkhodni Point, or Reef. The channel north of Ari Kamen and Toporkof is very dangerous and should be avoided. Farther south, on the same side, are two larger bays, Gladkovskaya and Lissonkovaya, but they are open and no landing can be effected in rough weather. On the east side is Staraya Gavan, the "Old Harbor," where there was formerly a settlement. The bay is small and narrow, with dangerous reefs on both sides.

These reefs are quite a feature of the Bering Island shores. In the northern portion they are mostly of volcanic nature, but in the mountainous portion they consist of stratified rock on edge in such a manner that many of them, especially at Tolstoi Mys and northward, when bare at low tide have the appearance of plowed fields with furrows of great length and regularity. On the stretch of coast just mentioned these reefs form a nearly continuous belt, one-fourth to one-half mile wide, and parallel to the beach. A narrow channel of somewhat deeper water, though only deep enough so that a large boat can be barely pulled and pushed through by low water, extends the whole length between the beach and the reef belt, which is covered by high tide. The continuity of the reef is only broken where some larger stream empties into a slight indenture of the coast, as, for instance, at Komandor, at Polavino, and at Buyan.

The main settlement is at *Nikolski*,[1] so named in honor of Mr. Nikolai Grebnitski, situated at the inner corner of the little bay east of Toporkof Island (pl. 17). The houses are built in several rows on the raised beach at the mouth of the Gavanskaya Reshka and partly upon the sandy slope of the adjacent hills, and being mostly frame structures are painted in many gay, if not always tasteful colors. Prominent also in this respect the new church, dedicated to St. Nicolas, raises its yellow dome over a grass-green roof, while the body is painted pink with white and sky-blue trimmings! The old church of St. Inakenti is still standing, dismantled and neglected.

---

[1] On some maps called Grebnitski Harbor, or Grebnitskoye Seleni.

At the western end of the village is located the new government building with offices for the administrator and the doctor, and next to it the new school-house, both rather large, but uninteresting, lead-colored structures (pl. 17b). In the center of the village is located the company's dwelling-house for the agent (pl. 18a), painted a friendly white and surrounded by the magazines, stores, stable, bath-house, etc. Beyond is the administrator's dwelling, unpretentious, but comfortable (pl. 18b). The sod-huts are relegated to the rear, and, hardly differing from the surrounding grass, are very inconspicuous (pl. 15b).

At *Saranna* (pl. 61) there is quite a village of small houses and huts for the women in summer, when they live there in order to put up the large salmon catch. A small frame chapel was being built last year on the brow of the hill back of the village.

The summer village at *Severnoye*, or the North Rookery, will be described under the head of the latter. There was formerly also a temporary village at Staraya Gavan, to accommodate the people during the planting and harvesting season, but a new one has been built in its stead at Fedoskia, not far from Nikolski.

SEAL ROOKERIES.

It was on Bering Island that Steller, in the spring of 1741, discovered for the first time the rookeries and breeding-grounds of the fur-seals, which he had previously observed traveling northeastward toward unknown regions. His classical descriptions, so well known to all naturalists, need not detain us here, except in so far as they relate to the extent and location of the rookeries. Unfortunately, his works contain very little bearing directly upon this question. In his "Beschreibung der Berings Insel" (Neuste Nord. Beyträge, II, 1793, p. 289) there are a few observations, however, which throw some light on the subject. On the 29th and 30th of April (new style) the shipwrecked crew had killed the first bulls just arrived. Steller at once concluded that they had found the breeding habitat of these animals and hoped for more to follow. He says:

In this hope we were not deceived, for numberless herds soon followed, filling the entire coast to such an extent that one could not pass by without danger to life and limbs; nay, in some places where they covered the whole shore we were often obliged to travel over the hills and rocky places. *These animals landed only on the southern side of the island,[1] opposite Kamchatka, consequently at least 18 versts from the nearest place to our dwellings.* * * * [This was a long way to carry the big bulls, the flesh of which, moreover, was very unpalatable.] But we soon discovered that another smaller kind of fur-seal, grayish of color, which arrived with them in still greater numbers, had a much tenderer and more palatable meat, without odor, which consequently could be eaten without nausea. *We discovered also a nearer road to these directly south from our dwellings*, scarcely more than half as long as the former.

From these quotations it is perfectly plain that at the time of the discovery of Bering Island there were no breeding-grounds or rookeries on the east side of the island; that there were well-filled breeding-grounds on the west side; that these were situated on the shore where now are located the few hundred females forming the Poludionnoye, or South, Rookery, and that vast numbers of bachelors hauled up in Lissonkovaya Bay, where there are none now, nor have there been any apparently within the memory of the natives residing on the island.

---
[1] Steller applies the term "south side" to the entire shore, which from our better knowledge of the topography of the island we would call the western shore. It is evident from various statements in his works that he did not visit the true northern shore between Cape Waksell and Zapadni Mys.

The destruction of this hauling-ground must be credited to the same parties who accomplished the extermination of the sea-cow in twenty-seven years.[1]

At the present day there are only two distinct rookeries on Bering Island, the principal one being located on the northern coast of the island, the other, a small affair, on the west coast.

THE NORTH ROOKERY. (Plate 7.)

The great North Rookery (*Severnoye lezhbishtche*) is situated on the northernmost prolongation of the island (Severni Mys; also called Cape Yushin) about 11 miles from the main village, Nikolski, and about 10 miles from the northwest cape, Zapadni Mys. The north plateau of the island recedes here from the sea, leaving a broad, level tundra, which slopes gently northward toward the sea, ending abruptly in a steep escarpment, about 30 feet high, between which and the water a flat beach, about 400 feet wide, extends all around the point.

From this beach a long, rocky reef, of volcanic origin, extends for half a mile nearly due north, ending in a somewhat isolated high rock, the so-called Sea-lion rock (*Sivutchi Kamen*). The terminal half of this reef is very low and, with the exception of the scattered larger rocks, under water at high tide; in fact, it requires very low water to be able to walk out to the Sea-lion rock. The basal half is formed by a slightly raised, long and narrow peninsula, about a quarter of a mile long by 400 feet wide, the central portion of which constitutes a hard, gravelly beach about 10 feet above mean tide, and gently sloping toward the water on both sides, and fringed, except at the base, by the rocky reef. The northern two-thirds of this gravelly central portion is covered with fragments of shells of mollusks and echinoderms, so that it appears quite white, for which reason this part of the rookery is often spoken of as "the sands"; the basal third is covered with a very rank growth of *Elymus mollis*, continuous with the fields of the same grass which line the inner portion of the beach up to the escarpment. The vegetation is now gradually extending in a wedge-shaped point northward over the central part of "the sands." Several isolated rocks surround the rookery on both sides, as well as numerous sunken reefs.

From the base of the projecting point thus described, which is specifically designated as the Reef Rookery (*Riforoye lezhbishtche*), the coast trends east and is fringed with the same rocky reef as the rookery itself; but the seals do not haul up on these rocks, and they form no part of the rookery. The bay thus inclosed is comparatively shallow and sheltered, forming the principal playing-ground of the pups. Here they learn to swim. Near the south shore the rocks mark off a series of shallow lagoons.

From the western side of the "Reef Rookery," the base of which is here marked off by a detached rock, called *Babin*, or Babinski Kamen, the coast trends south-southeast. The beach shows the same characteristics, viz, an inner grass-covered belt, followed by a narrow, pebbly belt more or less whitened by broken shells and fringed by an outer rocky reef, which by low water embraces innumerable very shallow lagoons.

The grassy belt is widest (fully 400 feet) toward the reef, and the escarpment is here nearly obliterated by a little creek coming from the south. Its mouth is usually dammed up by the pebbles and gravel thrown up by the sea, and the grassy belt in this locality is therefore intersected by numerous connected pools of nearly stagnant water.

---

[1] L. Stejneger, How the Great Northern Sea Cow (*Rytina*) Became Exterminated. American Naturalist, XXI, December, 1887, pp. 1047-1051.

Farther south the escarpment again assumes its precipitous aspect and approaches nearer to the beach.

About five-eighths of a mile from the base of the "reef" the rocky beach projects again a little and, as the coast line beyond takes a more southerly turn, a corner is formed which the natives designate as *Blizhni Mys*. Just before this "cape" there is an expansion of the gravelly part of the beach which, like "the sands" of the reef, serve the seal hauling up in this neighborhood as a "parade" ground. This portion of the beach is now called *Kishotchnaya*. The patch of breeding seals located here are known as *Kishotchnoye lezhbistche* or (rarely) *Blizhnoye lezhbistche*.

Beyond Blizhni Mys the reef fringe, as well as the grassy belt, again expands, the escarpment retreating from the coast, only to reapproach farther south at another promonotory which is well marked by two high, grass-covered, mound-like masses of rock, the so-called Great *Maroshishnik*, or Maroshnik, and Little Maroshnik. Beyond this point the coast forms another slight bay, fringed with reefs, like the foregoing, but not so wide. This is *Kisikof*, and as this is the last point where seals are known to have hauled up *regularly*, it may be regarded as the southern end of the great North Rookery.

The *killing grounds* are located on the gentle slope (about 3 in 100) above the escarpment, about 600 feet southeast of the base of the reef. The ground is here smooth and covered with a short, fine grass. The upper end is pitted all over with holes dug 4 to 6 feet deep and about 6 feet wide, used by the natives as "silos," into which they place the seal meat, intestines, etc., destined for winter food for the sledge-dogs. In addition, boxes and barrels are likewise scattered over that part of the ground, and in these the natives salt the seal meat for their own use (pl. 19a).

The *driveways* on this rookery are short and easy. From the reef the drive is scarcely three-eighths of a mile long, for the least part over the rocky beach, and for the greater portion through the shallow lagoon at the base of the reef and across the fields of rank grass. The ascent up the escarpment is scarcely 30 feet high, with an incline of about 35°. The road there is worn perfectly bare of vegetation and in wet weather is somewhat slippery, but not enough so as to cause a serious impediment to the drive.

The driveway from the southern end of the rookery is considerably longer, from Kishotchnaya, for instance, nearly three-fourths of a mile; but as it is partly over the same beach upon which the seals themselves haul up and travel about with ease, and partly over the inner grassy belt of the beach, no special hardship is involved. The killing-grounds are reached from the west side, where the escarpment is locally interrupted, and the gentle slope beyond extends down to the water.

The company's *salt-house* is located 500 feet north of the killing-grounds, at the extreme north end of the escarpment, and its reddish-brown walls and roof are visible all around for a considerable distance, being, in fact, the best landmark on this part of the island. It is a frame building, originally 45 by 26 feet, with a later eastern addition 20 by 24 feet. On the north side a plank "chute" and stairs lead down the escarpment to the beach below (pl. 21).

Southeast of the killing-grounds, about 1,200 feet from the beach, and between 60 and 70 feet above the sea, the mud-hut *village* of the natives, where the men live during the killing season, is located, and directly in front, north of the new huts, the only wooden dwellings of the place, one belonging to the Russian Government, in which the kossak and his family reside, the other (16 by 20 feet) built by the company for its employees. Formerly the company's "sealer" lived in a small frame-hut just east of the salt-house, but this is now used for storing salt in sacks, while the kossak occupied a mud-hut, or yurt, a little farther east (pl. 25b).

There has of late years been several distinct yurt or mud-house villages at this rookery. The first one was situated just back of the coast escarpment, west of the salt-house, and between it and the present driveway, scarcely more than an eighth of a mile from the rookery. This was inhabited until 1877. In 1878 Mr. Grebnitski ordered the village to be moved back and the new yurts were built an eighth of a mile southeast of and farther up on the hill than the former. The yurts, or barabras, were low and small and dark, musty and dirty, and have recently become entirely unfit for use. A series of new ones have now been erected and others are still being built immediately east of the former site, and these are in every way supplied with "modern improvements," inasmuch as they are comparatively large, dry, and provided with windows. They are built entirely above ground, and constructed of uprights rammed into the ground and covered on the inside with boards nailed on lengthwise. The walls and roof are then covered with a thick layer of sod (pl. 16a). On the whole, they are rather comfortable and warm, being certainly more suited to the climate and the wants of the people than the ordinary frame houses.

The appended map of this rookery (pl. 7) is the result of a traverse plane-table survey made July 9 to 19, 1895, in the intervals between the rain and fog. A base line, exactly one-fourth of a statute mile long, was carefully measured off on the level ground to the west of the salt-house. About 100 angles, from 14 stations, were measured. Another map of the same rookery was made by me in 1882-83, but on a considerably smaller scale, by means of an azimuth compass and pediometer. The new and more detailed survey confirmed the accuracy of the old map. There has never been published any map of this rookery.

THE SOUTH ROOKERY.

The South Rookery of Bering Island (*Poludionnoye lezhbishtche*) is now a very insignificant affair. As mentioned above, it is the only remnant of the countless numbers of seals which Steller saw on this side of the island. Situated at 55° 57′ north latitude, on the west coast of the island, halfway between Northwest Cape and Cape Manati and nearly 16 miles in a straight line from the village Nikolski, it occupies a narrow, curved beach under the steep bluffs of the coast escarpment, which here rises perpendicularly from 60 to 100 feet high. A beautiful waterfall in the next bight to the east forms a very conspicuous landmark (pl. 32b), and three-fourths of a mile to the westward is one of the most perfect natural arches, which I have named Steller's Arch (pl. 27b).

The *rookery beach* is hemmed in both at the west end and the east by projecting spurs of the escarpment, and at the corresponding corners long rocky reefs run out into the sea, inclosing and protecting a shallow bay which, in spite of the openness of the coast, forms a safe harbor for the pups. The beach itself, hardly 100 feet wide, consists of an outer pebbly and rocky portion with a rather steep incline toward the water and an inner narrow and level belt covered with very tall vegetation, mostly *Elymus* and *Heracleum*.

The breeding seals occupy part of the pebbly beach, also hauling up on the outlying rocks of the reef.

The *driving* is made along the beach toward the east, and although not long, the entire distance being about 2,000 feet, is somewhat harder than on the North Rookery, as the seals have to be driven mostly over sand and round loose stones. The ascent to the *killing-grounds* is steep and high, about 50 feet, leading from the boat landing up past the house, where the few natives live, and the small *salt-house* beyond (pl. 32a).

The accompanying map of the South Rookery (pl. 9), as the title indicates, is but little more than a sketch map. The time I had at my disposal was very limited, and did not suffice for a very accurate survey, or to measure off a reliable base line. The photographs I secured, however, testify amply to the general correctness of the map, and it is confidently asserted that the relative distances and angles are sufficiently accurate for all practical purposes. It is the first map published of this rookery.

B.—COPPER ISLAND.

GENERAL DESCRIPTION.

Copper Island (*Ostrof Miedni*), so called from the native copper, of which small quantities have been found from time to time near its northwestern extremity, lies between 54° 53' 30'' and 54° 33' 30'' north latitude and 167° 28' 30'' and 168° 9' east longitude (approximately). It is very mountainous, long and narrow, the length being nearly exactly 30 miles, the average width about 2 miles. The general trend is northwest to southeast, like that of Bering Island, from which it is distant only about 29 miles.

The northwestern extremity is formed by a projecting cape, continued in two characteristic and bold, detached rocks, the Sea Otter Rocks, *Bobrovi Kameni*. From this point to the southeast end, which is marked by several smaller conical rocks, the island consists of a backbone of peaked mountains from 1,000 to 2,000 feet high and connected by ridges varying from 500 to 900 feet high. Only in two places is this backbone broken, viz. near the northern end, where the Bobrovi Valley, between Pestshanaya Bay on the east side and Bobrovaya Bay on the west shore, cuts deep down to about 350 feet above the sea, so that Copper Island seen from a distance—for instance, from the opposite shore of Bering Island—looks like two distinct islands. The other place is near the south end. A very narrow and low neck only 900 feet wide and 75 feet high, very properly named *Peresheyek*, or isthmus, separates the mountains of the south end from the rest of the island.

The highest mountain on the island is *Preobrazhenskaya Sopka*, which rises precipitously above the main village. I have measured it with an aneroid twice, the height being 1,925 feet.[1]

Narrow, deep valleys cut into the sides of the island vertically to its axis. A kettle-shaped end with steep walls usually terminates these valleys, whence originate small creeks or rivulets which occupy the narrow bottom. The sides of the valleys are often quite smooth, the detritus consisting of small, sharp-edged pebbles, often forming long, unbroken slopes with angles from 30 to 40 degrees. The ridges between the valleys, if high, are usually very sharp and narrow.

The shores are mostly high and precipitous. Narrow beaches, covered with large bowlders of rocks fallen down from the cliffs behind, extend with many interruptions around the island, but the latter are so numerous as to make traveling along the beach for any distance impracticable. Cliffs and pinnacles, formed into most fantastic

---

[1] July 23, 1883, 1,921 feet; July 30, 1895, 1,929 feet.

shapes by the action of the waves, rise out of the sea all around the island, sometimes singly, sometimes in clusters. Occasionally large detached or half-detached rocks form more conspicuous landmarks, as, for instance, the Bobrovi Kameni mentioned above, the *Sivutchi Kamen* at the northern entrance to Bobrovaya Bay, and the one of the same name on the other side only a short distance east from the main village, the *Cape Matreya*, *Gladkovski Kamen*, both on the east side, and, most striking of all, perhaps, *Karabelni Stolp* at the rookery.

Outlying concealed rocks are few, except at the northwestern and southeastern capes, where dangerous reefs extend some distance into the sea. Otherwise the water around the island is bold, the farthest rock, to my knowledge, being off *Lebiazhi Mys*, is less than a mile from shore.

The rivers or brooks are necessarily all short and insignificant, hardly any one of them deserving special notice. A few of them, near their mouths, empty into small lakes, which have undoubtedly been formed by the sea throwing up material, thus damming off the inner end of the bay. Such lakes are *Pestshanoye*, just west of the main village; the lake at the end of *Zhirovaya Bukhta*, to the east of it; and *Gladkovskoye Ozero*, in the next valley beyond. The latter is not properly a lake, as the water is strongly brackish, the sea going in at high tide. There are many waterfalls, but on account of the insignificance of the streams, they are of little effect. A few, however, are quite picturesque; for instance, the one at Karabelni Rookery, figured on plate 45.

The entire western coast is very steep, with but few shallow indentations. On the eastern side the valleys are wider and deeper, and open into more or less deeply cut bays, none of which, however, offer sheltered anchorage for vessels much larger than a boat, and as the waves of the Pacific Ocean roll unchecked against the rocks and beaches, landing is often difficult or impossible even at the villages. Only the little rounded cove forming the harbor at the main village is an exception, it being well protected in almost all weather by a cluster of rocks off the entrance. But even this place is not always safe, as demonstrated by the fact that a tide-gauge, solidly built of timber in the most sheltered part of the cove and loaded with rocks, was thrown high on the beach by the surf during the winter of 1882-83.

The main village, called *Preobrazhenskoye*, or the "village of the Transfiguration," because of its church being thus consecrated (pl. 33), is situated on the eastern, or here more appropriately northern, side near the northwestern extremity of the island. Its neat, red-painted frame-houses and the handsome Greek church nestle cosily at the foot of a steep, high mountain, and it looks as if it might be a sheltered and pleasant place, but as a matter of fact it is not. The peculiar shape of the narrow valley at the mouth of which it is located compresses the winds and sends them howling down or up the cleft, while the precipitous walls, nearly 2,000 feet high on the east and south, shut out what little sunshine the island can boast.

Here the natives live all the year round, except during the sealing season, when the village is almost deserted. The company has here its stores and dwelling-house for the resident agent. The government has a large building (the office and dwelling of the assistant administrator), a drug-store, and a large school-house. The house in which the priest and his family live lies farther off, and is not distinguishable from the larger houses of some of the natives. The new church, which was built in 1895, at a cost of $9,000, is quite an attractive building, though entirely too large for the community.

The two "summer" villages in which the natives spend the few months of the sealing season are located on the east side, opposite the corresponding rookeries. The first one from the main village is *Karabelni*, openly situated among the low sand-dunes (pl. 34a). All the houses of the natives are small and poorly built huts, many of them being yurts or mud-huts. The salt-house and the government's house are the most imposing structures. Occasionally some of the families stay here until Christmas, or even the whole winter, but the Aleuts are too social a people to stand for any length of time such isolation for the sake of thrift or economy. The southern village is *Glinka*, picturesquely built on the slope of the steep coast escarpment (pls. 34b and 35); otherwise its general features are like those of Karabelni.

SEAL ROOKERIES.

The character of the Copper Island seal rookeries, owing to the precipitous nature of its coast and the narrowness of its beaches,[1] is very different from those on Bering Island. There is one quite notable similarity, however, viz, that none are situated on the eastern shore of the islands in spite of the fact that this side offers plenty of reefy and rocky places which might apparently answer all requirements. There are no records, to my knowledge, which would indicate that seals ever hauled up on the eastern beaches, and there is no reason to believe that they did.

There are two distinct rookeries on the west side of Copper Island, or, possibly we should say, groups of rookeries. However, while at the present day the various hauling or breeding grounds of each group are distinct and separate enough, they are manifestly only sections of the larger assemblage and are therefore most naturally and conveniently treated as such. These two main rookeries, named Karabelni and Glinka, corresponding to the summer villages of the same name situated opposite, on the east shore, are located in the southeastern half of the island, about 1½ miles apart.

KARABELNOYE ROOKERY

The northernmost of the two main rookeries is Karabelni (*Karabelnoye lezhbishtche*) located south of the village of like name and easily recognized by a very characteristic isolated rock, *Karabelni Stolp*, which rises a hundred feet perpendicularly out of the water at the western extremity of the rookery (pl. 38).

The "Stolp" is connected with the main beach by a low, flat, gravelly neck, the western portion of which is rocky and covered with water-worn bowlders.

The main coast itself is formed by a series of nearly perpendicular bluffs, the rocky sides of which rise above a narrow beach from 200 to 300 feet, and the only way to observe this rookery is from some exposed points on the top of these bluffs. From their projecting angles, in most cases, long rocky reefs run out into the sea, between which small coves with a narrow gravelly beach offer shelter for the breeding seals and their young. The bays thus included commence at a projecting bluff, between which and the sea there is no passage by high water, situated just west of the "Stolp," the first one between these two points being called *Martishina Bukhta*. Next, on the east

---

[1] So steep are the rocky walls behind the Copper Island rookeries and so close do the seals lie to them that falling masses of earth and rocks have occasionally caused the death of many of the animals. Thus it is recorded (Otchet Ross. Amerik. Komp. za 1849, p. 23) that on the 16th of October, 1849, during an earthquake, a rocky wall fell down burying a rookery on Copper Island. Another earthslide on one of the Gliuka rookeries in 1893 similarly resulted in the killing of many seals.

side of the "Stolp," comes *Bolshaya Bukhta*, as the name indicates, the largest of these bays, followed by three small ones, viz, *Staritchkovaya*, *Dalnaya*, and *Nerpitcha*. In Bolshaya Bukhta the hauling-ground is mostly coarse gravel with water-worn stones, up to the size of a fist, strewn over the surface and here and there with large bowlders which have fallen down from the overhanging cliffs. The grounds of the bays to the eastward, on the other hand, are stony reefs of the stratified rock of which Copper Island is mainly built up.

Nerpitcha Bukhta is easily recognized by a graceful waterfall, which overleaps the bluff in a fall more than 200 feet high. It must not be confounded with another waterfall, yet to be described, which forms the characteristic feature of the hauling-ground specifically named Vodopad.

Beyond Nerpitcha the bluffs again rise so abruptly as to allow no passage along the beach beneath them; hence the name of this projecting bluff—*Nepropusk*. Between this point and the next a long rocky reef represents the beach; but the bluffs become gradually lower toward the middle, where a little creek has cut a V-shaped valley and falls over the comparatively low escarpment in a beautiful cascade 65 feet high (pl. 45). From this waterfall the part of the beach between these points is named *Vodopad* and the cape terminating it to the east *Vodopadski Mys*.

This Vodopadski Cape, with its outlying rocks, is the extreme southern point on this part of the coast. It is the promontory seen farthest to the southeast from all points of the coast to the north of it and farthest to the northwest from all points south of it, although it projects but very slightly beyond a line through the westernmost of these points.

From Vodopadski Mys the coast trends a little northward again, being similar in character—viz, a narrow reefy and rocky beach at the foot of the steep bluffs. It is followed by a slight indentation, from which the ascent is so steep and difficult that it has received the name *Krephaya Pad* (the hard valley). It is followed farther east by another *Nepropusk*. Beyond this, a narrow strip of beach is called *Malinka Bukhta*, the "bay" being chiefly due to the projecting reefs at both ends. It is the last beach upon which seals have *regularly* hauled up at Karabelni, and is called the "little bay," in contradistinction to the large bay immediately to the east, which is often called Bolshaya Bukhta instead of *Serodka*—a practice to be discouraged, as it gives rise to confusion with the hauling-ground adjoining the Stolp.

A glance at the accompanying map (pl. 11) and the photographs of this rookery (pls. 38 to 40) will show how exceedingly difficult the taking of the skins must be. The bachelors are chiefly driven from the hauling-grounds at Karabelni Stolp, Vodopad, and formerly Krepkaya Pad and Malinka Bukhta.

From the Stolp the seals are driven northward along the beach of Martishina Bukhta beyond the promontory, which can only be passed by low water, on to the beach of the rather wide and gently curving *Stolbovaya Bukhta*. If the number of seals is so insignificant that the skins can be easily carried on the back and the meat is not wanted in Karabelni village, then they are driven across the little rivulet which here runs into the sea and are killed on the beach just west of it. The carcasses are left at the water's edge for the waves to carry off.

The *driveway* to Karabelni over the mountains is a long and very hard one, being fully $2\frac{1}{4}$ miles long.

In order to facilitate the ascent up the coast escarpment a *stairway* has been built of driftwood logs resting on pegs driven into the ground, as shown in the accompanying photograph (pl. 49b). The upper end of these stairs (68 feet above the sea) enters the little creek mentioned above and the driveway proceeds up the narrow valley. The kettle-shaped upper end of the valley, the sides of which form a slope of about 40 degrees, is separated from a similar kettle on the north side by a narrow saddle. This pass I have determined to be 643 feet.[1] The descent is steep, but not so high as on the south side, and the driveway now follows the bed of the little creek, as the narrow V-shaped valley affords no other road. The lower end of the drive, after it enters the grass-covered sandy plain back of the Karabelni village, where the killing-grounds are situated, is comparatively easy.

The *salt-house* was formerly situated at the front of the village, east of the river and of the large rock in the bay called *Urili Kamen*. The beach there is not very safe or convenient for loading the skins into the boats or landing the salt, for which reason a new one has been built at *Popofski*, the small "bay" just west of Urili Kamen (pl. 63a).

From Vodopad the driveway, if it is deemed necessary to take the meat to the village, is longer by at least a mile over the high plateau northeast of the rookery, besides being very severe in other respects. The grassy slopes of the valley opening at this point are very slippery and steep (about 30°), but the greatest hardship is caused by the exceedingly difficult ascent of the bluff before reaching the valley. The bluff here consists of the naked hard rock, and consequently steps built of drift-wood logs, as at Stolbovaya Bukhta, were out of the question. They had to be roughly cut out of the rock itself, as shown in the accompanying photograph (pl. 45), which will give a better idea of this extraordinary place than any description. It will be seen that the side next to the picturesque waterfall is nearly perpendicular, in fact so steep that the men can not follow the drive up on that side in order to urge the seals on and to prevent them from going down over the precipice. To remedy this a rope is stretched from the top down to the beach, as is plainly shown in the photograph to the right of the fall. When seals are driven, rags and scraps of paper are fastened to this rope, which is kept in constant motion so as to frighten them and urge them on.

It is hardly to be wondered at that the men prefer to let the seals carry their own skins up this road. The top of these stairs is 65 feet above the sea, and I found it pretty hard work to climb it without carrying anything.

At Krepkaya Pad and at Malinka Bukhta there is no possibility of getting the seals up alive; hence they were killed back from the beach and their skins carried across the mountains. At Krepkaya Pad the men alone did the killing and carrying, while Malinka Bukhta was reserved for the women, who did all the skinning and carried the skins to the salt house. Malinka Bukhta is reached along the beach from Serodka, but between it and Krepkaya Pad there is a *Nepropusk* which can not be passed.

The appended map of Karabelnoye rookery (pl. 9), was made in 1883, July 3 to 10. The angles were taken with an azimuth compass and the distance measured with pediometer. In 1895 my stay at the rookery was too short to make an independent plane-table survey, but a blue-print of the old sketch was placed on the table and a few necessary corrections made. A series of photographs taken at the time have also been used in verifying it.

---

[1] Average of 6 observations on July 3 to 8, 1883.

GLINKA ROOKERIES.

The southern, or Glinka, group of rookeries (*Glinkorskoye lezhbishtche*) is situated about 4½ miles southeast of Karabelnoye. They contain the most important hauling-grounds on the island, but at the same time the most inaccessible. The island is here very narrow, yet the mountains average even a greater height than farther north, and the passes between the short and steep valleys on the east and west sides are also very high. The mountains rise precipitously from the sea, bordered only by a very narrow beach of rocks and stones, hardly deserving the name. All the rocks are here stratified, with a very pronounced dip. The projecting capes run out into jagged reefs formed by the exposed broken strata standing nearly on end, while numerous outlying rocks and stones guard the approaches (pl. 47). Singularly formed rocks and pinnacles carved out by the never-ceasing breakers, and saw-tooth promontories mark the ends of the various bays.

The length of the whole beach of this rookery is about 6 miles, but this stretch is not occupied by a continuous line of seals. On the contrary, they are gathered in groups at certain points which, for some reason unknown to us, are preferred to others, although apparently equally suitable. These various seal-grounds are named as follows from west to east: Gorelaya, Lebiazhi Mys, Peresheyek, Urili Kamen, Post-shanoye, Pestshani Mys, Pagani, Zapadni, Sabatcha Dira, Palata, Zapalata, Sikatchinskaya, Gavarnshkaya, and Babinskaya Pad.

Of these, Palata (*Palatinskoye lezhbishtche*) is unquestionably the most important. It is named from the high and sharp promontory which extends farthest out into the sea on this part of the coast, and which somewhat resembles a large house with a steep, peaked roof. The top of it is fully 500 feet above the sea, and the walls are very steep, being in fact nearly perpendicular on the south side. This is *Palata* proper. A very jagged reef extends in a southwesterly direction from the foot of it, and to the northwest are several detached rocks. From one of these, two of the accompanying photographs were taken (pls. 48 and 49). On the north side this promontory is separated from the high mountain walls back of it by a narrow gully, which toward the sea expands into a somewhat open basin, the bottom and sides of which are lined with a pale-buff clay. The beach, a narrow strip covered with large rounded pebbles, extends northward under the clayey banks for several hundred yards, and continues in the same manner under the precipices of one of the higher mountains of this part of the island, rising to 1,400 feet. No particular feature, except a pile of rocks somewhat larger than usual, distinguishes this part of the beach, which is named *Sabatcha Dira*, the "dog-hole."[1]

From here to Pestshani Mys the character of the coast and beach is the same, except that about halfway the overhanging cliffs crowd the beach still more closely, with a small reef at their feet, thus forming a "mys," or cape. *Zapadni Mys*, probably so called because it is situated nearly due west from Glinka village. The gently curving beach between Zapadni and Pestshani Mys is called *Pagani*, the Unclean, for no obvious reason. At this place there is a break in the mountain wall behind, for above the coast escarpment a comparatively wide valley opens up, the drainage from which empties out at Pagani in three distinct streams.

---

[1] There are a number of places on Copper Island called Sabatcha Dira, but they are in all other cases actual holes through the rocks. I have been unable to see the application of the name to that part of the Palata rookery now so designated. Formerly there may have been such a perforated rock, now crumbled to pieces.

The accompanying photographs (pls. 46, 54a) show the character of this beach better than any description.

Pagani terminates at the northern end with *Pestshani Mys*. This is an exceedingly jagged cape of the saw-tooth type, the strata of the rock being nearly vertical and with an outlying detached rock, preventing further passage along the beach. The name, meaning Sandy Cape, has no reference to any characteristic feature of it, but is due to the fact that it forms the eastern termination of *Pestshanaya Bukhta*,[1] Sandy Bay, which extends from this cape northwestward. The western termination of this bay is marked by a slight projection of the beach and a low stony reef, which forms the great *Pestshani hauling-ground*. A comparatively large stream empties into the bay at its inner end, draining a grass-clad valley of considerable size compared with most other valleys in this part of the island, and the coast escarpment is unusually low.

Beyond this hauling-ground the cliffs again approach the sea, and the slightly curved narrow beach, covered with water-worn stones and loose rocks, turns outward in order to pass a slight but very jagged projection of the cliffs, in front of which a low isolated rock on the beach and another in the water beyond the low reef form another attraction for the seals. The rock on the beach, called *Urili Kamen*,[2] Shag Rock, gives this part of the rookery its name (pl. 54b).

The beach from here to the next cape is narrow and rough, covered with water-worn loose rocks from the foot of the steep slope at the back into the sea. This cape terminates in a large, semi-detached, roof-shaped, grass-clad rock, which obstructs the passage along the beach. A low but knife-sharp ridge connects it with the cliffs behind; hence the name of the place *Peresheyek*, or Isthmus, and that of the rock *Peresheyekski Kamen*.

From this point the last cape seen to the west is *Lebiazhi Mys*, which is easily recognized by a pair of cone-shaped twin rocks rising from the extreme end of the reef and several single ones of similar shape nearer the cape, as well as by two detached dangerous rocks situated seaward in the direction of the reef, the outer one fully a third of a mile from the cape. The bay between Peresheyek and this cape is called *Lebiazhaya Bukhta*, Swan Bay; hence the name of the cape. The beach is rocky and stony.

On the other side of Lebiazhi Mys the coast trends more northerly and is visible all the way to Vodopadski Mys, Karabelnoye Rookery. But we are here only concerned with the bay immediately behind Lebiazhi, as it is the last seal-ground at this end of the rookery. The character of the beach differs not from the seal-ground preceding it. Its name is *Gorelaya Bukhta*.

Returning to Palata we notice that from the extreme point of Palatinski Mys the coast trends more easterly. The abrupt walls of the cliffs are even more precipitous, and the beach, utterly inaccessible from the land side, is fringed by wide reefs surmounted by tall isolated rocks assuming the most fantastic shapes as pillars, pinnacles, towers, etc. Projecting corners hem in snug little coves for the breeding seals, while the outlying rocks and reefs break the force of the angry ocean and afford shelter in quiet pools for the growing pups.

---

[1] There are at least four different Pestshanaya Bukhta on Copper Island, a source of great confusion.

[2] Urili Kamen is a common name for various isolated rocks on Copper Island; for instance, at the West Cape of Glinka Bay and in the bay off Karabelni village.

The first of these coves, as the name *Zapalata* (behind Palata) indicates, is situated immediately under the perpendicular southern wall of Palata itself, and guarded on the east side by the pillar-shaped *Stolbi*. The beach itself is narrow, but smoothly covered with small stones rounded and polished by the water and of a very light pearl-gray color. This is, possibly, the most important of the breeding grounds, and is accordingly named by Colonel Voloshinof "Glavnoye Glinkovskoye Lezhbishtche" (Glinka Main Rookery). The name Zapalata, employed by the natives, however, is much preferable, not only because in common use, but also on account of its brevity and euphony (pls. 55, 56).

Sikatchinskaya follows on the other side of the "Stolbi" (pl. 57b), possessing the same main characteristics as Zapalata, merging eastward into *Gavavushkaya Bukhta*.

The end of the latter, or rather the beginning of the next bay, is marked off by a solitary, conical rock rising up in the middle of the reef. It is called *Babin*, and hence the name of the beach beyond, *Babinskaya Bukhta*, and the valley opening at this place several hundred feet above the beach, Babinskaya Pad. The beach is covered with the same water-polished, light-gray stones. This bay at its eastern end is blocked by a very rocky and rough reef, for which the natives only have an Aleut name, *Kalomakh*. This is the eastern end of the Glinka seal rookeries.

The main *killing-grounds* at this rookery are situated on the eastern side of the island, where the village and the salt-houses are located. Only of late years, when many drives have been so small that there were people (men, women, and children) enough to carry the skins on their backs across the mountains, and the meat was not wanted in the village for food, has it been the custom to kill the seals on the west side.

I have already remarked that the hauling-grounds east of Palata are utterly inaccessible from the land side. Formerly, when seals were plentiful, the bachelors used to haul up in great numbers on some of these beaches, notably at Babinski, and if the company's steamer, *Aleksander II*, happened to be at the island at a time when the weather and the waves on the west side of the island allowed boats to land there it was customary for the steamer to take the people around the Southeast Cape and land them at those hauling-grounds. The seals were slaughtered and skinned on the beach, while the pelts were taken on board the steamer and salted in the hull.

On the photograph representing Palata Rookery (pl. 50) a small patch of numerous white dots will be observed on the grass-clad hills near the extreme right of the picture. These white dots are sea gulls feasting on the carcasses of a small drive of seals killed here. It will be seen that this drive was neither long nor could it have been particularly severe. Not so the regular driveway from this rookery to the killing-grounds at Glinka village, a distance of nearly 2 miles over a ridge more than 1,200 feet high. The slopes to be climbed, or slid down, are in places 35° to 40°. They are partly grass-clad, and then very slippery.

From Zapadni and Sabatchi Dira the driveway is somewhat shorter and the pass over the mountain lower, *only* 760 feet, but the ascent is exceeding rough. The lower part follows the bottom of a narrow V-shaped valley—or rather gully—the bed of a short torrent filled with large bowlders, over which the seals have to struggle hard (pl. 58a). Higher up the slope becomes steeper and at the same time covered with a tenacious clay, hence very slippery. Steps have been cut in the ground to facilitate the ascent, but the clayey soil is soon smoothed down and made as slippery as before.

From Pagani the distance is about the same and the pass to be scaled but slightly higher (780 feet), but the ascent is not quite so steep nor nearly so rough, and the drive from this hauling-ground may be characterized as the least severe at this end of the island.

The seals hauling up west of Pestshani Mys used to have the longest of all the driveways on the island and one of the most severe as well. After being driven along the beach for some distance they entered the Pestshani Valley, where the river has cut down the coast embankment, and then had to climb the first ridge on the east side. If the drive was a large one—and in former days drives of 4,000 seals were not rare[1]— it took too long a time to ascend only in one place, so that one portion was driven over the ridge where it was only about 670 feet high, while the other had to climb at least 900 feet up. On the other side of this ridge was a descent into Pagani Valley, then another hill was ascended, and finally a third ridge, 780 feet above the sea, had to be climbed before the final descent into the Gilinka Valley took place. The length of this drive was about 2½ miles, and in warm weather it sometimes took two days to finish it.

This was finally found to be too great a waste of time and energy, and as more salt-house room was required it was decided to drive the seals the shortest way across the island, and as there was a good anchorage and a tolerably decent beach for landing boats, to build a new salt-house there. This is now known as the *Pestshani salt-house* (pl. 58c).

This change has shortened the drive from the rookeries west of Pestshani Mys from 2½ miles to 1½. In addition, there is now only one pass to climb, which my aneroid showed to be about 710 feet above the sea. The ascent is not very steep nor is the road particularly rough, but the final descent to the salt-house is simply a "slide." On the whole, it is now the easiest of the long drives at Gilinka. This, of course, does not mean that the drive is an easy one, and only a fraction of all the seals driven (in 1895 about one-sixth) gets the benefit from it.

The killing-grounds are located on the grassy slope near the beach, just north of the Pestshani salt-house. The killing-grounds at the Gilinka village used to be beyond the houses, but are now moved to near the beach a few hundred yards north of the village. In the latter there are two *salt-houses* close together. One of these has had an addition built to it, so that it is now twice its original capacity (pls. 35, 36).

The map of the Gilinka rookeries (pl. 13) is the result of a traverse plane table survey made during the few intervals from August 4 to 11, 1895, in which the rookeries were free from fog or rain. It was very difficult to find a level locality long enough for a suitable base line. After the map was completed, however, I measured off a line 1,000 feet long on the beach in front of the village and sighted it in on the map.

I had with me a sketch map which I had drawn from sketches and angles obtained in 1883. It was found fairly accurate, especially considering the fact that the fog during my visit in 1883 was so perverse that I never obtained a simultaneous sight of both sides of the island.

---

[1] In 1887 as many as 6,000 seals were taken in one drive at this place, according to Dr. Slunin.

2.—ROBBEN ISLAND.

DESCRIPTION.

Robben[1] Island, a literal translation of its Russian name, *Tiuleni Ostrof*, is situated in the Okhotsk Sea, 11 miles southwest from Cape Patience (*Mys Terpenia*), the end of the curiously long and narrow peninsula on the eastern shore of Sakhalin Island. The position is variously given as 48° 32′ north latitude and 144° 45′ east longitude, or 48° 35′ north latitude and 144° 44′ east longitude (recent Russian charts, while on the manuscript chart of the late Capt. J. Sandman I find given as "corrected longitude," 144° 30′ east).

Not having had an opportunity to visit the island myself, the following description is taken from a number of available sources. The accompanying maps (pl. 6) are copied from recent plans issued by the Russian hydrographic office in 1889.

The island is really hardly more than a large, flat-topped rock, trending northeast by southwest, long and narrow. The entire length of the reefy beach in that direction is about 2,100 feet, while the elevated portion, which rises abruptly to between 40 and 50 feet and tapers off to a point at both ends, measures only 1,400 feet in length. The width of this portion hardly exceeds 150 feet, while the reef surrounding it varies between 50 and 150 feet.[2] On the west side, near the southwestern end, there is a lower place, with somewhat sloping sides, upon which the company's salt-house and the barracks for the Aleut workmen and the naval guard are located. A rocky reef extends to the northwest, terminated by a large rock, the *Sivutchi Kamen*, about 10 feet high, a favorite resort of the sea-lions.

There is no harbor or convenient anchorage, and in bad weather vessels have to seek shelter under Sakhalin. Captain Sandman's manuscript map indicates "anchorage anywhere to northwest of island in from 10 to 20 fathoms; 13 fathoms, sandy bottom, 1 mile off, center of island SE. ¼ E.; end of South Reef S. by E. ¼ E.; end of North Reef and rock ENE. Nearer in rocky bottom."

There is no water on the island.

The climate is naturally more "continental" in its character than on either the Commander Islands or Pribylof Islands, having colder winters and warmer summers, but I am not aware that any regular observations have been published for the island. Mr. C. Carpmael, director of the Meteorological Service of Canada, has furnished a few figures, but they are apparently only based upon curves in the *Challenger* Report and are mere approximations. He states (Fur Seal Arb., VIII, p. 511) that according to these the mean temperature for May would be about 42 degrees, but thinks possibly the mean might be as low as 40 degrees. In June it is "probably about 48 degrees." In July "probably a little under 60 degrees." In August "it must be nearly 60 degrees." In September "it must be a little below 55 degrees." In October "about 44 degrees."[3]

---

[1] Not Robbin Island, or Robin Island, as it is occasionally written.

[2] These figures are taken from Shamof's map (pl. 6). Lieutenant Egerman, I. R. N., gives the following dimensions: Length 1,960 feet; width about 300 feet; height 48 feet (Morskoi Sbornik, 1881, No. 11, Lots. Zam., p. 8). Capt. J. G. Blair says "1,960 feet long, by 175 feet wide, and in places 46 feet high" (Fur Seal Arb., III, p. 194).

[3] According to Shamof (Ausland, 1885, p. 537) the mean temperature at Cape Patience, Sakhalin, was 52.2° F. for June, and 62.4° F. for July, 1881.

The mean temperature of the surface of the water around Robben Island is given by Makarof as 13 degrees centigrade (middle of August).

These temperatures are considerably higher than the corresponding ones at the Commander Islands, and lend color to the statements by Captain Blair and Capt. G. Niebaum, that the Robben Island seals can be distinguished by experts from those on the Commander Islands, and that they do not mingle with them, being a separate and distinct herd (Fur Seal Arb., III, pp. 193, 204).

Very little is known about the movements of the Robben Island seals, except that they migrate southward. I am informed by Capt. D. Greenberg, however, that sealers who are said to have followed up the migrating herd assert that these seals come up the Gulf of Tartary and pass through La Perouse Strait into the Sea of Okhotsk. The feeding grounds of the Robben Island seals seem to be unknown.

The knowledge of the condition of the rookery is also highly fragmentary. When the first sealers arrived there they found the whole beach surrounding the island so occupied by seals that there was no place to effect a landing without driving the seals off. At present the few remaining seals congregate on the very narrow beach on the southeast side of the island.[1] The bachelors are now hauling up on both sides of the breeding females, and so close that many females are caught in the drives.

The various estimates of the number of seals on this island may be somewhat more accurate than similar figures from the other seal islands, because of the small extent of Robben Reef and the ease with which the rookery can be watched. Thus, in 1871, when Hutchinson, Kohl, Philippeus & Co. took possession of the place, Mr. Kluge found that "there were not over 2,000 seals to be found on the entire island." Capt. G. Niebaum, who visited it at the same time as the representative of the firm, states as follows: "The rookeries were also very small, and contained at that time, of all classes, about 800 seals, as I ascertained by a careful count, and, in addition, a small number in the waters adjacent."[2]

In administrative respect Robben Island is under the jurisdiction of the administrator of the Commander Islands and is included in the lease of the latter. In fact, Robben Island is regarded as a dependency of Bering Island, as the men of the killing gang are taken from that island and the money for the Robben Island seals goes to the Bering Island natives. Since 1885 the government has stationed a force of 20 sailors and an officer of the navy on Robben Island, in order to protect it against

---

[1] The breeding-ground, according to Dr. Slunin (Promysl. Bog. Kam. Sakh. Komand., p. 12), occupies about 4-5 sazhen by 70-100 sazhen (a sazhen being equal to 7 feet).

[2] Dr. Slunin (Promysl. Bog. Kam. Sakh. Komand., p. 13) has been able to utilize certain reports by some of the naval officers in charge, from which a few interesting facts are noted: "According to the reports of Lieutenants Rosset (1887) and Brumer (1892) the arrival of the first bulls depends upon whether the ice has disappeared along southern Sakhalin or not; but whether there is any ice present in the Bay of Terpenia or at the mouth of the Taraika is apparently of no significance. Thus, in 1891, the bulls arrived very slowly; on June 5 (old style) there were in all 28 males, 65 females, and one pup; in 1892 the ice also remained late on northern Sakhalin, and on May 15 (old style) there was not one seal on the rookery, the first bull arriving on the 16th of May (old style). In 1893 the first bulls appeared on May 17 (old style) at the coast, although broken ice was lying along the eastern side; the temperature of the water was 2.5° C. Ice was covering the deep water of Terpenia Bay. In 1891, at the end of the period of birth, there were on July 3 (old style) 5,000 females and 4,000 pups, showing one-fifth of the females to be virgin. Lieutenant Brumer notes the following special circumstance: In July and the beginning of August (old style) there were about 15,000 to 17,000 seals, but in September the inhabitants of the rookery had increased considerably."

Dr. Slunin himself, in the beginning of May (old style), 1892, calculated the number of seals on Tiuleni to be from 13,000 to 16,000 all told, allowing 3 square feet to each animal, large and small (op. cit., p. 17). In 1892 the first bulls arrived about May 16 (old style), and the first females May 20 (op cit., p.27). This is contrary to what he states on p. 18, where it is said that in 1892 the bulls arrived about June 15-18 (old style), and the females came ashore on June 26.

the raiders, but apparently with but poor success, judging from the history to be related further on. This failure is partly due to the fact that on account of the severity of the season the guard has been taken off before the middle of October.

As remarked above, the island is included in the lease of the Commander Islands, and Hutchinson, Kohl, Philippeus & Co. took possession of it in 1871. The Robben Island part of the business was attended to chiefly by the schooner *Leon*, Capt. John G. Blair; mate, Mr. E. Kluge. The name of the schooner belonging to the new company is the *Bobrik* (pl. 59b), Capt. D. Grenberg, master, who for many years was first mate on the old company's steamer *Aleksander II* (pl. 59a). The skins have hitherto been shipped to London via San Francisco.

HISTORY OF ROBBEN ISLAND.

The history of this little reef is very interesting and highly instructive as showing how nearly impossible it is to extirpate the seals, either by harsh measures on shore or by excessive raids from marauding vessels.

The existence of seal rookeries on Robben Island was probably first discovered by some of the numerous American whalers frequenting Okhotsk Sea in the early fifties. In a recent statement Capt. G. Niebaum alludes to these early visits as follows:

From information gathered from various sources I learn that Robben Bank was first visited and exploited by whalers about 1852 or 1853, and that in two seasons they obtained some 50,000 or 60,000 skins, almost completely "cleaning it out." I understand that for several years thereafter the occasional vessel which touched there found the rookeries practically deserted. (Fur Seal Arb., III, p. 203.)

Captain Scammon (Marine Mammalia, pp. 150–152) gives an account of a visit of a New London bark to Robben Island in 1854 or 1855, which it may be well to reproduce here:

In the midst of the Crimean war an enterprising firm in New London, Conn., fitted out a clipper bark, which was officered and manned expressly for a sealing voyage to the Okhotsk Sea. The captain was a veteran in the business, and many thought him too old to command, but the result of the voyage proved him equal to the task. The vessel proceeded to Robben Island, a mere volcanic rock, situated on the eastern side of the large island of Saghalien. Many outlying rocks and reefs are about it, making it dangerous to approach and affording but slight shelter for an anchorage. Here the vessel (of about 300 tons) lay, with ground tackle of the weight for a craft of twice her size. Much of the time fresh winds prevailed, accompanied by the usual ugly ground-swell, and in consequence of her being long, low, and sharp the deck was at such times frequently flooded; nevertheless, she "rode out the whole season, though wet as a half-tide rock," and a valuable cargo of skins was procured, which brought an unusually high price in the European market on account of the regular Russian supply being cut off in consequence of the war.

Robben Island was thus "practically cleaned out"; the whaling industry also came to an end, and the very existence of seals on the lonely rock was almost forgotten.

At the breaking up of the great Russian-American Company in 1869, many enterprising citizens of California and Alaska turned their attention to the Pribylof Islands and the Commander group; the Kuril Islands and the Okhotsk Sea attracted the attention of Captain Limachevski. With a schooner manned by Aleuts (Kadiak Islanders?) from Urup Island, the station of the Russian-American Company on the Kuril Islands, he sailed, in 1869, to Robben Island. During the 14 years of rest since the Crimean war the seals had again multiplied to such an extent that they were occupying the entire beach all around the rock, as in the days when first discovered.

THE RUSSIAN FUR-SEAL ISLANDS. 55

The Urup Aleuts, who had never had any experience with the driving of fur-seals, were afraid of the vast numbers which blocked the way, so that no landing was effected, and Limachevski had to sail away.

In 1870, however, the seals did not fare so well. In that year at least two schooners raided the island. Mr. D. Webster, of Pribylof Island fame, arrived there in the schooner *Mauna Loa*, and the number of skins taken on Robben Island was probably more than 20,000.[1]

The island was "practically cleaned out" again, so that when the representatives of the lessees of the Russian Seal Islands arrived on Tinleni in 1871, "there were not over 2,000 seals to be found on the entire island." Capt. G. Niebaum, a member of the firm, landed there in August, and seeing the depleted state of the rookery ordered that no killing should take place there that year, nor, in fact, until "such time as seemed prudent to resume, so as to give the rookeries opportunity to recuperate, leaving strict orders to the guard ship to protect them against molestation." The result of this wise order was that in 1873, not more than two years after, the rookeries had so far recovered that sealing could be commenced again on a small scale, and about 2,700 seals were taken that year by the company, "knowing that the killing of the useless male seals would accelerate the increase of the herd. From this time forward the herd showed a steady and healthy growth,"[2] and would probably have continued so had it not been for the unparalleled boldness of the seal pirates. They fitted out in Japan and sailed under various flags, British, German, Dutch, United States, etc., and from about 1879 paid special attention to searching for hitherto unknown seal rookeries on the Kuril Islands and elsewhere in the Okhotsk Sea, as well as raiding those already well known. Robben Island, being conveniently located, poorly protected by a single schooner and a few Aleuts, and absolutely unprotected later in the season, after the company had finished the legitimate catch, was particularly exposed to the ravages of these marauders. The total number of seals indiscriminately slaughtered by them on that lonely rock will never be known, nor, probably, the names of all the vessels that took part. The following few particulars, however, will give a good idea of the slaughter and the methods.

In 1880 the company's schooner *Leon*, Captain Blair, landed at Robben Island with the Aleut workmen on June 13 and found there already two schooners, the *Otsego* and the *North Star*, though they had been unable to do anything, as the seals had not yet arrived. During the summer schooners were scarce. On June 22 the *Vladimir* touched there; on July 16 the *Stella* came around, and on July 20 the *Flying Mist*. On September 4 the company's steamer *Aleksander II*, Captain Sandman, called and took off the 3,330 skins. Sandman records in his log that he found "on shore a considerable number of pups and females, but very few killing seals." After the lessees' vessel left, however, things became lively. When Capt. A. C. Folger arrived in the schooner *Adèle* he found 11 schooners already assembled there, and he states (Fur Seal Arb., VIII, p. 662) that "altogether we got 3,800 seals; we killed them all or drove them away." It is possibly to the raids of this year that W. F. Upson refers (*tom. cit.*,

---

[1] Webster, according to the British Bering Sea Commission, put the number of skins he assisted in taking at 15,000, but they add that "Kluge's estimate of the number taken was 10,000." When reading this report on Bering Island last summer, Mr. Kluge stated to me that he understood Webster's catch in 1870 to have been about 20,000, and that he did not "estimate" 10,000, as alleged by the commissioners, he not having been there at the time. (Rep. Brit. Bering Sea Commn., p. 80).

[2] Niebaum, Fur Seal Arb., III, p. 203.

p. 724) when he states that he "was on the first schooner that raided Robben Island, the *Matinée*, fitted out by H. Liebes, T. P. H. Whitelaw, and Isaac Leonard," of San Francisco.

In 1881 a number of schooners again hovered around the island, waiting for the guard-ship to leave, even as late as November. About the first of that month Mr. E. P. Miner arrived in the *Janie Cushman* and met three other schooners there. "We went ashore and clubbed the seals. Our schooner's share was 800 skins." (Fur Seal Arb., VIII, p. 704.) Those four schooners, therefore, probably secured about 3,200 skins.

This feature of the schooners raiding in concert is well worth noticing. Captain Folger corroborates it: "We worked together, and the schooners would divide up." The latter also mentions how the schooners succeeded in eluding the vigilance of the guard-ship and making raids during its absence:

> We had the guard [i.e., the Aleut workmen] in our pay, and when the *Leon*, which had been sent there to guard the place, would go away, lights would be put out, and we would come over from Cape Patience, where we had men on the lookout constantly, or if we got impatient the fastest sealer in the fleet would go there and be chased by the *Leon* (a sailing vessel), and the others would make the raid. (Fur Seal Arb., VIII, p. 663.)[1]

The experience of the authorities with the raiders in 1881 led to more vigorous attempts to protect the rookeries. The first step was the issue of the consular warning referred to in detail elsewhere in this report (chapter on Raids of Commander Island Rookeries, p. 120), and to enforce it a stronger force of natives was sent to the island in 1882. They were well armed and under the command of a non-commissioned kossak officer. The proclamation and the presence of patrolling men-of-war had evidently some restraining effect upon the pirates in so far as the Commander Islands were concerned, but the result was only that the raiders concentrated their efforts on Robben Island. At least 13 schooners hovered about that rock in 1882, and, emboldened by the previous success, they actually carried the island by armed force. As the greatest loss to the island usually was inflicted after the guard-ship had left in autumn, most of the raided seals being females and young ones of both sexes, it was determined that the guard should winter there, and the men consequently remained when the *Leon* sailed. Shortly after, 6 schooners anchored off the island and each landed 10 well-armed men. The Aleuts, thus outnumbered, did not dare resist, and were locked up in the house. The crews of the schooners then quite leisurely went about the clubbing of the seals. It is probably to this raid that E. P. Miner, schooner *Otome*, refers when stating that the raiders "landed and killed about 12,000 seals" (Fur Seal Arb., VIII, p. 704). The natives, being thoroughly intimidated and seeing the smoke of a steamer, took to their boat and made for it. It proved to be Philippeus's supply steamer *Kamchatka*, on its return trip along the Okhotsk coasts. The men were taken to Korsakovski, a port near the south end of Sakhalin, and wintered there.

This is the story of the kossak and natives. On the other hand, it has been asserted that they were bribed. So far as the result is concerned, it matters very little which story is the true one. The rookery was now becoming so depleted by illegal, reckless, and indiscriminate slaughter that it was seriously considered by the authori-

---

[1] So bold did the schooners become that when Lieutenant Shamof, of the cruiser *Razboinik*, in 1884 sent to guard Robben Island, landed near Cape Patience, Sakhalin, on May 21, he found there two sheds containing about 15,000 pounds of salt, etc., three skiffs, and a whaleboat, and six Japanese, the whole outfit belonging to a schooner from Japan, of which a certain Johnson was said to be the captain (Ausland, 1885, pp. 536–537).

ties whether it would not be the better policy to kill off the few remaining seals and to abandon the island. If the seals were not killed by the company they were taken by the raiders, extermination was sure to follow, and it was only a question who were going to have the skins, the legitimate lessees, who were paying for the privilege and acting under contract with the legal owner of the island, the Russian Government, or the pirating poachers, who knew well that they were doing lawless acts, and who, moreover, also knew that their penalty for the criminal business, if caught, would be confiscation and, possibly, hard work in the mines of Siberia. Under these circumstances it is hardly to be wondered at that the decision was to disregard the distinction between sex and age in the killing by the lessees, as it was done by the poachers. This was undoubtedly done in 1883, and it is quite possible that some of the men, when more seals had been clubbed than the little gang could properly skin, in their zeal may have slashed the skins to prevent the raiders who were continually hanging around, among them the schooners *North Star*, *Otome*, *Helene*, and *Adèle*, from profiting to the extent of even having the seals clubbed for their benefit. It is utterly unjustifiable to characterize the proceeding as "barbarous" in contradistinction to that of the poachers. The number of seals thus killed has been grossly exaggerated. Some of the poachers have estimated it to be from 12,000 to 20,000 seals, but it is pretty safe to say that there were not nearly so many seals at that time on the island, all told. The number mentioned by another of the poaching captains (Fur Seal Arb., VIII, p. 664), viz, 3,500, is undoubtedly much nearer the mark.

Notwithstanding all this, enough seals hauled up on Robben Island in 1884 to justify the lessees in continuing the regular killing that season. They were particularly encouraged to do so since the Government had stationed a man-of-war, the *Razboinik*, to guard the rookery. Four seizures were made, among them the German schooner *Helena*, Captain Gohler, which had "raided that island five years." Others escaped, like the *Felix*, which got 500 skins (Fur Seal Arb., III, p. 358). The killing of other classes of seals by the company on shore, however, was brought to a stop by Col. Nicolai Voloshinof (since deceased), who visited the island that year on a tour of inspection.

The Government, seeing that energetic means had to be taken if the seals were to be protected at all on Robben Island, in 1885 stationed a regular naval force of 16 sailors of the Siberian flotilla and 1 officer on the island, which was removed, however, before the middle of October. The company that year obtained less than 2,000 skins, but the schooners, late in autumn, made additional hauls; thus the *Penelope*, Capt. E. P. Miner, on her part alone got "about 800 skins" (Fur Seal Arb., VIII, p. 702). Captain Blair, of the *Leon*, estimated the number of seals on the island that year to be about 6,000.

For four years, 1886 to 1889, inclusive, the company refrained from taking any skins on the island; but there were still some left for the raiders, who appear to have visited the rock every year. The British Bering Sea Commission states that "these schooners must have obtained at least 4,700 skins" (Rep., p. 89). In 1890, the last year of the lease of Hutchinson, Kohl, Philippeus & Co., 1,456 skins were secured by them.

With the lease of the islands by the Russian Seal Skin Company the regular killing was again resumed in 1891, but the poor result led to the abandonment of the attempt in 1892. In 1893 the rookery had recovered sufficiently to yield the company 1,500 skins; 1,000 were taken in 1894, and 1,300 in 1895.

In all these years the raiders continued to prey upon the island in the autumn, with but scant danger of being captured. In October, 1891, however, Captain Brandt, commanding the *Aleut*, upon returning to the island unexpectedly, captured two schooners, the *Arctic* and the *Mystery*, both fitted out in Yokohama but flying the British flag and having 1,500 seal skins on board (Brit. Behring Sea Comm. Rep., p. 89).

The latest raid on Robben Island was undertaken last autumn. On October 29, 1895, the British schooner *Saipan*, sailing from Yokohama early in October, ostensibly on a shark-fishing expedition, landed 17 of her crew on Robben Island. She sailed away, promising to return in eight days. In the meantime the Russian transport *Yakut*, which did patrol duty around the Commander Islands during the summer, arrived and found the 17 men with a great number of slaughtered seals. They were arrested and brought to Vladivostok, where she arrived about November 6. The schooner returned to the island too late, and thus escaped capture.

In addition, there is no doubt that the Robben Island herd must have suffered somewhat from pelagic sealing proper, though the extent can not be known.

Capt. D. Greenberg, of the *Bobrik*, in 1895 reported that females were present in fair numbers, and that the proportion of bulls to females was about 1 in 40. The weight of the skins taken was good, and yearlings were quite scarce. He also mentioned having observed an unusual number of dead pups.

Number of skins taken by the lessees of Robben Island from 1871 to 1895.

Year.	Seals.	Year.	Seals.
1871	0	1885	1,838
1872	0	1886	0
1873	2,694	1887	0
1874	2,414	1888	0
1875	3,127	1889	0
1876	1,528	1890	1,456
1877	2,949	1891	450
1878	3,140	1892	0
1879	4,082	1893	1,500
1880	5,330	1894	1,000
1881	4,207	1895	1,300
1882	4,106		
1883	2,049	Total	14,009
1884	3,819		

3.—OTHER ISLANDS.

Omitting all references to breeding rookeries on the mainland of Kamchatka as based upon hearsay, and in all probability resting on misidentification of young sea-lions, it may be well in the present work to mention those localities in the Okhotsk Sea, besides Robben Island, where seals are said to haul out to breed.

ST. IONA ISLAND.

This is a small island, about 2 miles in circumference, situated in 56° 25′ north latitude and 143° 16′ east longitude, 120 miles north of the northern extremity of Sakhalin Island and a little more than 150 miles east of Port Ayan. It is said to be about 12 feet high and to have a crowd of detached rocks lying off its west side.[1]

[1] "*St. Iona Island*, in lat. 56° 22½′ N., long. 143° 15½′ E., is merely a bare rock, about 2 miles in circumference and 1,200 feet high, surrounded on all sides, except the west, by detached rocks, against which the waves beat with great violence, and which probably extend a considerable distance under water. With the island bearing north, distant 12 miles, Krusenstern had 15 fathoms water, but when it bore west, about 10 miles, no bottom could be obtained with 120 fathoms." (China Sea Directory, IV, 1884, p. 178).

William Hermann, a seal-hunter of San Francisco, states that in 1890 his schooner got 283 seals on the island of St. Iona; that, altogether, 700 seals were obtained there that year by three schooners, and that in 1891 he was there again, and got 551 seals in the schooner *Arctic*:

These were got hauled up on the rocks, and were first discovered by Captain Pine, of the *Arctic*, in 1889. Eight years ago Captain Peterson, of the schooner *Diana*, of Yokohama, was there, and there were no seals there (Fur Seal Arb., VIII, p. 709).

This last paragraph does not necessarily mean that we have to do with newly formed rookeries on St. Iona. In the first place, it is not stated at what date the island was visited; in the second, the seals may have been easily overlooked. I will mention an instance to show this. In 1881 Capt. J. Sandman, in the *Aleksander II*, in passing the Kuril chain was looking for the possible existence of fur-seal rookeries on the uninhabited islands. His attention was particularly drawn to Srednі Island, quite a small and insignificant affair. He happened to approach it from the Pacific side, and seeing nothing but sea-lions went away. Imagine his chagrin when he heard that Mr. Snow landed on the island that same season, taking several thousand seals. They were located on the Okhotsk Sea side.

SHANTAR ISLANDS.

It has been supposed upon the "very categorical statement" of the captain of the *Walter L. Rich*, and of Captain Powers, that fur-seals occur at the Shantar Islands (a numerous group of large and small islands in the Shantar Bay, 55° north latitude and 138° east longitude), and it is quite possible that such is the case.[1] I am also told that seals have been taken on a small island close to the Okhotsk coast.

It is believed that both the company and the Russian Government possess more definite information about these various islands than has been given to the public, but that it has been withheld so as not to invite raids by sealing schooners. In the spring of 1895 the authorities in St. Petersburg granted the Russian Seal Skin Company the right to take seals on all the islands, known and unknown, upon the payment of a stipulated tax and upon condition that a Government officer accompany the vessel dispatched by the company.

---

[1] "*Shantarski Islands* lie off the western coast of the Sea of Okhotsk, about 150 miles northwest of Cape Elizabeth on Saghalin island, and although the largest island (Great Shantar) is 35 miles long, east and west, and about the same distance broad, it does not appear to afford any port or shelter; though its southwest point projects to the S W., so as to form a bay on the south side of the island. Between this bay and the nearest point of the continent, 14 miles distant to the southwest, are two islets surrounded by rocks and reefs. Soundings of 30 to 40 fathoms over a bottom of stones will be found at 8 to 10 miles to the eastward of the group. The tides run from 1½ to 2 knots an hour.

"To the southward of the south points of Great Shantar island are some small islands which have not been examined.

"*Fekshptoff Island.*—At 6 miles from the west side of Great Shantar is Fekshptoff Island, 20 miles in extent, NE. and SW., and 10 miles wide, but it has no port nor shelter" (China Sea Directory, IV, 1884, p. 178).

III.—SEAL LIFE ON THE COMMANDER ISLANDS.

HISTORICAL AND GENERAL.

The northern fur-seal (*Callotaria ursina*) was known to the natives of Kamchatka and the invading Russian promyshleniks long before the islands to which they resort to breed were discovered. The seals were seen to arrive in spring, on their way north and east, and to return in autumn, and the correct conclusion was formed that the seals went to some unknown coast to bring forth their young.

The discovery of Bering Island revealed this unknown coast. Steller, the naturalist of Bering's expedition, had a whole spring season on the island in which to study their habits, and that he made good use of it is evidenced by the account he gave of these animals in his famous memoir, "De Bestiis Marinis," published in 1751 in St. Petersburg.[1] In this paper, written in the Latin language and finished on Bering Island for publication, he established the salient points in the natural history of the fur-seal. Two figures, one of a bull (fig. 1) and one of a female (fig. 2, pl. XV), probably made by the artist Berckhan, as shown by Dr. E. Büchner (Mém. Ac. Imp. Sc. St.-Petersb. (7), XXXVIII, No. 7, pp. 12–13), accompany the descriptions. Fig. 2, at least, is a fairly characteristic representation of a bull, and superior to several figures published much later.

Steller described in some detail the external and internal anatomy of the fur-seal, or sea bear, as he called it, and gives a pretty accurate account of their migrations and their habits on the island during the breeding season. He stated that they are polygamous, each bull having "8, 15 to 50 females"; describes the harems and the bravery of the bulls fighting for the possession of the females; the birth of the one pup shortly after the arrival of the mothers; the nursing and the play of the pups; the long fast of the bulls on the rookery, etc. In fact, he covered nearly all the essential features of their lives. Later researches have made but few corrections, and the additions have been those of detail and elaboration.

Such detail and elaboration was to some extent furnished by the venerable "apostle of the Aleuts," Ivan Veniaminof, who gathered his information on St. Paul Island, Pribylof group, more than eighty years later than Steller. A very precise and concise account, both of the natural history of the animal and of the sealing business, communicated by Veniaminof to Admiral von Wrangell, then chief manager of the Russian-American Company, was published in 1839 by the latter in the German language,[2] and was thus made easily accessible to the scientific world of his day. His somewhat more voluminous account in the Russian language did not appear until the following year.[3] He carefully distinguishes the various classes of seals—the *sikatchi*, or old bulls; the *polusikatchi*, or young bulls; the *holustiaki*, or bachelors; the *matki*, or mother seals; the *kotiki*, or pups, and the yearlings. The sikatchi in spring arrive first on St. Paul Island, about April 20 (old style; May 2 new style), "even if the

---

[1] Novi Comment. Acad. Sc. Imp. Petrop., II, pp. 289–398; pp. 331–359 relate entirely to the fur-seal.
[2] Statistische und Ethnographische Nachrichten über die Russischen Besitzungen an der Nordwestküste von Amerika. Gesammelt von dem ehemaligen Oberverwalter dieser Besitzungen, Contre-Admiral v. Wrangell. St. Petersburg, 1839, 8vo XXXVIII + 332 pp. and map; pp. 39–48 treat of the "Seebär, *Phoca ursina.*"
[3] Zapiski ob Ostrovakh Unalashkinskago Otdiela. St. Petersburg, 1840, 2 vols.

island is still beset by ice,"[1] and take up the same place as the previous year, being extremely fat upon their arrival. They pass most of the time sleeping, before the arrival of the females, when the sikatchi tries to get hold of as many as possible for his harem, in which he succeeds not without bloody contests with other males. "From 1 to 150 females have been observed with one sikatch, the number depending simply upon his bravery. He is the unrestricted lord, the guardian and protector of his harem. He takes no food whatever when staying ashore."

The polusikatchi and holustiaki arrive later and congregate in large companies upon the grounds which are usually separate and more distant from the sea than the breeding grounds. The females commence to arrive on May 26, rarely on May 21, shortly before giving birth to their single pup, the season for the delivery being from the end of May "through the whole of June, and even as late as July 10." The kotiki arrive usually by southerly winds, but not with the same regularity as the others, all not having arrived even by the middle of June, "as there are instances of yearlings having arrived as late as July." The sikatch comes together with the female some time after the birth of the pup, but only once; he "is able to cover from 21 to 25 females in 24 hours." The pups "feed exclusively upon the milk of their mothers until leaving the land. The female never suckles her young while in the water, but coming ashore for that purpose attends her offspring in a resting position." The pups do not go into the water until they are 30 to 35 days old, becoming familiar with the water when 40 to 50 days of age. "The color of the pups when born is black, but from September 10 changes to gray, the old hair being cast off." The seals leave the island (St. Paul) gradually, beginning about October 5, and always with north and northwest winds, the young ones remaining longest. A few old bulls may occasionally be seen in November, or even December, but none in January or February. "Very rarely 2 or 3 sikatchi show themselves again in March, but always for a very short time only."

I have thought it worth while to give the above short summary of the natural history as it was known in 1840, since it has been asserted that from the time of Steller to about 1870 "the scientific world actually knew nothing definite in regard to the life history of this valuable animal." Not even the pictorial representation of the northern fur-seal in that period was so bad as it has been made to appear, as will be plain from an inspection of Choris's drawing of a fur-seal rookery on St. Paul, published in 1822 as pl. XV of his "Voyage pittoresque antour du Monde" (Fol. Paris, 1822) of which I append a greatly reduced copy on pl. 59.

Since Veniaminof's account, no original contributions to the natural history of the fur-seal, of any magnitude, appeared until the studies of Scammon, Bryant, and particularly Elliott were given to the public in the early seventies. These, with the

---

[1] The arrival of first bulls on Bering Island rookeries are reported for a few years as follows:

Date.	No. of bulls arrived.	Locality.
1879, May 5	2	North rookery.
1880, April 27	3	Do.
1881, May 20	2	South rookery.
1882, April 19	4	North rookery.
1883, May 23	2	South rookery.
1884, April 27	2	North rookery.
1885, May 19	1	Do.

On Copper Island the first bulls, 7 in number, were observed in 1885 on May 13.

bulky literature which sprang up as part of the "Fur Seal Arbitration" case, are too well known to need any further comment in this place.

The natural history of the Commander Islands seal is essentially that of the Pribylof Islands seal. Even their migrations, although along entirely different and distinct routes, show parallel phenomena. The route of the Commander Island herd, as we have seen, was known to Steller in a general way, but it is only recently, since the pelagic sealers are following the migrating herds, that the routes have become known in detail. Mr. C. H. Townsend, the naturalist of the United States Fish Commission steamer *Albatross*, has made a special study of this branch of the subject and has kindly furnished me with the following notes relating to the migrations of the Commander Islands herd as shown by the records of the pelagic sealers:

Pelagic sealing off the coast of Japan usually commences about the middle of March and lasts until the middle of June. The seal herd appears to be massed off the coast between the latitudes of Yokohama and Cape Noishap (the eastern point of Yezo Island) in March, April, and May. In March sealing commences off Hondo Island (Nipon); in latitude 36, where seals are also of common occurrence in April, but they are then moving slowly northward. In May the best sealing is found south and east of Yezo Island, Cape Yerimo (the southeast point of Yezo) being a favorite sealing-ground. In June they are usually a little farther north, being taken generally off the eastern coast of Yezo and the most southerly of the Kurils. They are also taken in June off the more northerly Kurils, but the herd is then farther off shore and more scattered.

In the Japan region proper, sealing is carried on from the coast out to a distance of about 300 miles, while in February straggling seals have been taken as far south as the Bonin Islands. Seals occur in the Sea of Japan, catches having been made at several points there and in La Perouse Straits by the schooner *Penelope*, in a voyage around Yezo Island during the past season.

Sealers crossing the Pacific in the latitude of Yezo Island pick up seals at many points between Japan and the longitude of 180. In June and July scattered bands of seals, presumably of the Commander Islands herd, occur 500 or 600 miles south of the western Aleutian Islands.

The charts accompanying my report on the fur-seal fishery for 1895 (Senate Document 137, part 0, Fifty-fourth Congress) show the positions where seals were taken by 20 vessels sealing off the coasts of Japan and Russia during the past four years.

LATITUDE IN THE PHENOMENA OF SEAL LIFE.

It can be safely said that most of the points in the life-history of the fur-seal have been cleared up, in so far as they can be cleared up by direct observation, but the recent activity for information in this matter resulted also in a vast accumulation of misinformation gathered by and from persons either untrained in scientific methods, inexperienced in this particular subject, or prejudiced in favor of some pet theory, or biased by political considerations. This unnatural history of the fur-seal has caused doubts and confusion in the minds of those who have to trust to the literature for their information as to the truth of even some of the most easily observed and most firmly established facts. Renewed investigations have, therefore, become desirable.

Aside from the mass of downright misinformation, a good deal of harm has been done by the often too sweeping generalizations based upon a few isolated facts and caused by ignorance of the true relations of the latter as exceptions and not as rules.

It must not for one moment be imagined that the lines are as tightly drawn in nature as in many books and reports. It will probably be possible to cite more or less isolated occurrences contrary to nearly every habit of the seals as generally outlined. These exceptions are not frequent enough nor important enough to affect the general result, and it may be confidently asserted that the investigations which have of late been carried on by the American Bering Sea Commission and quite recently by the

United States Fish Commission have brought out correctly the main facts relating to the life-history of the seals.

We have frequently seen, however, that the various exceptions alluded to have been brought forward in the controversies relating to this theme as particularly essential, thus obscuring the main questions, while, on the other hand, conditions have been described and depicted as so uniform and stable that it has been easy for the opposite side to controvert these assertions, thus throwing doubt upon the correctness of the whole argument and the soundness of the conclusions. It may be useful, therefore, to review a few of these questions.

A protracted stay at the rookeries reveals two facts. The one which probably first impresses the observer is the curious stability of the general outline of the groups of breeding seals, especially if the comparisons be made at frequent intervals during the earlier part of the season. The masses of seals assume certain definite shapes which in many cases have no apparent relation to the nature of the ground upon which they are lying. Thus, on the North Reef Rookery on Bering Island, a very peculiar feature of the distribution of the breeding seals this summer was a narrow band of seals which extended obliquely across the northern end of the "parade-grounds," cutting off from the latter a small oval portion, visible in most of the photographs (plates 19, 21, 22) and also indicated in the map (plate 8), and connecting the masses of seals on the western side of the reef with those on the eastern side. I have walked over the territory thus curiously occupied many a time, but I have failed to find any difference in the ground which will account for this belt or answer the question why the seals do not also occupy the bare oval island it surrounds.

To appreciate this *general* stability of the outline, it is necessary to have had an opportunity to observe the rookery for some length of time. A person who had only a few days at his disposal for examining the same rookery might, on the other hand, be impressed by the fact that on two different days, or at different hours of the same day, the outlines thus referred to present entirely different aspects, and if he offered photographs in evidence of this fact he might seemingly prove the instability of these lines. Thus, the "band" of seals on the North Reef Rookery above alluded to did occasionally entirely disappear, particularly during the warmer portion of bright, sunny days, or after the rookery had been disturbed by a recent drive (see pl. 26).

Nevertheless, this "band" was a very *characteristic* feature of the seals on that rookery. Single photographs are therefore of no particular value for comparison *from year to year unless they are taken by a person familiar with the characteristic distribution and the view is selected by him for that particular purpose.* The main reliance must, therefore, be placed upon the observer, and his statements must be received in accordance with his known experience, accuracy, and intelligence.

PROPORTIONATE NUMBER OF SEXES AND AGES ON ROOKERIES.

A question which of late has been given considerable prominence is that of the relative number of breeding females and old bulls on the rookeries. Upon this, and upon the closely connected one as to the number of females a bull is able to serve, there has been a great diversity of opinion.[1] My experience this summer leads me to

---

[1] While maintaining that the value of the guesses as to the number of females a bull is able to serve is of necessity very dubious, I may mention that Mr. Klnge, who for eight years spent the summer upon Tinleni Island with the seals practically under his very eyes the whole season, informed me this summer that "he does not for a moment believe that twenty-five females to a bull are in the least too many," though he did not venture to guess at the maximum.

the belief that, *on the whole*, a bull is able to take care of as many females as he can keep around him. There is undoubtedly great individual differences in this respect, some bulls being stronger than others, but I think it can be safely asserted, *as a rule*, that the procreative power of the bull is in direct proportion to his general physical strength. I think it also sound to assume that, *as a rule*, a bull physically strong enough to live through the winter gales and the vicissitudes of his winter wanderings and to return to his place on the rookery is also strong enough to fulfill his duty there. I have purposely emphasized "on the whole" and "as a rule," because I can easily imagine individual cases of, for instance, accidentally castrated bulls, or old feeble ones who might have the good fortune to meet with unusually favorable conditions during their winter migrations, etc., and because I am quite willing to admit that a number of such bulls may be found on each rookery. These exceptions, however, do not materially alter the above propositions as relating to the whole population of the rookery.

The train of reasoning which led me to the above conclusions is as follows: Some of the most noteworthy of my observations this summer on the Commander Islands establish the facts (1) that the decrease in the killable seals was most marked on Copper Island; (2) that there was a full complement of pups as compared with breeding females on both islands; (3) that there was an ample supply of bulls, old and young, on Copper Island, while on Bering Island they were much less numerous as compared with the number of females. I was informed that the latter condition was not peculiar to the present year (1895) alone, and it is also particularly mentioned in Mr. Grebnitski's report for 1893. It would therefore seem as if the different proportions between the sexes on the two islands have had no visible influence upon the number of pups born.

The soundness of the above deductions may receive corroboration, or the reverse, by observations on the South Rookery on Bering Island in 1896. On that rookery the disproportion between the two sexes was excessive in 1895. According to reliable information, the number of bulls on the whole rookery did not exceed five.[1] Judging from what I saw of this rookery during two visits, I should place the number of breeding females at about 600, possibly only 500. It would be a comparatively easy matter to observe this year whether the number of pups born be very markedly small in proportion to the number of females hauling out.

On the large rookeries it is difficult, if not impossible, for various reasons, to correctly estimate the average proportion between the bulls and the females, and particularly so on Bering Island, because the bachelors to so great an extent haul up between the breeding females. Mixed in among the latter in this way, it is next to impossible at long range to say, with any approach to accuracy, what the proportion between these two classes is.[2] In general, the difficulty lies in the fact that the individual harems differ so greatly in size. Thus, during the visit to Kishotchnaya Rookery, Bering Island, on July 9, Mr. Grebnitski counted several harems which contained all the way from 12 to 23 females, or more. But there is still another serious difficulty, which is due to the constant going and coming of the females, so that

---

[1] When I visited the rookery on August 17 the bulls had already left. It was rumored in the village that there had only been one bull, but Nikanor Grigorief, the native in charge of the killing there, informed me that the actual number was five.

[2] It is held by some that the natives have such a marvelously keen eye and discriminating power as to enable them, at least, to make such an estimate. At one time I accepted this as a matter of faith, but my experience last summer to be detailed further on has convinced me that the natives are not particularly gifted in that respect. As a matter of fact, their estimates are about as much guesswork as that of the white people, only that from their greater familiarity with the ground and the seals, they are apt to guess more closely.

the number of females in the individual harem fluctuates between 0 and the maximum, according to the time of day or condition of weather. Thus, on the 16th of July, on the same rookery, I counted a harem having 16 females, which, upon a recount a few hours later, contained 23, "while some of the other bulls were entirely deserted."[1]

I have above alluded to the difficulty of discriminating at a great distance between the females and the killable bachelors when mixed on the breeding ground. The difficulty is not confined to these two classes alone. The experts profess to be able to separate the bachelors into yearlings, 2-year-olds, 3-year-olds, 4-year-olds, and 5-year-olds, and in the descriptions and discussions we find these classes mentioned in such a way as to lead to the impression that they are easily recognized on the rookery or the killing-ground, but nothing can be further from the facts. With hundreds of dead seals before me, I have been unable to draw any line between the various ages, nor has anybody present been able to point them out to me.

I have submitted elsewhere in this report a series of weights of skins (p. 109) which shows beyond a question that there is an unbroken series of all sizes from the smallest to the largest. The whole question resolves itself into a mental sorting of the killable seals into a number of classes, calling the smallest two-year-olds, the largest five-year-olds, and roughly distributing those in between among their respective classes. The yearlings, however, form a fairly well-marked class by themselves, as do, of course, the bulls—features not apparent in the tables of skin weights alluded to, from the fact that these classes are not killed.

The fact that even the natives are not always able to tell the females from the bachelors on the rookeries was curiously proven to me one day at Glinka, Copper Island, when Aleksander Zaikof and the chief, Sergei Sushkof, had a somewhat heated controversy over the question whether a certain body of seals on the Urili Kamen Rookery consisted of bachelors or females. Both of the men are among the most experienced and intelligent on the island. Yet it was only because Sushkof had been stationed the whole season at Glinka, while Zaikof only arrived with us the day previous, that he was regarded to be in the right.

But even at closer range it is sometimes difficult to distinguish the sexes. On the killing-ground, where the teeth of the seals are easily seen, there is, of course, no special difficulty, and mistakes are seldom made; not so in the drives, however.

During a small drive at Glinka, Copper Island, August 8, 1895, about 300 seals were made to cross the mountain pass (about 800 feet) in three main divisions, no less than 30 grown men taking part in the driving. Halfway up one of the men declared that there was a "matka" in the drive. It was questioned, but upon closer scrutiny he was found to be right. It was not until the final sorting before the killing took place that several females were discovered in the flock.

As an additional indication of the lack of definition of the different classes of seals as expressed in their sizes, I append a few tables of measurements taken from the freshly killed animals.

---

[1] The number of animals and the proportion of the sexes on North Rookery, Bering Island, during July, 1893, as quoted by Dr. Slunin (Promysl. Bog. Kam. Sakh. Komand., p. 9), from the official journal of the overseer (*offitsialni dnevnik nadziratelia*) are worse than useless. The numeration by the overseer in question is the worst kind of guesswork, if not entirely fictitious. Dr. Slunin's remark that the conclusions to be made from those figures would be strange (*stranni*) is certainly appropriate.

Measurements (in millimeters) of fur-seals (Callotaria ursina), Bering Island, North Rookery, July 30, 1882.

No.	Sex.	Total length.	Fore legs.	Hind legs.	Girth behind fore legs.	Nose to eye.	Nose to ear.	No.	Sex.	Total length.	Fore legs.	Hind legs.	Girth behind fore legs.	Nose to eye.	Nose to ear.
1	Male	1780	495	555	910	105	212	12	Male	1250	390	400	780	82	165
2	do	1660	465	475	920	95	205	13	do	1205	325	410	775	82	175
3	do	1560	480	495	880	95	180	14	do	1200	292	380	760	75	165
4	do	1550	390	480	890	92	204	15	do	1185	300	385	750	68	152
5	do	1430	436	465	790	83	175	16	do	1180	330	415	810	85	180
6	do	1390	390	470	860	85	180	17	do	1170	345	400	750	83	166
7	do	1380	400	455	795	85	175	18	do	1140	315	395	700	75	165
8	do	1345	360	455	800	90	175	19	do	1125	350	385	730	85	184
9	do	1340	370	440	823	90	180	20	do	1100	300	355	710	75	168
10	do	1330	360	440	870	82	185	21	do	1035	255	340	620	73	155
11	do	1260	405	450	710	85	183								

Measurements (in millimeters) of specimens of fur-seals collected for United States National Museum at North Rookery, Bering Island, August 20, 1883.

	No. 2519 male.	No. 2520 male.	No. 2521 female.	No. 2522 male.	No. 2523 male.	No. 2524 male.	No. 2525 male.	No. 2526 female.	No. 2527 pup.	No. 2528 pup.	No. 2529 pup.
Total length	1495	1930	1283	1495	1475	1285	1085	1025	800	800	785
From nose to end of outstretched hind feet	2505	2450	1650	1935	1935	1655	1300	1255	1040	1030	965
From nose to armpit	1125	980	685	780	775	660	605	520	410	427	375
From nose to eye	110	98	67	78	90	80	72	60	55	50	52
From nose to ear	214	213	168	183	173	156	154	148	120	120	111
Distance between eyes	98	104	70	83	72	71	70	70	59	55	54
Distance between ears	183	173	138	150	140	138	120	125	99	104	98
Length of ear	52	52	45	53	53	47	39	46	38	42	32
Length of longest mustache bristle	195	113	125	186	177	105	95	87	70	67	66
Length of fore limb	530	540	345	500	515	395	300	305	255	268	220
Width of fore foot	215	223	123	160	165	125	107	117	100	89	85
Length of hind limb	615	597	415	485	507	420	350	295	216	275	210
Width of hind foot at tarsus	130	135	95	112	113	85	80	70	65	67	60
Width of hind foot at end of toes	250	285	170	245	202	177	100	155	135	138	125
Average length of toe flaps	230	230	162	190	196	161	115	102	88	85	84
Length of tail	55	50	53	55	55	47	46	57	25	30	29
Distance between tips of outstretched fore limbs	1770	1740	1205	1445	1370	1085	960	855	705	720	650
Girth of neck behind the ears	580	598	405	475	470	405	360	355	330	332	404
Girth over the shoulders	1150	1205	750	950	930	820	680	600	455	480	465
Girth behind fore limbs	1260	1155	780	850	790	740	625	565	450	425	445
Girth in front of hind limbs	475	480	280	380	365	285	245	225	197	195	168

Measurements of two gray pups, taken at North Rookery, Bering Island, October 20, 1883.

	No. 1697. Male, 38 pounds.	No. 1696. Female, 30 pounds.
	Mm.	*Mm.*
Tip of nose to end of tail	885	865
Tip of nose to fore flippers	425	375
Fore flippers	265	263
Hind legs	275	243
Tip of nose to eye	55	42
Tail	27	20
Girth behind fore flippers	630	570
Ear	38	35

VIRILITY OF BULLS.

While there is thus shown to be a certain instability in the rookery outlines and quite an uncertainty as to the various classes and stages of the seals, except in a *general* way, there is observable a similar lack of strict adherence to the habits as described by many writers, though these may upon the whole be correct. No doubt, for instance, many of the old bulls on the rookery, especially early in the season, stand up bravely without retreating, even against a number of men, but it is also true that a good many of them do not. Lest the more cowardly conduct of some bulls should be charged to an alleged lack of vitality in those of the present generation, I will only quote what I wrote immediately after my visit to the North Reef Rookery, Bering Island, on June 5, 1883:

Between 200 and 300 old bulls were scattered all over the ground, some sleeping, some fighting; others rose up, somewhat uneasy at our approach; others, again, galloped away as fast as their short feet would carry them, plunging headlong into the water. A few would make a bold stand for some moments and roar at us, but they soon turned, seeking to escape. None of those we approached very closely would keep their position.

I may cite another instance from a date much later in the season, but yet at a time when the females required the full attention of the bulls and on a rookery where the latter were plentiful and vigorous. The observation was made in Sikatchinskaya Bay, Palata Rookery, Copper Island. Mr. Grebnitski had landed on a rock in the rookery to take a couple of photographs, while I, with the men, remained in the boat. The following is an abstract from my diary of August 3, 1895:

It was a sight never to be forgotten. The females from all around rushed into the water pellmell, while the old bulls were running to and fro trying to keep them back, though in some cases taking the pame themselves and following the example of the females, who made the water fairly boil around the boat by their jumping. On the nearest rocks hundreds of black pups were huddled together as close as they could stand, fearing to go into deep water; but finally driven into it by the advance of the photographing party, they swam with the utmost ease. Of all the many seals covering the rocks around us when we first arrived, only two kept their places. These were an old bull and a matka in heat. Our boat was lying within 20 feet of them, yet they did not mind us, and the courting—the female did the courting—went on, although our presence evidently acted somewhat depressingly on the male, who anxiously kept an eye upon us, while yet unwilling to leave the female. Occasionally he screwed up enough courage to face us and roar defiantly, but as we approached to within 10 feet and I got up in the boat to fire my camera at him, he suddenly thought that discretion is the better part of valor, and plumped headlong into the water on the other side of the rock. He came out and up on the rock, however, a few minutes later and shook the water out of his fur, but the female had apparently become disgusted with him, for, in spite of our retreating, she went into the water shortly after he had returned to her. He then also left for good.

DO ALL BACHELORS HAUL OUT?

The general impression, as derived both from the printed reports and oral communications, seems to be that the vast majority, if not all, of the bachelors haul out on the beaches during the season. It would, of course, be impossible to say whether each individual bachelor does haul out at least once during the season, or whether some of them stay in the water throughout the entire year, but my observations lead me to believe that only a smaller portion of the whole body of bachelors haul out *at any one time*. That a good many of the seals in the water in the immediate neighborhood of the rookeries are bachelors, I know from personal observation, for the two sexes are more easily distinguished at a distance while in the water than on the rocks. These probably all haul out at some time or another. But the question is, does the bulk of the bachelors met with on the feeding-grounds and far away from the rookeries during the breeding season also haul out? I am inclined to believe that they do not, for the following reason:

While it is true that the great rookery on Bering Island was never before "raked and scraped" for the last bachelor seal as it was during the past season, yet it is not denied that a similar difficulty in gathering the requisite number of killables has been going on for a couple of years, though not to the same extent. Now, if intelligent and honest persons, at the close of the season of 1894, had been asked, while viewing that rookery, whether there were, say, 18,000 bachelor seals (outside the pups of that year) in sight or within a comparatively short distance, they would be obliged to answer no. The question then becomes pertinent: Whence, then, came the 9,000 bachelors killed in 1895 on that rookery (hardly any yearlings showed up at all) and the probable other 9,000 that perished during the winter by being killed by the pelagic sealers, or otherwise? The bulk of these 18,000 must have stayed away from the immediate neighborhood of the island, and as bachelor seals are not known to haul out in great bodies very far from the breeding-grounds there is every reason to conclude that they stayed at sea.

To fully weigh this answer, it is necessary to remember that the bachelor seals, especially the younger classes, have no functions to perform on land during the breeding season. I do not believe that a single good reason can be advanced in defense of a proposition that the hauling out of the bachelor is of any advantage *to the individual*. Nor does it seem probable that all the bachelor seals are subject to a very *pressing* desire to go ashore until the sexual instinct is awakened. The hauling out on dry land by any immature seal is, therefore, only the result of the habit having been inherited. It is therefore likely to be of very varied intensity, and there is nothing intrinsically improbable in admitting that this habit in some, or even in many, is only awakened at the approach of sexual maturity. It must, furthermore, be borne in mind that the bachelor seals require an abundance of food no less than the females. The *nursing* of the young makes it imperative for the latter to visit the distant feeding-grounds, but also to return regularly to the rookery. The bachelor seal, on the other hand, in contradistinction to the old fat bulls remaining the entire season on the rookery, needs a big food supply because he is *growing*; but different from the female, he has no individual business on the rookery. Of course, while there is no advantage to the individual bachelor in hauling out, there is an advantage to the species, inasmuch as it tends to strengthen the inherited habit which insures the return of the necessary number of breeding males at a later age to their respective rookeries, but this proposition does not involve any necessity for *all* to do so.

The above observations and reflections, which are chiefly submitted in order to emphasize that it is necessary to allow for a certain latitude in the habits of the seals, I am now going to follow up with a series of special observations upon certain phases of fur-seal life which I made during the investigations of last summer. They are in part corroborative of observations made by investigators in other localities, particularly the Pribylof Islands, while, in part, opposed to the opinions held by some other observers. In so far as this diversity of opinion affects certain theories only, my deductions will stand or fall upon their own logic; but where there is a disagreement as to the facts I beg to remind my readers that the facts, as here set forth, only relate to the conditions found on the Commander Islands and more particularly on Bering Island. If the facts observed by me differ from those established by others, it does not necessarily follow that one of the two observations is erroneous. I will again recall the fact of the bachelors mixing among the females and the consequent driving of the latter on Bering Island in order to show there are differences between the conditions there and upon the Pribylof Islands.

FOOD OF SEALS AT THE ISLANDS AND EXCREMENTS ON THE ROOKERIES.

The question as to what animals furnish the bulk of the food of the fur-seals can not be solved positively on the rookeries. My investigations last summer corroborated those of twelve and thirteen years ago and tally with those of others, viz, empty stomachs with a few stones in them, and occasionally a few beaks of cephalopods or very rarely the backbone of some unlucky fish. Since, however, as I have already pointed out, the bachelor seals on account of their growth must necessarily take a great deal of food during the summer, the above negative result does prove pretty positively that the seals on the Commander Islands must, *as a rule*, obtain their food so far from the islands that it is thoroughly digested before they return to the hauling-grounds.

I emphasize again the "as a rule," because there are single observations to the contrary. Thus, I was informed on Bering Island that once on the South Rookery a flock of bachelors was so full of octopods that they vomited up quantities of these mollusks while being driven.

It is true the statement that the bachelor seals must necessarily feed because they are in a stage of continued growth is a purely theoretical one, and it has been seriously denied that they feed during the season to any much greater extent than the old bulls. In support of this contention is quoted the observation by the British Bering Sea Commissioners (Rep. Brit. Comm., p. 42) as to the absence of excrementitious matter upon the rookeries. Though my observations, more particularly on the Commander Islands, do not agree with theirs, or Bryant's, I am not going to dispute their accuracy on that account, but I do maintain that their negative result does not prove anything, while my positive observations to the contrary do prove that the seals take nourishment throughout the season. And now for my facts.

Anyone examining the carcasses on the killing-grounds immediately after the killing can not help observing that a good many of the dead seals at the moment they were slain had voided a greater or less quantity of ocher-yellow excrement of a creamy consistency. This observation I have not only made on the Commander Islands at every killing I have there witnessed (and the unpleasantness of handling the seals thus soiled has very vividly impressed my mind), but also on St. Paul Island during the only drive it was my privilege to follow there, viz, on June 26, 1895. Here is the entry relating to the latter observation:

Mr. True afterwards opened a number of stomachs without finding any food in them, and I opened one, which had just voided a quantity of fluid excrement, with similar result. Quite a number of seals voided excrement of like nature.

On the 2d of August, 1895, Mr. Grebnitski and I landed and established our camp at Babinski Padjom, Glinka Rookery, Copper Island, on the former hauling-ground of the bachelors. A few half-bulls only were located at the eastern end of the bay, all that was now left of this rookery. Here are the words of the diary:

After supper I went over to the eastern end of the bay, where the polusikatchi above alluded to had been lying (for upon our settling down in their neighborhood all of them sought safety in the sea). The entire narrow and steep beach which lines the precipitous cliffs (300 feet and more), forming the coast here consists of rounded stones of various sizes, from that of a marble to that of a man's head, but averaging perhaps that of a fist, and of a light-gray color. On this pearl-gray ground the station of each half-bull was clearly marked with a brown stain, and all around patches of semifluid excrements were found in various stages of drying up and disintegration. The freshest excrements were of a blackish-brown color and of a very penetrating and disagreeable odor, while the dried ones were of a pale drab color. In spite of the humidity of the climate things on the beaches dry up remarkably fast and thoroughly, but I suppose it is partly due to the perfect drainage of the sandy or pebbly beaches. * * * The fact is that the excrements contain comparatively few solids and are easily dissipated.

This observation is particularly conclusive because it showed at the well-defined station of each half-bull (hauling up much after the fashion of the old bulls) a quantity of fecal matter in the various stages of disintegration, from that of the semifluid, nearly fresh excrement, to the dry and odorless "chip." Taken as late as August 2, yet a considerable time before the close of the season, it has a very important bearing upon the question.

The third and last entry in my diary in regard to this matter is dated August 22, and relates to what took place during the big drive on that date on the North Reef Rookery, Bering Island, which was witnessed by the officers, including the surgeon, Dr. Lloyd Thomas, of Her British Majesty's ship *Porpoise*. It reads as follows:

There was another matter to which I called the special attention of the English gentlemen while we were on the rookery, viz, the presence—and very offensively smelling presence—of semifluid excrements on the rocks, particularly mentioning the opposite observation of the British commissioners. In fact, the fecal matter was making it very slippery in places.

The argument derived from the alleged absence of excrementitious matter on the rookeries is, consequently, disposed of. It may be well to add the remark that it is more than probable that most of the feces are voided at sea before hauling up, and that, in conjunction with their fluid nature, this explanation accounts satisfactorily for the fact that its presence on the rookeries is not more obvious.

As already remarked above, observations on the rookeries are not apt to furnish positive data as to the nature of the bulk of the food of the Commander Islands fur-seals. That they eat cephalopods is proven by the occasional presence of the beaks in their stomachs, as well as by the above-quoted instance on the South Rookery (p. 69). It is also possible that Mr. Grebnitski's suggestion is correct, that the presence of pebbles in the stomachs is largely to be accounted for by assuming that they are swallowed together with the octopods holding on to them. That they also eat fish, at least occasionally, is also unquestionable. But the following facts will as unquestionably show that salmon and cod, at least, do not furnish any portion of the *regular summer* diet of the Commander Islands seals worth mentioning:

It may not be very much to the point to observe that three species of salmon (*Oncorhynchus*) abound in all the rivers on Bering Island, and that the fur-seals are not observed to feed upon them at the mouths of these rivers; but the fact that the largest salmon river of the island, the Sarauna River, is situated less than 7 miles from the largest seal rookery without the seals coming over there to feed upon the enormous numbers of salmon ascending that river, is proof conclusive. The river and the fishing establishment of the natives at Saraunna have been described elsewhere in this report, so that it will suffice in the present connection to recall the statement that the annual catch in that river alone varies between 20,000 and 100,000 salmon.

As for the codfish, it is only necessary to state that they are common right off the great North Rookery of Bering Island. On September 16, 1895, we were anchored in 10 fathoms of water less than a mile from Sivutchi Kamen and within hearing of the roar from the rookery. A single cod line over the side of the steamer for a couple of hours brought up three-fourths of a barrel of codfish.

EFFECT OF DRIVING.

One of the questions to which I paid special attention during the past summer was that of the effect of driving upon the vitality of the seals. It has been variously asserted that the repeated driving of the male seals on the Pribylof Islands has resulted in the weakening of the procreative power of the bulls and the consequent degeneration and partial decrease in the number of seals on the rookeries. It has also been hinted that the difference in the methods of driving the seals on the Pribylofs and on the Commander Islands might account for the apparent lesser diminution of the seals on the latter islands. The question is, therefore, one of the utmost importance, and it was in order to specially make a direct comparison between the methods employed on the American and the Russian side that I asked to be enabled to land on St. Paul Island and witness a drive there before proceeding to the Commander Islands. It is, therefore, pertinent to submit a description of this drive, which, thanks to the assistance of the agents of the company and of the United States Treasury, I had an opportunity to follow on June 26, 1895.

It would, of course, be hazardous to base any far-reaching conclusions upon one single drive. As Mr. F. W. True was going to follow up similar studies on St. Paul Island during the whole of the following season, he kindly assented to accompany me on the present occasion, so that he might afterwards inform me how the drive we were going to take part in might compare for severity with those which were to follow later, and which I myself would not be able to inspect.

At 9 p. m. on June 25, in company with Mr. Stanley-Brown, the general agent of the company, we started for Polavina Rookery in a buckboard drawn by a pair of strong mules. The road was to a great extent still covered with snow and water, compelling the driver to pick his way in the dark over hills and marshes. After a trying ride of two hours, during which it was a wonder that we were not upset and spilled by the roadside or into the water which surrounded us on all sides, we arrived safely at the hut, where we found a party of nine Aleuts who had preceded us. After a fitful slumber on the benches in front of the cooking stove, we turned out with our gang at 2 o'clock the next morning and proceeded to the hauling-ground, where we could hardly discern the various objects in the hazy gray light of the early morning. I quote now from my diary, written a few hours later:

We move stealthily along the margin of the breeding-ground, which is occupied by angrily bellowing bulls, a few—a very few—females, and still fewer pups, cutting off a small herd of bachelor seals that are skirting the inner edge of the breeding-grounds. At the end of the latter we make a sudden spurt, Mr. True and I running at full speed with the Aleuts for the water's edge, thus cutting off another crowd of bachelors—I estimate in all about 1,000. Then the driving begins by dividing the herd in two (unintentionally) uneven sections, which are driven easily, without special urging, over very even ground.

The seals are of very unequal sizes, there being quite a number of large half-bulls in the flock. In driving, the various sizes become somewhat sorted, inasmuch as the younger and more agile seals keep well to the front, while the large and fat half-bulls bring up the rear. Occasionally a few of these are cut out and left behind—probably in all about 50. No other cutting out or culling is undertaken while the driving is going on, and is practically impossible as long as the seals are driven in as large flocks as these. On the other hand, the driving gang is too short-handed to manage a large number of small sections, as on the Commander Islands. After a moderate drive overland for about three-quarters of an hour, the seals enter a series of shallow lakes, and now the progress is rapid. At 5 a. m. the herd is halted just outside the salt-house at Rocky Point, and the drive is over.

It is noticeable that the seals are nearly as fresh at the end of the drive as at the beginning. The younger seals are quite active; they walk about unconcernedly, and stand well up on their legs, while the big ones commence to fight each other immediately upon the halt being made. Only one single seal dropped voluntarily out of the line on the road, viz, a large and particularly fat half-bull that got tired very early.

The killing gang arrived from the village in two boats a little after 7 a. m. Six men with nicely finished oaken clubs did the killing while the others were skinning. Mr. True and I took the tally of each of the first ten "pods" of seals as they were separated off from the big herd to be killed. These "pods" consisted of from 15 to 40 seals, averaging about 25. Of these the killing gang clubbed to death those which appeared to come within the required size; the others, being either too large or too small, were allowed to escape to the beach close by. About 50 per cent were thus turned away, about one-half consisting of too small seals, the other half of too large ones. The killing was over at 10.30 a. m., about 500 skins having been secured. It is to be noted that no female was observed among the seals driven.

On the whole the affair was conducted with care, although a certain hurry in order to get through as soon as possible was quite manifest. This haste, probably due to a desire to be back in the distant village before dinner, was responsible for the less deliberate way in which the "pods" to be killed were cut out from the main herd. This resulted in great worry and consequent heating of the remaining seals, which made it necessary to drive them repeatedly into the ice-cold waters of an adjacent pond in order to cool them off. This necessity was rather startling in view of the chilliness of the atmosphere and the long rest enjoyed by the seals between the drive and the killing.

Apart from its length—about 2 miles—this drive must be characterized as very easy. An inspection of the ground over which the drives from some of the other rookeries must travel impressed me, however, with the fact that not all the seals on St. Paul Island are let off as easily. Mr. True also informs me that this impression is correct, and that the drive we witnessed in company was rather easier than the average.

I will now submit a description of a few characteristic drives observed by me on the Commander Islands. The first one (which took place during the palmy days of the business on these islands) occurred on July 13, 1883. A thousand seals were to be taken from the Pestshani hauling-grounds (p. 49), Glinka, Copper Island, to finish up the catch of the season.

We started out at 4 o'clock in the morning from Glinka village. The weather was very disagreeable. A wet, gray fog concealed everything, preventing us from seeing 20 paces ahead. The thermometer indicated +43° F. The path, which in two places rises to over 800 feet above the sea, with a drop of 500 feet and another rise of nearly 200 feet between them, was slippery in the extreme, as the protracted rain had softened the clayey ground. After a very tiresome walk of nearly an hour we halted on top of the third hill, where we had a pretty good view of Pestshani hauling-ground, as the fog had lifted somewhat by this time. The projecting point of the beach, so named, was densely covered by a black mass of bachelor seals, which here haul out by themselves in large numbers apart from the breeding-ground. When the last of the gang of about 20 men had arrived the line of action was decided upon, the chief assigning to each man his duty, and the whole crowd ran or slid down the steep, grassy descent about 700 feet in one continuous slope.

We approached the compact mass of bachelors rapidly. The nearest animals showed signs of uneasiness upon our coming within 50 feet of them. The chief then ordered "Go ahead," and we all made a rush to cut the big herd off from the sea. Those located near the water's edge were successfully intimidated along the whole line and prevented from seeking safety in the sea; they fell back upon those behind, thus effectually barring them, and soon the whole mass was surrounded and slowly moving away from the water until stopped by the precipitous walls of the coast escarpment. The flock thus secured consisted of about 2,000 bachelor seals of various ages. As rigorous orders had been received not to accept skins under 8 pounds, the sorting would have to be very careful, hence the necessity of a large number to select from.

The whole regiment of seals were now divided into companies, which were driven slowly along the escarpment to the steps built of driftwood (see fig. b, pl. 58). These were ascended with but little difficulty. Altogether, ten companies were formed, each driven by two men. A space of several hundred yards was allowed between each section.

The progress was slow, averaging less than a mile an hour. There was consequently good opportunity to sort out any undesirable seals. Thus a number of undersized youngsters were allowed to escape early in the drive. Before ascending the 700-foot slope mentioned above, a halt was made. Soon, however, the climbing began. As may well be imagined, the ascent was very laborious. The angle of the slope was at least 35 to 40 degrees, and the smooth grass and slippery clay made it almost impossible to get a hold with the feet. The poor animals slid backward over and over again, and when they finally succeeded the ground was made smoother and more difficult for those to follow. Moaning, and blowing, and steaming, they press their smooth fore-flippers hard on the elusive clay, and drag the hind part of the body after, while the men beat the ground with their long staves in order to stimulate the animals to further effort. It happens rather frequently that a seal loses his balance, and after a series of bounding somersaults lands at the foot of the hill, accompanied by the laughter and merriment of the Aleuts. I expected every time to see it lie dead with broken back or neck, but every time the involuntary acrobat arose unhurt, looked around in a dazed manner, as if surprised at finding himself so suddenly alone, away from his comrades and tormentors, and scampered away as fast as possible toward the sea.

About halfway up the hill even the larger seals commenced to give out and refused to move farther, from sheer exhaustion. As it would not do to leave these behind, a knock with a club on the head finished their unhappy existence. In a minute, or a minute and a half, the skin had been ripped off from the quivering body and thrown into the knapsack which each man carried on his back. Having arrived at the top, the survivors were given a long rest. The remaining 2 miles of the march were easier, though the last ascent was hard enough on account of the tired condition of the animals. An hour of rest was given before the final killing, to allow the animals to cool off.

This drive can easily be traced on the map (pl. 13 , as it followed the dotted line between the Pestshani hauling-ground and Glinka village.

With slight modifications the above description applies to most of the drives on Copper Island during the days of plenty, though the present one was one of the hardest, as it was the longest. A shorter route was afterwards devised, as detailed under the description of the Glinka rookeries (p. 51). Of late years there has not always been enough animals to make it worth while to drive them from Palata over the 1,000-foot pass, and many of the small drives are killed not far from the beach, and the skins carried in knapsacks across the mountains to the salt-houses on the other side of the island. At Karabelni the carcasses were even skinned right on the beach, not 1,200 yards from the breeding-grounds, so that the waves carried them out to sea and occasionally threw them up again on the rookery amongst the living seals. However, even nowadays the seals are driven across the island every time their meat is wanted for food, or whenever the drive consists of so many seals that it is practically impossible for the people to carry all the skins on their backs, as testified by the 700 decaying corpses on the killing-ground at Pestshani salt-house, which I photographed on August 6, 1895 (pl. 58c).

To complete the picture of the driving on Copper Island, I may describe one of these small drives, the principal object of which was to obtain fresh meat for the natives. It is thus recorded in my diary for August 8, 1895 (pl. 58a):

> The weather was just right for ducks and fur-seals, and consequently we started out this morning at 6 a. m. in a drizzling rain. There was no help for it. The drive could not be postponed, and as I was going to photograph, rain or no rain, the cameras were taken along. The weather might possibly be better on the other side of the mountains, but it wasn't.
>
> As indicated yesterday, all the rookeries had to be scraped in order to make even a small drive, and since I could only be in one place at a time, I selected to go with the party taking the drive at Zapadni. Here altogether about 250 animals were finally gathered together, and the driving started in three divisions. This could easily be done, for there were certainly enough people to attend to each division, there being no less than 30 full-grown men and about half a dozen boys. What a difference from former days, when 2 men or boys were all that could be spared for divisions of about 200 seals each! Most of the animals were killable bachelors, a few females and undersized bachelors having

been separated out, as the drive went on, before the steep ascent was reached. Thus far I have only with certainty discovered one female driven across the mountain.

The road was very wet and slippery, both from the long grass and the smooth clay which here forms the chief material covering the underlying rock, and the ascent was consequently a very laborious one. The middle part of it is very steep, and in one place steps have been cut in the ground so as to facilitate the climbing. The altitude of the pass forming the highest point on this drive is about 800' [760 feet].

The seals soon commenced to give out, and the men then resorted to all sorts of goading them on, short of killing, in order to get as many of the seals as possible alive to the killing-ground at the village, since they wanted the meat badly. Only when a seal could absolutely go no farther, after having been urged on by being poked and beaten with the sticks, only then it was killed and skinned. But not even then in all cases, for if it was a small and therefore particularly tender animal, it was grabbed by the hind legs and dragged along [pl. 62a] until some steep declivity was reached, down which it was then flung. Yet a good many had to be killed along the road. Little girls and still smaller boys arrived now with big skin bags on their backs [pl. 62b] to carry home the skins and choice parts of the meat. The last division, as well as about one hundred seals from Palata Rookery, reached the level ground behind Glinka village at 10 a. m. and were given a rest there.

At 11 o'clock the final drive in four divisions was begun toward the killing-ground near the beach (not 300 yards) west of the village. Down the steep embankment (fully 60 feet high) the numerous drives have worn a deep channel-like rut in the slippery clay, and down this chute the animals came rushing as if it were a toboggan slide [pl. 63b]. They slid down in bunches together, and became piled up at the bottom in big heaps. As they were now driven over the sand of the beach, a few undersized seals and a solitary matka or two were sorted out and allowed to escape into the water, but the final culling was done on the killing-ground. Altogether 47 undersized animals were thus driven over the mountains and finally permitted to go back into the sea.

These young animals let loose on the sandy beach afforded great sport for the younger generation of future seal-killers, if seals there be left when they grow up. Four little tots, five to six years old, with sticks in their hands, tried to drive into the water two young seals too tired to advance further and asking nothing but to be allowed to lie down and rest. The seals resented the attack, and the four little fellows hit them over the head and the snouts with their sticks, as they had seen their parents do with the big ones, and finally succeeded in driving them into the sea.[1]

The above descriptions give a fair idea of drives on Copper Island as they were and as they are. They demonstrate the tremendous difficulties and the hardships on the seals. A glance at the maps of the Copper Island rookeries and a study of the descriptions I have given of them in another chapter must convince anybody that there is nothing even approaching them on the Pribylofs.

Not so on Bering Island. There the drives are short and easy on the seals. The killing-ground is located scarcely more than 500 yards from the main rookery, and right in front of the summer village where the men live during the sealing season. The longest drive ever taken is only 1½ miles long; the road is over level ground, mostly covered with grass, and the ascent up the coast escarpment is easy and only 30 feet high.

A grave feature of the Bering Island drives, however, consists in the mixing in of females and pups with the bachelors throughout the season. I have elsewhere in this report treated of this side in detail, but it may not be superfluous to give an account of one of the largest drives last summer on North Reef Rookery, Bering Island, which took place August 22.

It being necessary to wait for low water, we did not start until 7 o'clock a. m. The morning was raw (about + 50° F.) and dark, a drizzling fog enveloping the scene and

---

[1] I am sorry to say that a good deal of unnecessary suffering was caused the animals simply for the fun of it. The people can hardly be blamed. They are certainly not particularly cruel by nature, but on the other hand they evidently have no idea of such a thing as cruelty to animals. They have grown up from babyhood among these scenes, and their feelings are naturally blunted. It must not be forgotten, however, that in the midst of our own civilization more cruelty to animals is practiced in a single day than in a whole season on the seal islands.

making successful snap-shot photography an impossibility. We proceeded, Indian file, to the rookery and in short order drove off nearly all the grown seals located on the reef itself, over 4,000 animals all told. Most of these were females (about 3,000) and bachelors (about 1,000). As it was late in the season, only 8 bulls were caught. As many pups as possible were allowed to escape into the sea, and they availed themselves of the opportunity offered to go off in large flocks. Nevertheless, about 300 pups were driven off to the killing-grounds before they could be released. The whole breeding-ground not located on outlying rocks—and it was now low water—was gone over and swept absolutely clean. Not a living seal, except a few pups too weak from starvation to move, was left on the "Reef."

As usual, the seals were driven in squads of 200 to 300. The length of the drive was only 650 yards and in the cold morning entailed no hardship on the seals. On the killing-ground they were again collected into two large herds. The segregating of the "pods" to be killed was done very quietly and deliberately, without worrying the entire herd. Only about 190 grown males (too large and too small) were allowed to escape, or 20 per cent of all the males driven. Whatever injury the driving might inflict would consequently be trifling so far as the male element was concerned.

But how about the females? More than three times as many females were driven and returned to the sea as there were bachelors to be killed. How did it affect them? Did they suffer much physically? Does the driving of the females seem to have any influence upon their return to the rookery?

These and many related questions will find an answer in the notes and remarks which I wrote down on the spot during an earlier drive on the same rookery, viz, on July 19, 1895.

A separate tally of the number and kind of seals driven is submitted elsewhere (p. 110), and some of the following notes refer to the "pods" therein enumerated, by "pod" meaning each little flock of seals taken out of the big herd to be killed. Each pod usually consists of bachelors, females, bulls, and pups. The killing gang attempt to hit as many of the bachelors on the head with their clubs as possible, while the other classes are allowed to escape. Occasionally the club glances off and hits the wrong animal or, more rarely, a mistake is made in the identification of the animal clubbed. The following remarks are transcribed from the diary without any attempt at classification:

Female seals were accidentally hurt, more or less severely, during the killing. I noted the more severe cases as follows:

In pod 4, 1 stunned; soon recovered and scampered off.

In pod 18, 1 so severely stunned that a man carried her off by the hind legs; recovered in fifteen minutes.

In pod 25 the most severe case occurred; she was perfectly unconscious for a long while; finally sat up, but could not be induced to move; at 2 p. m. I found her still in the same place in a dazed condition.

In pod 31 a female was also badly hurt and bleeding, but not so severely as one in pod 35, which received a very big scalp wound; both ran away with the others, however.

In pod 7 a yearling was so badly hurt that it was thought best to kill him.

In pod 28 a pup was hurt, but I don't believe it was done by clubbing; it was probably injured in the crush. At 2 p. m. I found it still unconscious in the place where it first fell, but as I roused it by lifting it up by the hind flippers it came to and in a little while ambled off.

Returning to the killing-grounds at 7 p. m., I found there a lonely pup roaming about aimlessly. As I saw the other pups escape with and follow the various pods of females, I am inclined to believe that this was the same pup which was hurt and which I was speaking of above. If so, it was very lively now and made a furious resistance when Abraham Badaef made an attempt to grab it by the hind legs. This he had to be very careful about, for a bite of even such a little fellow—probably not so very many weeks old—might be serious enough; but he finally succeeded and carried the pup off to the beach, where it was left to take care of itself.

I watched the handling of the seals very carefully in order to ascertain the amount of injury they might receive during the affair. The natives were certainly not very particular, much less so than those on St. Paul Island when Mr. True, Mr. Stanley-Brown, and the Treasury agent were observing them, but I can not say that I was much impressed with the severity of the hurt that could have been inflicted. The animals are as soft and pliable as cats, and while there is a good deal of excitement, even panic, and the wildest possible scramble one over the other, none of them seemed to mind it in the least. The whole mass of more than a dozen females would occasionally be piled up on top of a little mite of a pup, but he would immediately pick himself up upon being released and plunge into the seething mass with renewed vigor. The scramble was very suggestive of a game of football, and I feel certain that the seals were less injured externally and internally than the average football player; and as for the exertion, excitement, and fright of the drive having any influence upon the procreative powers of the bulls, as well might it be asserted that the football players impair their virility and render themselves impotent by playing the game.

Many incidents might be quoted to show how little the seals mind the drive and how soon they forget its hardships. On Bering Island I have repeatedly observed half-bulls in a drive trying to mount females in heat during intervals of rest. Another observation is so highly interesting in many ways that I quote it from my diary of July 15, 1895, North Rookery, Bering Island, as follows:

This evening I made a very suggestive observation. While working along the escarpment just west of the salt-house, I came across a small flock of seals left over from yesterday's drive. They had not returned to the sea, but had located on the very extreme northern point of the escarpment, a considerable distance from the rookery [about 250 yards] and 30 feet above the sea. I was quite surprised at finding the flock to be a "harem" consisting of 1 bull and about 20 females. I could not count their number exactly, as I did not want to disturb them, but there were about 20 females, and I heard at least 1 pup, though I did not see it. I took up my position some distance off and watched them. Several of the females were in heat and were alternately teasing the bull, getting him by the throat, but he was kept too busy running around trying to keep the harem together, as some of the females were evidently anxious to return to the rookery. He, on the other hand, was plainly well satisfied with the location and intended to hold it. * * * Now, these animals were driven yesterday and not let go until after they had reached the killing-grounds [only 220 yards away from their present location]. In view of the above observation, it seems absurd to assume that the driving had injured them in the least. Nor can this bull be accused of sleepiness—yet bulls are few on the rookery—for he was kept very busy indeed.

His vigilance did him no good, however, for the females escaped to the rookery during the night, and the place was entirely deserted when I visited it next morning.

It is certainly very significant that on Bering Island over a thousand pups are yearly driven to the killing-ground, there to be released, without any visible harm coming to them worth mentioning. If these newly born seals can stand to be driven three-fourths of a mile from Kishotchnaya and to be repeatedly trampled upon by the larger ones piling up four high, or more, on top of them, it stands to reason that the vigorous holustinki—or even the females—*as a whole* can suffer but little injury from the same cause.

Before leaving this subject it may be well to recall the following points:

On Bering Island the drives are easy, while on Copper Island they are exceedingly severe. Yet on Copper Island the bulls and half-bulls are plentiful, while on Bering Island they are comparatively scarce. The severity of the driving, therefore, does not seem to bear any relation to the relative plenty or scarcity of mature bulls on the rookeries.

Again, on Bering Island breeding females and pups are always mixed with the bachelors in the drives. This, on the other hand, does but seldom happen on Copper Island, even nowadays. Yet the female seals on Bering Island are proportionately more numerous and do not appear to be less vigorous or less prolific than on Copper Island. Moreover, the productivity of the Copper Island rookeries has evidently suffered more of late years than those of Bering Island. The driving, therefore, does not seem to be responsible for the depletion of the rookeries.

DOES THE FEMALE SEAL NURSE HER OWN PUP ONLY?

The question whether the mother seal nurses her own pup only, or whether she will allow other pups to suck her promiscuously, has been causing quite a controversy. To persons who have not studied the question on the rookeries with the closest attention it seems an absurdity to suppose that a female seal, after an absence of a day or more, during which her pup has been mingling with the thousands of other pups and roaming all over the rookery with them, should be able to find it and recognize it. During my visit to the islands in 1882–83 the question was not up, and I had paid no special attention to it. On thinking of the multitudes of pups which I had seen podded together in those days I was, therefore, on theoretical grounds, strongly inclined to side with those who deny that such a search and recognition takes place, and I so expressed myself to Mr. True when we talked this matter over on our way to the Pribylof Islands. I resolved, however, to pay special attention to this question. The great difficulty lies in the impracticability of so singling out a number of *mothers with their young* and so marking them that they could be individually recognizable at a distance and for several days at least. Only in this way would it be possible to gather proof conclusive to others than the observer himself, particularly to persons who might not be willing to accept his other observations as final.

My observations on the rookeries, however, have been sufficient to convince me that I was wrong in doubting the ability of the mother to find and recognize her individual offspring among thousands of pups of identically the same appearance. Some of these observations noted down in my diary follow here in the very words written down on the spot.

Kishotchnoye Rookery, Bering Island, July 16, 1895.—Old bulls are certainly scarce and of holustiaki I have thus far seen none. Pups are very plentiful, and the females do not appear to have been barren when they arrived. The pups are already "podding," and the two backward extensions on either side of the "parade" consist chiefly of pups.

The matki come and go, especially those that are wet and apparently just in from the sea, while the dry ones [meaning those with the fur dried from having been longer ashore] lie still, sunning and fanning themselves.

Right in front of me, about 200 feet away, is a small group of 6 dry matki and close to them a pod of about 50 pups. About 20 feet to the left is a lonely sikatch; then another similar group of dried matki and pups. The dry mothers are silent and lie down sleepily; the bull has not changed his position, his nose sticking right up into the air, during the last hour; he probably sleeps. Occasionally a wet matka [i.e., with wet fur] comes ambling up from the sea, and fighting her way through the harems next to the water's edge finally reaches this group, which is located at the posterior left hand horn of the breeding-ground—the very edge of the rookery. Such a matka will stop occasionally, shake her head and bleat (apparently in anger); a few pups will rush at her; she noses them; finally shows her teeth, bleats, shakes her head and ambles away to repeat the performance at the next pod. A matka with only a large wet spot on the hind quarters [she had consequently been a considerable time out of the water] came up in this fashion to this pod, and after nosing about in the midst of it finally grabbed a pup by the skin of its neck, much to the disgust of the pup, apparently, and carried the little one off, part of the way holding it in her mouth, part of the way pushing it ahead between her fore flippers. In this manner she brought it through several pods of pups and groups of females down to an old sikatch, a distance of fully 150 feet, where she lies down, but I can not see whether she is nursing the pup, as she is down in a hollow. I see, however, that the pup tries to escape—probably wants to go back to play—but is brought back every time.

Some of these wet matki will stop several minutes in front of four or five pups and nose them repeatedly, as if in doubt, before they go away.

There is a remarkable individual variation in the voice of the females.

At 1 o'clock p. m., I moved to the northern end of the rookery. Among the notes written down there I find the following:

The pups were very active, running to and fro, but I could not discover that any of them went very far away from where I saw them first. On the other hand, females hauling out of the water were constantly traveling all over the rookery, calling and bleating.

Later in the season similar observations were made on the little South Rookery, Bering Island (August 17, 1895). The notes then written down also contain some reflections of a general nature upon the question. It is hardly necessary to add that upon further reflection I still adhere to the opinion then expressed—an opinion which may possibly have some weight, written as it was in plain view of the seals it refers to. That part of my diary reads as follows:

I was able to get very close to the grounds, which were occupied by mothers and pups only. A good many of the latter were in the water, but there was also quite a large pod of smaller pups at the posterior edge of the herd (near the place where I was watching). I was again impressed, as before on Kishotchnaya, by the action of the females and pups when the former haul up from the water and go in search of the young to nurse it. The ground is here so small that it is a comparatively easy task for the mother to find its young, and I consequently observed several dripping-wet cows nursing pups. The mother in coming out of the water made straight for the pod of pups and the usual performance of pups rushing up and, upon being nosed at critically, refused, whereupon her search continued, was gone through.

So much is absolutely certain, that the females do not nurse the pups promiscuously. I am thoroughly convinced by what I have seen that the mother wanders considerable distances and spends much time in searching for her own individual child. Whether a mother who had searched in vain for a long time, and whose milk was pressing her very strongly, might not finally give in to the importunities of a particularly hungry pup is a question which it will probably never be possible to answer definitely, but I think such cases [if they occur] are the exceptions; the rule is certainly the reverse.

To the above I need add but little by way of argument. Persons who reject it on purely theoretical grounds have adduced much testimony to show how some other animals do not discriminate between their own young and those of other mothers, but anyone who has studied the habits of wild animals will know how utterly futile such an argument is, and how absurd it is to conclude from one species what are the habits of another.

I may finally, however, call attention to the fact that the opinion here held has of late received strong confirmation. I refer to the thousand of starving pups of late years found on the rookeries; for if the females were willing to nurse the pups of other mothers as well as their own there would seem to be no reason at all why any pups should starve to death.

MORTALITY OF PUPS.

The above reflection leads me to the question of the mortality of pups on the rookeries. With the reports of the appalling loss of pups on the Pribylof Islands fresh in my mind, one of the first inquiries I made on Bering Island, upon my arrival, naturally was whether any unusual mortality had been observed there.

The answer came from an authoritative source that—

> No abnormal mortality had been observed among the pups on the Commander Islands. A few are killed on the rookeries by the old bulls stepping on them, or otherwise, and others are caught in the breakers and surf and are thrown on the beaches. The skins of these are all utilized and their number on each island averages about 200 a year.

This was also the opinion of everybody I spoke with.

On August 1 and 2, 1895, Mr. Grebnitski and I visited the Karabelnoye Rookery on Copper Island, i. e., the eastern end of it, particularly the beach near the "Stolp" and the first breeding-ground. On the 1st of August we found "two dead pups, one with the placental cord still attached, but too much decomposed to make an examination of the cause of death possible."

The next day we visited the same place again:

> A few more dead pups were seen on the rookery this morning, all decomposed. They are easily accounted for, and the native was undoubtedly correct who stated that he had observed that the great number of sikatchi [remember, there were plenty of bulls on the Copper Island rookeries] caused so much fighting among them that many pups which came in their way got trampled upon and killed. The number, however, is plainly insignificant.

On August 22, 1895, in company with the captain, Mr. Francis R. Pelly, and several of the officers of H. B. M. S. *Porpoise*, I attended a large drive on the North Reef Rookery, Bering Island, the same of which I have given a description previously in this report (pp. 74–75). In order to fully appreciate the account which is to follow, it is necessary to remember that this great rookery covers a long rocky reef and that low tide (the difference between high and low water being about 4½ feet) uncovers a long stretch of rocky beach which forms the favorite roaming and playing ground for the pups. (Compare photographs 19b with 22b.) It should also be borne in mind that, as I have stated previously, it was extreme low water at the time we went with the natives on the rookery to take the drive.

When all the animals had been driven off, I remained behind to investigate. On the rookery ground I was startled by the great number of dead pups. I was wholly unprepared for this, because at the great distance from which it had become necessary to watch the rookeries here the small bodies of the dead seals have not been noticeable; in fact, I do not see how in the binocle they could have been distinguished from sleeping ones.

Those lying in a windrow along the high-water margin of the rookery were most conspicuous. These had evidently been washed ashore. A good many of them were in an advanced stage of putrefaction—some entirely flattened out and without hair. But an equal proportion had evidently died more recently, being in good condition. There was another class of pup carcasses, viz, those which were lying dead upon the higher portion of the breeding-ground, away back from the water's edge. These were mostly all in good condition and appeared as if they had died within a few days.

When the seals were driven off, as many pups as possible were allowed to escape into the sea, and they availed themselves of the opportunity offered to go off in large flocks. But there was a considerable number of pups staying behind singly, which upon our approach, made but feeble attempts at getting away. Evidently something was the matter with them. Upon a closer examination they were found to be very weak, and their thin, pinched appearance was at once noticeable. They were starving: their shoulder blades and ribs and hips were sticking out in strong contrast to the rounded and plump forms of those scampering off with the others. Upon handling the carcasses, both in the windrow and on the higher ground, the same state of affairs was apparent, viz, extreme leanness and emaciation.

After the rookery had been completely cleared I took my notebook and walking along the beach (starting at the south end, west side) began to count the number of dead pups, making a distinction between those in good condition and those in an advanced stage of decay. I had gone about half way round and counted about 200 of the former class and 150 of the latter, when the starshena arrived and said he had orders from the kossak, Selivanof, to ask me to leave the rookery at once.

It was evident later that Selivanof was uneasy because he thought that the number of dead pups might in some way become charged against the management, for he tried to make the whole thing a small affair and explained to me that the number of dead pups was due to their being trampled upon by the sikatchi. But for three very good reasons this theory does not hold: (1) There are now very few sikatchi on the rookery at all, entirely too few to be able by any possibility to even kill a small fraction of the pups which have recently died; (2) if this trampling caused the death of so many pups, how many might we not expect in a drive like the one to-day, in which hundreds were trampled upon, not once, but over and over again, yet not a single dead pup was found in the wake of the drive; (3) this explanation does not account for the emaciated condition of the bodies of the dead ones.

Seeing the necessity of complying with the order to leave the rookery, I could not finish my count. I am pretty positive, however, that the following estimate is not much out of the way. I may preface it by saying that the number of dead bodies on the east side appeared to be about double that on the west side.

Dead pups on west side, counted, about	350
Dead pups on east side, estimated, about	700
Dead pups on high ground, estimated, about	200
Total	1,250

In leaving the rookery I took from the high ground two bodies, which seemed quite fresh and from which, therefore, it would seem possible to determine the cause of death. In lifting the second body up by the hind flippers I was somewhat startled to find it still gasping, though it was much too weak to give any signs of life when lying on the ground. I carried it up to the killing-ground, where the rest of the company had congregated, but the pup had died before I reached them. The other pup had died apparently during the previous night.

The doctor on board the *Porpoise*, Surgeon Lloyd Thomas, kindly consented to attend the post-mortem. On viewing the opened bodies he agreed with me that death was due to inanition—lack of food. They were starved to death. There was not a trace of fat left in the tissues under the skin nor on the muscles. The extreme leanness of the carcasses was very noticeable. Both of us afterwards commented upon the plumpness of the average pups as they appeared in the drive.

I satisfied myself while on the rookery that the fresh bodies in the windrow were in the same condition, and the fact that they were thus thrown up on the beach by the sea signifies nothing, for we had had no severe weather as yet, and it is therefore impossible that these pups could have been killed by any "surf nip."

It may be well to remark right here that the fact that these bodies were found in a windrow at high-water mark does not imply that they died in the water or were killed by the sea. I have explained above that at low water a long stretch of beach is bared, upon which the pups roam about and play. Naturally, a good many of the starving pups died there at ebb tide and their emaciated bodies were thrown up by the rising tide. It may even be reasonably supposed that these hungry pups would attempt to keep as close as possible to the water's edge, to beg nourishment of the females landing.

On the 16th of September I had another chance to inspect the North Rookery. My experience was as follows:

Very few seals were seen on the rookery, only a few thousands all told; the "sands" were almost entirely deserted, nor were any seals to be observed in the sea. Those on the reef were cows and pups, the majority of the latter now gray. One or two old bulls were seen and half a dozen large four or five year olds mingling among the females, apparently playing sikatchi. I found a great number of dead pups; there were at least twice as many as on August 22. All, or nearly all, were lying in windrows. Curiously enough, there were no very fresh bodies which might have been killed by the recent northerly swell; all I saw were dead at least one week. It was also notable that nearly all were black, only here and there a gray one.

After all, the absence of fresh bodies does not signify much. I have no doubt that most of them were eaten or carried off by the blue foxes. Since the decrease in the number of seals killed the natives on Bering Island have utilized every seal carcass, salting the best parts for their own use and putting the rest, including the entrails, into holes in the ground for winter food for the sledge-dogs. The foxes in the neighborhood of the rookery, instead of feasting on the carcasses on the killing grounds and elsewhere, are therefore reduced to making a precarious living out of what they can snatch from the rookery. There being now only a few old seals on land, the foxes and their young, at this time nearly full grown, naturally clean the ground very early every morning of every pup dead during the night. The flock of large sea gulls (*Larus glaucescens*), always present on the rookery, also dispose of many bodies. It is therefore perfectly safe to assert that a great many more seal pups have died than any census based on the dead bodies present on the rookeries will account for.

It may be observed in the present connection that the bodies of even grown seals disintegrate and disappear with amazing rapidity. The combined efforts of the foxes, the birds, the staphylinid insects, and the fly larvæ reduce a carcass in very short order to a skeleton. During the winter the bones become scattered. If they are lying on or near the beach the furious winter surf sweeps them away; if they are farther away the decaying rank vegetation covers them up. During the winter the waves wash over the entire "reef" and the "sands" as well, and not a trace of the starved pup carcasses will be found on the beaches the next season.

It is a curious fact that the natives and the kossak in charge of the rookery were trying to make light of this state of affairs, although the very fact that the latter prevented me from finishing the count is evidence enough that he was aware of it. As mentioned in the abstract from my diary, he suspected that the great mortality might be charged against management. I have shown that his argument that the pups were being trampled to death on the rookery has no foundation in fact, but I did not mention, however, his answer to my question why he thought so. It was to the effect that the flattened condition of the dead pups showed that they had been trampled upon. Now, it is quite true that these half-decomposed bodies present a very much flattened appearance, but that is not surprising when we consider the amount of cartilage in their skeleton. Moreover, there is no doubt that they have been trampled upon, but that took place *after they were dead*. After I had demonstrated to Selivanof and some of the natives that the pups had died from starvation and not from any injuries received, there was evidently a load taken off their hearts, and lamentations over the great number of dead pups were heard all around. I mention this incident chiefly to show how little dependence can be placed upon the observations made by the natives, and more particularly upon their deductions, or the explanations they see fit to make.

From the above it may be regarded as well established that during the past season an unusual mortality took place among the seal pups on Bering Island, and that they died of starvation. There seems but one reasonable explanation of this phenomenon, viz, that they starved because their mothers were killed, and as they were not killed on the island there seems to be no other logical conclusion but to assume that they were killed by the pelagic sealers.

ALLEGED CHANGES OF HABITS.

During the recent discussions relative to the habits of the fur-seals and to the seal fisheries, it has been asserted by various persons that the habits of the seals have undergone, or are undergoing, material changes. Curiously enough, such changes have been alleged by both sides, but while one side attributes certain alleged changes to the disturbance of the seals on the rookeries, the other side insists that certain other alleged changes are due to the interference of the pelagic sealers.

It must not be forgotten that the habits of the fur-seals at the present time are the result of a long evolution, which dates back possibly millions of years. The habits of the North Pacific and South Pacific seals in most essential points are alike, and as these seals belong to very distinct species it is practically certain that these habits were formed before these species had emerged from the common ancestral stock. This separation probably dates back to the time when the North Pacific seals became geographically shut off from intermingling with the southern forms. From that early period the differentiation of the local habits of the former must have gone on for ages, until now there is inborn in every seal an instinct which is the inherited accumulation of the doings of tens of thousands of generations repeated every year.

It must, moreover, be borne in mind that the fur-seals are gregarious animals. Such animals always act in flocks; their habits are the habits of the flock. Individual deviation from the habits inborn does not materially affect the habits of the whole community. To effect a change in the habits of such a species it would be necessary not only that the bulk of each yearly class should change their habits in the same way, but also that the causes should continue long enough to allow the change to be transmitted to the offspring through an unknown number of generations. This is particularly true where, as in the present case, the disturbing causes mainly affect the male sex.

The first detailed description of the habits of the northern fur-seal, after Steller's account, is, as I have shown (p. 60), by Veniaminof in 1839. The next by Bryant (1870) and Elliott (1874). No change of habits is alleged up to that time. In fact, these changes are supposed to have taken place during the last five to ten years.

The theoretical considerations presented above have not been submitted with any intention of overriding by *a priori* reasoning any statement of alleged facts, though it is believed that its soundness is unassailable. It is only my intention to show the utter improbability of any change of habits within the short period in which man has interfered with the fur-seal in order to demand strong proof in support of the alleged changes. In view of that improbability we can not accept a change of habit as the explanation of certain phenomena unless demonstrated beyond peradventure, or no other reasonable explanation can be furnished. Much less can we be expected to admit such changes simply upon hearsay evidence or speculations of a general nature.

Now, for the alleged changes in so far as they have had reference to the habits of the Commander Islands seals.

The decrease in the number of killable seals on the rookeries has been attributed to their having been driven off to seek other haunts. It is alleged that they are staying at sea and that they are forming rookeries on the Kamchatkan coast.

The evidence in support of these contentions are of the most indefinite kind. On a couple of occasions fur-seals are *believed* to have hauled out at certain uninhabited rocks on the eastern coast of Kamchatka. In the first place, the accounts are so devoid of details that it is impossible to attach much importance to them. In the second place, granting that fur-seals do haul up there occasionally, what scintilla of proof is there that they have not done so always?¹ As a matter of fact, I heard these rumors of fur-seals hauling out on the coast of Kamchatka during my first visit, in 1882–83, and I know positively that Captain Sandman contemplated a trip to go in search of the alleged rookeries as far north as the island Karaginski. Nearly the whole eastern coast of Kamchatka, for a distance of more than 400 miles, is almost entirely uninhabited and very seldom visited by man.

The other evidence offered is the fact that lately the sealing schooners have been found taking fur-seals during the summer months off certain capes in Kamchatka, notably Cape Shipunski. Here the same objection obtains. What proof is there that seals might not always have been taken there in summer? Moreover, is it certain that the seals taken there by the schooners represent the bulk of the "killables" of the islands? On the contrary, it is probable that these locations of schooners indicate the feeding-grounds of the females, as hinted at in another chapter of this report. Krashenninikof's statement that "none of them are to be seen [on the east coast of Kamchatka] from the beginning of June to the end of August," only relates to the immediate coast itself and not to the open sea, where pelagic sealers make their catches.

The explanations offered of these alleged, but utterly unproven, changes of habits are diametrically opposed to each other. Those postulating that the regulated driving and killing of the bachelor seals on shore is causing the decrease of seals on the islands, explain that this interference with the seals has led them to seek other haunts—in this case the coast of Kamchatka. There was never any evidence that seals were driven away from any place frequented by them habitually and took up their abode habitually in some other place. Elliott (Monogr. Pribyl., 1882, p. 109, footnote), it is true, in speaking of the "rapacious hunters" that were drawn to the Commander Islands, states as follows:

They appear, as near as I can arrive at truths, from the scanty record, * * * to have killed many and harassed the other fur-seals entirely away from the island; so that there was an interregnum between 1760 and 1786, during which time the Russian promyshleniks took no fur-seals, and were utterly at loss to know whither these creatures had fled from the islands of Bering and Copper. When they (the seals) began to revisit their haunts on the Commander islands, I can find no specific date. * * * I think, therefore, that when the fur-seals on the Commander islands became

¹They apparently did so occasionally more than 150 years ago, if Krashenninikof's statement, that "they seldom come ashore about Kamchatka," means anything.

so ruthlessly hunted and harassed, shortly after Steller's observations in 1742, then they soon repaired, or rather most of the survivors did, to the shelter and isolation of the Pribylov group, which was wholly unknown to man.

As will be shown in the historical part of this report (p. 90), the seals, as a matter of fact, never fled from the islands of Bering and Copper, and Elliott's statement rests on a misapprehension. In the very year 1786, when Pribylof first discovered the islands which now bear his name, there returned to Kamchatka two vessels, loaded with fur-seal skins which could only have been taken on the Commander Islands, viz, one belonging to Protassof, "the cargo consisting chiefly of fur-seals," and one belonging to Shelikof, with no less than 18,000 seal skins. Pribylof, with his cargo of over 31,000 seals from the new islands, did not return until several years later.

The other explanation offered by some of those who ascribe the decrease of the seals on the rookeries to the interference by the sealing at sea, rests on an assumption that the sealers, by stationing themselves at intervals across the path of the seals on their northward migration, actually cut the seals off from the islands, thus forcing them to go elsewhere, or, in the case of those finally reaching the islands, materially delaying them on the way. It would seem that to anyone who has seen the way in which seals travel during their migrations it would be plain that it would be impossible for many times the number of sealing schooners now in existence to effectually block the progress of the migrating herds. It may well be that the positions of the schooners if plotted on the charts would show them to thus stretch across the path of the seals (it has been so asserted in Russian reports), and the large marks on the chart may well convey such an impression, but at sea the thing is quite different.[1]

This last explanation hints at the other alleged change in the habits of the seal, viz, an increasing lateness in the arrival of the bulk of the seals and a corresponding lateness in many of the phenomena of seal life on the islands. It is utterly inconceivable, however, that the sealers can even delay the bulk of the migrating herds *materially*, and the explanation, therefore, would not explain, even if the allegations of the increasing lateness of the phenomena alluded to could be substantiated, and in my opinion they can not.

A glance at the table of seals killed on North Rookery, Bering Island, during the season of 1895 (p. 110) shows that nearly one-third of the total number of skins was obtained between the 22d of August and the 13th of September (the skins being shipped September 16); in other words, during 1895 nearly one-third of the skins was taken after the time when the skins were usually shipped. Thus, in 1894 the skins were shipped August 27; in 1893, August 22; in 1892, August 24. The earlier records to which I have had access are rather incomplete, but from 1877 to 1882 the seal skins were shipped from the North Rookery, Bering Island, on the following dates:

1877	Aug. 26	1880	Aug. 20
1878	Aug. 16	1881	Aug. 13
1879	Aug. 29	1882	Aug. 16

It will be seen that even in the palmiest days of the rookeries, long before the advent of the pelagic sealers, the shipping dates do not differ materially from those

---

[1] For the contemplation of those who believe in the schooners being able to cordon the sea so as to actually intercept the seals, I submit the following: In the latter part of July, 1892, to the end of August, numerous schooners killed seals south of Copper Island. If the position of the daily catches of eight of them be plotted down on a chart, it will be seen that they covered pretty evenly an area of 13,000 square nautical miles (roughly speaking). As their combined catch amounted to about 4,000 skins, it is plain that they secured about one seal on every 3 square miles (see map, pl. 1).

of the years 1892 to 1894. The lateness of the catch in 1895 is therefore abrupt and exceptional. There is a great deal of difference in the dates upon which the hunting ceases, even in former years. Thus, on Gliuka, Copper Island, the catch was all in on the following dates:

1877	June 30	1880	Aug. 7
1878	July 12	1881	July 30
1879	Aug. 1	1883	July 13

But the lateness of the Bering Island season of 1895 is not explainable in that way either, for no amount of backwardness of the season would account for the catch after the middle of August. The summer of 1895 was certainly a cold and late one, and the snow was in places lying down to the water's edge the entire summer; but the season of 1879 was also late, according to the records, and the "year remarkable for much snow," yet the sealing season closed on both islands on August 2. There must consequently be some other reason for the lateness in 1895.

Here is where the plea comes in that the killable seals in 1895 arrived later on the rookeries than in former years. In answer to this I would like to ask the question: Is there anybody familiar with the North Rookery, Bering Island, who would deny that it would have been feasible in any previous year to have obtained there 2,670 skins between August 13 and September 13, if an attempt had been made to "scrape and rake" the rookery to the same extent as in 1895? However, the table of the seals killed on that rookery in 1895 (p. 110) directly disproves the alleged late arrival of the killables, for it will be seen that the proportion of the killables to the other classes of seals driven was decreasing toward the latter part of the season, instead of increasing. Thus, before August 12 the average proportion of killed seals to those escaping was as 1 to 2.2, while after that date it fell to 1 to 3.75.

The following table shows how exceedingly variable the first arrival of killables on the rookeries really is:

First drives on Bering Island, North Rookery.

Date.	Number of skins.	Date.	Number of skins.
1877, June 29	911	1890, May 25	41
1878, June 3	3	1891, May 29	51
1881, May 31	221	1892, June 1	5
1882, June 8	512	1893, June 24	830
1883, June 19	1,532	1895, June 13	110
1889, June 19	1,103		

The true and only explanation of the exceptional lateness of the season on Bering Island lies in the fact that killable seals, especially the younger classes, had become very scarce, and that, consequently, in order to get as many skins as possible—the company and the natives being equally eager to make up the threatened deficiency—seals were killed until the advanced staginess of the skins put a stop to it, as proven by the fact that in the last drive, in which 194 seals were killed, 51 were more or less stagy.

This statement recalls the other change alleged to have taken place. It is asserted that the skins become stagy later in the year now than formerly.

In order to fully weigh this allegation it is well to call to mind the fact that there are very few detailed and definite observations upon this point so far as the Commander Islands are concerned. Nowhere do we find any series of observations concerning this question continued through a number of years. It can not be too often emphasized that there is a great latitude of date in the events of seal life,[1] and assuredly the beginning of the stagy condition of the skin is no more bound to a rigid observation of the calendar than the other phenomena. Moreover, we do not at all know the causes which are responsible for these fluctuations; we do not know the conditions which accelerate the advent of the stagy season or postpone it. Possibly cold and damp weather may retard it. In that case we might expect the skins to become stagy somewhat later in 1895. The only definite record, so far as the Commander Islands are concerned, that I am aware of is the statement by the British Bering Sea Commission (Rep. Behring Sea Comm., 1893, p. 50) that "In 1891 we found the 'stagy' season was just beginning on the Commander Islands on the 1st of September." In 1895 there were 14 stagy skins taken in the drive on September 10. The "beginning" must, therefore, have been somewhat earlier—enough to show that in this respect 1895 is not extravagantly late.

The lack of reliable information concerning the beginning of the stagy season in earlier years is easily explainable by the fact that the killing season was over long before there was any suspicion of staginess. The question then was not at all "When does the stagy season begin?" but, on the contrary, "When does it end?" The reason of this was that the natives were anxious to begin the autumnal catch as early as possible, in order to get fresh meat, which they had been obliged to be without since the end of the killing season. Thus I find in the records of Bering Island station for 1878 that on October 13 it was contemplated to take a drive in order to get fresh meat. The "chief wished first to ascertain how skins looked at present, supposing they were too stagy yet," and accordingly went himself to the rookery, whence on the 16th he returned with 9 skins, reporting that "far was good." The drive was therefore made and 520 seals taken on October 18.[2]

The explanation of the fact that nowadays many phenomena appear to happen later is easy enough. During the years of plenty very little attention was paid to them except in the most general way. Such a thing as detailed observations and records throughout the season for a number of years sufficient to furnish exact data for reliable deductions were (and, as a rule, are yet) unknown. This is particularly true of phenomena happening after the finishing of the catch. But now, in the days of threatened commercial extinction, when the rookeries and the seals are under constant and anxious inspection, many things appear unusual and new. The killing season being extended in order to fill the required complement of skins, the impression easily takes hold that the phenomena particularly noticed during the thus belated season are themselves likewise belated.

[1] The first arrivals on Bering Island rookeries are shown in the following statement:

Date.	Rookery.	Arrivals.	Date.	Rookery.	Arrivals.
1879, May 5	North	2 bulls. 1 bachelor.	1882, April 19	North	4 bulls.
1880, April 27	do	3 bulls.	1883, May 23	South	2 bulls.
1881, May 20	do	2 bulls.	1895, May 10	North	1 bull.

[2] The difference from the Pribylof Islands will be noted, as in the latter the natives were allowed to take seals for food in the stagy season. (See, for instance, Fur Seal Arb., v, pp. 714, 715.)

FEEDING-GROUNDS OF COMMANDER ISLANDS SEALS.

It was formerly held by those who had anything to do with the Russian fur-seals that the females only went a comparatively short distance from the islands to feed. This assumption was based upon no observed fact whatsoever, and was only a general expression of the total ignorance of the true location of these feeding-grounds.

When the Canadian sealing fleet, in 1892, in a body resorted to the Commander Islands, after having been excluded from the eastern portion of Bering Sea, an inkling of the truth was felt, and undoubtedly to some extent influenced those who were responsible for the 30-mile zone fixed in the Russian-British *modus vivendi* of 1893. But it was not until the logs of the more successful schooners had been published and their positions at noon every day, with numbers of seals taken during the past 24 hours plotted on the charts, that the true status of affairs was made clear. It was then manifest that the bulk of the catch was taken on a comparatively limited area south of Copper Island, approximately bounded by 52° 30' and 54° 30' north latitude, and by 165° and 170° east longitude. The richest hauls, however, were made within a much more restricted area south and south-southwest, and on the line between this area and the rookeries of that island. As a matter of fact the overwhelming majority of the skins were taken more than 30 miles distant from the island, and most of the skins that were taken closer in were secured by those of the schooners that found it more tempting to raid the rookeries from a safe distance. The time of the season during which the fleet operated that year was chiefly during the months of July and August. There is, therefore, not the slightest doubt about the correctness of regarding the area as above limited as the feeding-grounds of the seals frequenting the Copper Island breeding-grounds (pl. 1).

The season of 1892 failed to throw much light upon the question where the Bering Island seals go to feed during the same months. The *Vancouver Belle* made a reconnaissance to the northeast and north of Bering Island, at a distance varying between 20 and 100 miles, but obtained only a few (13) stray seals, and hastened back to the Copper Island grounds. The *Maud S.* made a similar trip of exploration around Bering Island with a similar result (27 seals). The experience of the fleet, however, demonstrated pretty clearly that the Bering Island seals do not go to the Copper Island grounds to feed. It seems that the *Henry Dennis* was on or near the Bering Island feeding-grounds, for between August 1 and 7 she took 189 seals in a restricted area a little more than 100 miles due northeast of the Bering Island North Rookery.

The experience of 1895 seems to show that the Bering Island feeding-grounds are somewhat more distant and more extensive than the Copper Island ones, for the *Jane Grey* took 65 seals between August 16 and 21 about 25 miles from the Kamchatkan coast, east of Cape Afrika, while the *Ida Etta* obtained 180 skins between August 20 and September 4, 20 to 30 miles northeast and east from Cape Nagikinski, as detailed elsewhere in this report.

IV.—THE RUSSIAN SEALING INDUSTRY.

HISTORICAL.

Even before the discovery of the Commander Islands, in 1741, the fur seals were known to and hunted by the natives of Kamchatka. Krasheninnikof (Hist. Kamtschatka, 1764, p. 124 seq.) refers to this catch as follows:

> The sea cats are caught in the spring and in the month of *September*, about the river *Shupanova*; at which times they go from the *Kurilskoy* island to the *American* [i. e., Commander Islands] coast; but the most are catched about the cape of *Kronotzkoy*, as between this and the cape *Shupinskoy* the sea is generally calm, and affords them properer places to retire to. Almost all the females that are caught in the spring are pregnant; and such as are near their time of bringing forth their young are immediately opened, and the young taken out, and skinned. None of them are to be seen from the beginning of *June* to the end of *August*, when they return from the south [!] with their young. * * * They seldom come ashore about *Kamtschatka;* so that the inhabitants chace them in boats, and throw darts or harpoons at them, which stick in their body; to this harpoon is fixed one end of a rope, and the other is in the vessel; and by this rope they draw them towards the boat; but here they are to be particularly cautious whenever they chace one, if he comes near, not to suffer him to fasten upon the side of the boat with his fore paws, and overturn it; to prevent which some of the fishermen stand ready with axes to cut off his paws.

In later times there has been no such regular catch of fur-seals on the Kamchatkan coast, for the reason that now the whole region from the Bay of Avatcha to the mouth of the river Kamchatka is entirely uninhabited.

Following the discovery of the Commander Islands numerous vessels were fitted out to hunt fur-bearing animals on these islands and, later, to lay in provisions of sea-cow meat for use in their protracted journeys to the Aleutian Islands farther east (see Stejneger, American Naturalist, 1887, pp. 1049-1052). It does not seem, however, as if the fur-seal skins were in demand. The skins were not particularly valuable; the sea otters and blue foxes were still numerous; the men had more pressing and profitable things to attend to; the drying of the seal skins was both laborious and precarious in the damp climate; in brief, it did not pay to bother with the fur-seals at that period. Later, however, all this was changed. The more costly furs were getting scarce and the enterprising Russian merchants, now following upon the heels of the promyshleniks, or hunters, had found a profitable market in China for large quantities of the cheaper fur-seal. Foremost among these merchants was Grigori Ivanovich Shelikof, whose name, from 1776 on to his death in 1795, was connected with the fur trade and colonization of that part of the world. He seems to have been the first to pay special attention to the skins of the fur-seal, and was for a long time the only one who gathered them in large quantities.

The discovery of the Pribylof Islands, with their countless numbers of fur-seals, did not seem to have made any difference in this. On the contrary, the increased supply seems to have created an increased demand. Under the pressure of a fierce competition a senseless slaughter of the fur-seals was carried on until the whole business was threatened with destruction, from which it was alone rescued by the formation of a dominant company, which soon swallowed up the smaller concerns and obtained a monopoly of the entire trade of the region.

By the establishment of the great Russian-American Company, in 1799, Shelikof's enterprise was merged into the larger concern, and the Commander Islands became part of what was from now on in reality a Russian colony. The supply of fur-bearing animals must have become practically exhausted on the Commander Islands by that time, for the islands were abandoned and vessels touched but seldom, scarcely one in five years. In 1826, during the second term of the Russian-American Company, a new district, the district of Atkha, was formed, consisting of the Commander Islands and the western portion of the Aleutian chain from Attu to the island of Yunaska, consequently including the Near Islands, the Rat Islands, and the Andreanof group. The agency was located on Atkha Island.

Shortly afterwards the permanent colonization of the Commander Islands was undertaken, and Aleuts and half-breeds from the Andreanof Islands and from Attu were transferred to the new settlements on Copper and Bering islands. This was accomplished before 1828, in which year Admiral Lütke, in the corvette *Seniavin*, visited the latter island and communicated with the inhabitants of the settlement at Saranna, on the north coast.[1]

Very little is known concerning the islands and the seal industry on the islands during their occupancy by the Russian-American Company. Its jealousy of both foreign and domestic interference caused it to keep all details of its dealings secret, and as the islands were entirely away from the ordinary line of travel, scarcely any outside information is to be had. The overseers were probably unimportant, possibly uneducated, persons, and the reports of the inspectors occasionally visiting the islands are probably buried in the St. Petersburg archives of the company.

There can be no doubt that the alarming decrease in the Pribylof catch, which in ten years dropped from 60,000 skins to less than 20,000, caused the company to colonize the Commander Islands in order to work the seal rookeries there. In 1821 this decrease was threatening enough to make the board of administration of the company suggest stopping killing on the Pribylofs altogether for one season, if certain islands which were supposed to exist north of the Pribylof Islands should be found to be fictitious or not to harbor the hoped-for fur-seals (Fur Seal Arb., VIII, p. 323). The discovery was evidently not made, and the reoccupation of the Commander Islands resulted.

It seems, however, that the Greek war of independence against Turkey had a depressing effect on the fur market of Europe, and it is therefore not improbable that the Pribylof Islands were capable of filling the demand until the restoration of order in that part of the world, about 1830. By this time the annual yield of the Pribylofs had fallen to 16,000, and shortly after even as low as 6,000, the average during the ten years from 1832 to 1841, inclusive, being less than 9,700 skins a year. As I have shown elsewhere, this was not nearly enough to satisfy the demand, which probably averaged in the neighborhood of 25,000 during this period, and the deficiency was probably made up in the Commander Islands.

With the destructive methods then in vogue, it is not to be wondered at if the Commander Islands were unable to furnish an annual quota of, say, 14,000 skins for any considerable length of time. The close season which Chief Manager Etholin asked for and probably instituted in 1843 was therefore very necessary. From this

[1] This fact shows that Dybowski's statement that the settlements were not established until 1830 (Wyspy Komand., p. 36) is erroneous.

time until the end of the régime of the Russian-American Company the yield of the Commander Islands was very insignificant. It is true, the reports were in 1859 that the rookeries were again crowded, a condition evidently due to the improved methods, especially the prohibition of killing the females, but as the Pribylof Islands showed the same favorable conditions and could easily supply the demand, there was no inducement for the chief management in Sitka to incur the increased labor and risk at the more distant islands, and it is probable that the Commander Islands were only worked enough to supply the kind and quantity of skins demanded for the Siberian (Kiakhta) trade, a comparatively insignificant amount (5,000 to 6,000 a year).

In a general way the condition of affairs on the Commander Islands during this period must have been very similar to that on the Pribylofs, though from their remoteness from the seat of the general management and their comparative insignificance the criticisms of the company's dealings which were current probably applied with still greater force to the Commander Islands.

Once a year the islands had communication with the outer world. A small vessel brought supplies, etc., from Sitka and carried away the dried skins.[1] In the earlier days, after the recolonization of the islands, the skins were apparently shipped to one of the ports in the Okhotsk Sea, but this was changed later, so that all the furs were first sent to Sitka, whence they were reshipped the following year. This method, however, involving additional cost and risk, was discontinued in 1854, and the vessel which brought the supplies and inspectors was henceforth ordered to proceed with the skins to Ayan, on the Okhotsk Sea, by way of the Kuril district (Fur Seal Arb., VIII, p. 349). Occasionally some of the vessels of the semi military navy of the company would call at the islands on their cruises of protection against the foreign—chiefly American— fleets of whale ships which infested the waters in those days, and even landed on and raided the islands.[2]

When finally, in 1868, the Russian-American Company abandoned the management of the islands, the so called "interregnum" commenced. The islands were placed under the jurisdiction of the Petropaulski district, and the first thing the ispravnik, or official, of that place did was to issue a proclamation declaring the natives to be free men[3] and giving them liberty and power to regulate all their affairs, including the catch of the fur-bearing animals. It seems that only a non-commissioned officer, Teterin, was left in charge.

Quite a number of foreign merchants, among them the Russian vice-consul at Honolulu, Mr. Pfluger, but mostly American citizens, prominent among whom was the so-called "Ice Company" of San Francisco, flocked to the islands, their schooners bringing all sorts of trade goods, necessities and luxuries of life—particularly the latter—

---

[1] I am not aware that skins were ever salted on the Commander Islands during the time of the Russian-American Company.

[2] Note, for instance, the case told by Tikhmenief (Istor. Oboz. Ross. Amer. Komp., II, p. 131?) to the effect that " in 1817 one of the whalers came to Bering Island, and on the captain being told that he must not capture sea-lions on a neighboring small island (evidently Ari-Kamen), he ordered the overseer of the island to be turned off his ship, and immediately went on shore with his men with the evident intention of disregarding the prohibition. It was only when active steps were taken to resist them that the whalers left, but before going they cut down a plantation, which had been grown with great trouble, the island being without other trees or shrubs." It is curious to reflect that the British case at the Paris Tribunal has taken this incident as a proof that "traffic in fur-seal skins was carried on by a United States whaler at Bering Island" (Fur Seal Arb., IV, p. 66). There never were fur-seals on the island referred to, though, on the contrary, it formerly abounded in sea-lions (sivutch), the only animal mentioned by Tikhmenief.

[3] During the régime of the Russian-American Company the natives were practically serfs.

and, not to be forgotten, plenty of alcohol. In return they brought away as many pelts as they could induce the natives to secure. The rivalry between the traders was very sharp and the natives had high carnival most of the time as a consequence. Gambling and drinking prevailed to a fearful extent, and the natives were willing to sell anything and everything for whisky. The drunken debauches were carried on right on the rookeries, and it is authoritatively stated that, as the skins of the female seals were higher priced, because of their finer fur, quite a number of this class were slain. Besides, drunken men would not be very apt to discriminate as nicely as necessary to distinguish the females from the bachelors. It is also authoritatively asserted that a count of the skins taken was never kept, neither by the natives nor by the police authorities in Petropaulski. The figures presented elsewhere, giving the total export of skins for the period as from 60,000 to 65,000, are, therefore, only guesses and are probably underestimated rather than overestimated. At least one of the vessels, with its valuable cargo of furs, was lost. As a result of this reckless slaughter the rookeries were nearly ruined in those three years.

In 1871 there was a wholesome awakening. Hutchinson, Kohl & Co., a San Francisco firm which had already acquired extensive property and trading rights in Alaska, had opened negotiations with the authorities at St. Petersburg for a lease of the islands on practically the same conditions upon which the Alaska Commercial Company leased the Pribylof Islands of the United States, and the contract was signed February 18, 1871, but was kept a profound secret until the following summer. In the meantime the Ice Company, ignorant of the lease and in anticipation of a profitable season, had dispatched a large cargo of merchandise to the islands. Shortly after the representative of the new company arrived with the lease and took possession. As the lease not only included the monopoly of taking the furs but also of trading with the natives, there was no other choice for the Ice Company but to sell out to its successful rival at a ruinous price. So well had the secret been kept that even the ispravnik at Petropaulski, who was still to retain jurisdiction over the islands, did not know of the lease and the impending change until it was presented to him by the company's representative alluded to.

With the taking of possession by the new company a new order of things commenced. The firm's name was altered to Hutchinson, Kohl, Philippeus & Co. It had been necessary, in order to obtain the lease from the Russian authorities, to include at least one Russian subject in the firm, and Mr. Philippeus, a Russian merchant having great trading interests in Kamchatka and neighboring districts, was paid a considerable amount for the use of his name in this connection. Nominally, therefore, the company was Russian, but practically it was American. Their vessels were flying the Russian flag, but they were American property. In 1872 Hutchinson, Kohl & Co. sold their interest and property in Alaska to the Alaska Commercial Company of San Francisco, members of which also acquired a controlling interest in the Russian company. From that time on until the expiration of the lease in February, 1891, the management of the company's affairs on the Commander Islands and Tiuleni Island were in the hands of the celebrated firm, with headquarters at 310 Sansome Street, San Francisco.

The management now became practically identical with that on the Pribylofs, and an employee from the latter was sent over to the Commander Islands to teach the natives the improved methods of taking the seals and curing the skins adopted on the former. It is, therefore, unnecessary to go into details concerning this part of the industry, which has been described so often in connection with the Pribylof Islands.

The affairs as I found them in 1882 were managed in the following way:

On each island there was a local agent and storekeeper,[1] who had general charge of affairs, except the management of the taking of the skins, and who kept the books and accounts. The sealing business proper was attended to by a sealer for each rookery, who accepted the skins brought by the natives to the salt-house door and superintended the salting, bundling, etc. During this period these overseers were not natives, except Mr. Fedor Volokitin, a "creole," who represented the company at the South Rookery, Bering Island. The general management of the business was in the hands of Mr. John Sandman, the captain of the company's steamer *Aleksander II*.

Practically, the whole administration of the business rested with the company, not even a maximum limit as to the number of skins to be taken being contained in the lease. The function of the Government official stationed on the islands was chiefly confined to seeing that the company did not overstep its contract, that the regulations for the protection of the seals, as well as the natives, were enforced, to supervise the killing, keep account of the number of skins taken, to receive and distribute the money for the skins to the natives, etc.

The skins were taken by the company's steamer from the islands to Petropaulski in installments and there reloaded before shipment to San Francisco. One of the reasons for this arrangement was that Petropaulski is the only port of entry in that part of the Russian Empire, and as the skins were to be shipped to San Francisco, a foreign port, clearance paper had to be obtained in Petropaulski, while at the same time the insurance companies would only assume the risk from the sailing from the latter port. At this place, therefore, Hutchinson, Kohl, Philippeus & Co. maintained quite an extensive establishment. Large warehouses and a wharf were built on the spit in the outer harbor near the extreme end of the Nikolski peninsula, while in the town itself a large and commodious house for the accommodation of the resident agent and his family was erected.

This position as resident general agent in Petropaulski was held to the expiration of the term of Hutchinson, Kohl, Philippeus & Co. by Mr. Joseph Lugebil, who extended the company's hospitality in a manner pleasantly remembered by all who had the good fortune to visit Petropaulski during that period.

Under the lease the company was to keep a general store for the sale of articles of food, clothing, etc., to the natives on each of the Commander Islands. The merchandise was imported free of duty, but the company was only allowed to charge San Francisco wholesale prices plus a certain fixed percentage as compensation for freighting and storing the goods. The company decided about the kind and quantity of goods to be brought, while the administrator appointed by the government saw to it that the prices charged were not in excess of the contract and that the quality of the goods was satisfactory.

---

[1] On *Copper Island:* Mr. Alexander Kostromitinof, who succeeded Mr. C. F. Emil Krebs. The latter served from 1871 to 1881. Mr. Emil Kluge followed after Mr. Kostromitinof until the fall of 1891, when he was succeeded by Mr. A. Cantor.

On *Bering Island:* Mr. George Chernick. He died on the island in the fall of 1887. Mr. F. Volokitin tending the station during the following winter. In the spring of 1888 Mr. Kostromitinof was transferred from Copper Island, being relieved in 1890 by Mr. Julius Lindquist. He was succeeded in about a year by Mr. Waldemar Paetz, of St. Petersburg, whose term expired in 1895, Mr. Emil Kluge being then transferred from Copper Island.

The original lease stipulated a price of 2 silver rubles ($1.33) per skin accepted by the company, but in a subsequent supplementary contract the tax, from 1877 on, was reduced to 1.75 rubles ($1.17) for the first 30,000 skins. The natives received for their work 1 ruble (66⅔ cents) per skin for the first 30,000, and one-half ruble (33⅓ cents) for each skin over 30,000. The company had to pay a yearly rental of 5,000 rubles, and to contribute a considerable amount toward the support of the natives.[1]

There being no serviceable buildings left by the old company, Hutchinson, Kohl, Philippeus & Co. had to build a number of houses on both islands to accommodate their goods and their men. Salt-houses were erected on all the rookeries, and near each a small frame-hut for occupancy by the company's "sealer" during the killing season. In the main village on Bering Island several large stores and warehouses, a cow stable, boat-house, bath-house, besides two dwelling-houses were built, as well as similar though somewhat smaller structures in the main village on Copper Island. These are all frame-houses built of California or Puget Sound lumber by an American head carpenter with the assistance of native workingmen.

Although under no legal obligation to do so, the company gradually built and presented to nearly all the families on both islands commodious frame-houses, mostly with 4 rooms, similarly built, the natives receiving full title to them.

By careful management the seal rookeries, which at the beginning of the company's term scarcely yielded 30,000 skins annually, toward the end produced about 50,000 a year, the annual average between 1880 and 1889 being nearly 45,000. Among the entries in the diaries of the company's agents during this period are many like the following: "Natives say there are a good many female seals this year, and holostiaks, too" (Bering Island, July 23, 1877). "Assistant Starshena (chief) has been on South Rookery: reports that both holostiaks and females are double in quantity as has been before, but not many old bulls. On the North Rookery there are more seals, too" (Bering Island, August 12, 1877). "Natives report good many thousand seals more this year than ever before" (Bering Island, August 2, 1880).

The lease of Hutchinson, Kohl, Philippeus & Co. expired in February, 1891, and as the new lease was awarded to a new company, the old company's steamer *Aleksander II* was sent, early in the year to take off the fall catch of 1890, consisting of 5,800 skins.

The new company, into the hands of which the sealing industry of the Commander Islands and Tuleni now passed, was incorporated in St. Petersburg under the name "Russkoye Tovarishtchestvo Kotikovikh Promislof,"[2] or the "Russian Seal Skin Company," as the name of the firm is officially rendered in English.

By the new contract the mutual relationship of the government, the natives, and the company was materially changed, considerable power being placed in the hands of the administrator, while the direct dealings of the company with the natives were greatly reduced. The gradual americanization of the natives under the régime of Hutchinson, Kohl, Philippeus & Co. was undoubtedly distasteful to at least one of the inspectors, whose opinion with the St. Petersburg authorities must have been of great weight, as there is now a manifest tendency toward a rerussification of the business and its methods.

---

[1] The text of the contract, with supplement, is printed in Shornik Glavn. Off. Dokum. Upravl. Vost. Sibir., III, ii, Append., pp. 1-8.
[2] Russian Company for Fur-Seal Hunting (lit. transl.).

The tax to be paid for skins was raised considerably. Under the present contract the company pays to the Russian Government 10.38 "metallic" rubles (gold) per skin taken, one-half to be paid in St. Petersburg in the month of May, in advance of the sealing season. This advance payment, from 1891 to 1894, was made on a basis of 50,000 skins to be taken. In the meantime Russia had agreed with England not to take more than 30,000 skins a year, hence from 1895 the advance payment was made on a basis of only 30,000 skins. The other half is paid at the end of the season, when the amount of the catch is known. The amount which the Russian Government pays the natives for their work, 1.50 rubles per skin, is usually paid at the islands by the company at the end of the season and deducted from the draft of the balance due in St. Petersburg. It will be seen that by this arrangement the Russian Government is amply protected, but in addition the company is obliged to deposit Imperial Russian bonds with the Government in St. Petersburg to an amount equaling that of the advance payment.

The entire sealing business is exclusively in the hands of the local administration, and the company has nothing further to do with it but to receive the skins at the side of the vessel, except that it accepts or rejects the skins immediately upon their being brought from the killing-grounds and superintends the salting of the skins, for which purpose it also furnishes the salt. The administrator, therefore, has unlimited power to determine how many seals are to be taken, and also how, when, where, and by whom they are to be taken. The Government undertakes the driving, killing, skinning, salting, bundling, and delivery. The administration takes the temporary receipt for the skins issued by the company's overseer at the salt-houses and finally the agent's receipt when the skins are received on board the company's vessel. The skins are then brought to Petropaulski, where the ispravnik can not give clearance papers without first receiving the certificate of the administrator of the islands that the company has complied with the Government requirements.

Like Hutchinson, Kohl. Philippeus & Co., whose establishments both on the islands and in Petropaulski the Russian Seal Skin Company acquired, the latter has the exclusive right to keep a store on each island in which to sell to the natives such staples and articles as are necessary for their existence and comfort. The company is not allowed to bring such articles as it may deem thus necessary, but the administrator each year makes out a detailed list of quantities and qualities, specified in the minutest details, which goods the company, upon his requisition, are obliged to bring during the year and to sell to the natives at a certain stipulated percentage over the certified market price, the Government showing a decided preference for Russian goods. Should any of the goods thus ordered remain unsold on the company's hands the loss falls upon the company. As a rule, the company sells for cash to the natives, unless the administrator expressly authorizes a family head to take goods on credit, in which individual case the amount is specifically limited. At the first distribution of money for work or furs the amount is paid and the debt canceled before new sales can be made.

For the privilege of thus trading the company has to pay all the various license and guild fees to which the Russian merchants are liable, in this case amounting to many hundred rubles.

STATISTICS.

Having thus given a brief résumé of the history of the fur-seal industry on the Russian side, as it is revealed in the scanty records, it may be well to present, in chronological order, such statistics as I have been able to bring together showing the number of fur-seals taken at various times on the Commander Islands. Unfortunately, many of the figures submitted are only hypothetical, some even highly problematical, but I have accompanied them with a running comment which it is hoped is sufficiently explicit to show how the estimates were made.

It is not probable that any great slaughter of the fur-seals took place during the first period. Bassof and Trapeznikof returned from the Commander Islands in 1746 with a cargo of furs, among which are mentioned 2,000 fur-seals (Bancroft, Works, XXXIII, p. 100), but in the returns of the other expeditions between 1743 and 1750 no other mention of seal skins is made. As sea otters and blue foxes are mentioned frequently, it is evident that the fur-seal skins were of but little importance and value. It is also probable that in those days only the pups were taken, for it is specifically stated that Yugof's cargo of fur-seals, when the vessel returned in 1754 from Copper Island, consisted of 1,765 black pups and 447 gray ones (Neue Nachr. Neuent. Ins., 1776, p. 22). Tolstykh, likewise, in 1750 returned from Bering Island with 840 "young fur-seal skins or *kotiki*" (*ibid.*, p. 26), and Vorobief in 1752 is said to have brought to Kamchatka, probably from the Commander Islands, "5,700 black and 1,310 gray young fur-seals or *kotiki*" (*ibid.*, p. 27). Drushinin in 1755 returned with 2,500 seals taken on Bering Island (*ibid.*, p. 32). These, as well as the 2,000 brought by the *Vladimir* in 1767 and the 630 in Popof's *Ioann Pretecha* in 1772, were also probably young.

As I have shown elsewhere (Amer. Natural., XXI, Dec., 1887, p. 1053), the sea cow on the Commander Islands had become nearly extinct in 1763. The sea-otter had also been killed off there to such an extent that the hunt had become unprofitable, and the blue foxes likewise. As the fur-seal skins were of comparatively little value, there were no inducements for the fur-hunters to visit the islands after that time as frequently as before. It is certain enough, as shown above, that the fur-seals had not left the Commander Islands, or become nearly extinct there, as alleged by Elliott, as there are records of vessels having actually visited the islands between 1760 and 1786, bringing plenty of seal skins back. As a matter of fact, it was during this very period that the heaviest slaughter of fur-seals took place on the Commander Islands. It appears that Shelikof was the first trader to deal extensively in fur-seals, and his name is not mentioned until 1776. It is stated that up to 1780, consequently in four years, he had imported 70,000 fur-seal skins. It is furthermore stated that his vessel, *Sv. Ioann Rylskoi*, returned in 1786 with 18,000 fur-seals. In the same year Protassof returned with a "cargo consisting chiefly of fur-seals." Panof's vessel, *Sv. Georgi*, which also returned in 1786, had less luck, having secured only 1,000 seal skins. As the Pribylof Islands were not discovered until that year (the first cargo from there did not arrive in Okhotsk until 1789), the bulk of the fur-seal skins brought to Kamchatka must have come from Commander Islands (see Bancroft, Works, XXXIII, pp. 185-191). There is *record* of about 100,000 skins having been taken between 1760 and 1786, while from 1746 to 1760 the skins brought to Kamchatka probably did not exceed 20,000.

For the early times, between the return of the first cargo from the Pribylof Islands to 1841, the year of the expiration of the second term of the Russian-American Company, there are absolutely no accessible records as to the number of seals taken at

96 BULLETIN OF THE UNITED STATES FISH COMMISSION.

or shipped from the Commander Islands. Elliott states (Monogr. Pribyl. Group, p. 70) that from 1797 to 1861 the statistics of skins taken from the Pribylof Islands include "about 5,000 annually from the Commander Islands," but I have reasons for believing that this statement is erroneous. As I have shown elsewhere, there was no regular population on the Commander Islands until after 1826, and as vessels touched at the islands at great intervals only, an annual catch of 5,000 skins from the Commander Islands is out of the question. This is also plain from the figures given by Veniaminof and Von Wrangell. The former, according to the table presented by the British Bering Sea commissioners (Rep., p. 132), gives the total number of seals killed on the Pribylof Islands from 1826 to 1832, inclusive, as 137,503. This agrees fairly well with the statement by Baron von Wrangell, the chief manager of the Russian-American Company during that period, that the total number of skins exported from the colonies from 1827 to 1833 amounted to 132,160. This number is clearly meant to include all the skins exported from the whole colony, and would include any and all from the Commander Islands, if skins were then taken there, for he expressly remarks that his statistical figures date from the incorporation of the Atkha district, which included the Commander Islands, under the colonial management (Stat. Ethn. Nachr. Russ. Besitz. Nordwestk. Amer., p. 24).

The fact that the Commander Islands were not subject to the central management located at Sitka until 1826 leads me to believe that the few Commander Islands skins taken are not reported in the figures before that date, but that they were received direct either at Petropaulski or Okhotsk.[1]

But even Veniaminof's figures are not beyond suspicion. In his "Zapiski," published in St. Petersburg in 1840, vol. I, chap. XII, he writes as follows (according to Elliott, Monogr., p. 165): "The company on the island of St. Paul killed from 60,000 to 80,000 fur-seals per annum, but in the last time (1833?) [Elliott's interpolation], with all possible care in getting them, they took only 12,000. On the island of St. George, instead of getting 40,000 or 35,000, only 1,300 were killed." Now, if we examine the table of his figures, as presented by Elliott (Monogr., p. 143), we find no year between 1817 and 1837 in which 12,000 seals were taken on St. Paul (13,200 in 1833), nor 1,300 on St. George.

[1] To show how very unsatisfactory the statistical figures of the early days as collated by the British Bering Sea Commission are, I may mention that they estimate the number of fur-seals killed on the Pribylof Islands from 1786 to 1833, inclusive, as follows:

1786 (according to Shelikof)	40,000
1787-1806 (Rezanof's estimate)	1,000,000
1807-1816 (approximated from Tikhmenief at 47,500 annually)	475,000
1817-1833 (Veniaminof)	543,230
Total, 1786-1833	2,058,230

This number is 1,120,323 skins short, for Baron von Wrangell, who undoubtedly had pretty reliable information to go by, states that "since the discovery of the islands St. Paul and St. George, from the year 1786 to 1833, 3,178,562 fur-seals were killed there" (Stat. Ethn. Nachr. Russ. Am., p. 48). These I should be inclined to distribute as follows:

Fur-seals killed on St. Paul Island, 1786-1833:

1786 (according to Shelikof)	40,000
1787-1798	1,035,467
1799-1816 (Bancroft's figures from 1799-1821, 1,767,540, minus Veniaminof's figures from 1817-1821, 267,484)	1,499,856
1817-1833 (Veniaminof)	543,239
Total (Von Wrangell's figure)	3,178,562

In the same table and report it is stated (p. 133) how the figures for the years 1861 and 1862 are obtained: "1861.—Bancroft's total for years 1842-1861 (both inclusive) is 338,600. The total for years 1842-1860 (both inclusive) is 308,901. This being deducted from total for 1842-1861 gives the number of seals taken in 1861." In their table, however, the total for 1842-1860 is not 308,901 but 318,901.

While thus the figures relating to the Pribylof Islands are dubious and unsatisfactory, there are next to no records in regard to the catch on the Commander Islands between 1787 and 1862. In fact, there is hardly a scrap of available history to be found on the subject during that period.

There is no reason to doubt, however, that the slaughter of the fur-seals on the Commander Islands after 1787 was as enormous as on the Pribylofs, proportionately (where, according to my calculation, the average annual killing was 86,511.)[1] The result of this *indiscriminate* wholesale slaughter undoubtedly brought the rookeries to a very low ebb, for we find the Commander Islands practically abandoned shortly after the establishment of the Russian-American Company, and a permanent population was not again established until after 1826, by which time the rookeries must have recuperated to some extent. The same old method of killing the young ones, and not even sparing the females, must soon have brought on the inevitable result of depletion, for we find that the chief manager of the colonies, Capt. I. A. Kuprianof, as early as 1839, had conferred with the baidar-steerer Shayashnikof as to when, in his opinion, it would be possible to begin taking a full catch on St. Paul Island in order to *establish a close time for sealing on* St. George and *the Commander Islands*, and that Captain Etholin, his successor as chief manager, in 1842 asked permission to institute a close season on the Commander Islands, a permission that was granted the following year (Fur Seal Arb., XVI, pp. 76, 114).[2]

Shortly after, the prohibition to kill females was enforced, and as a result of both measures the seals were again increasing, so that in 1859 the chief manager could write to St. Petersburg that, according to the reports of the officials of "even those of the Commander Islands, the seals have increased in numbers on all accessible places to such an extent that the areas occupied by them appear crowded." It is evident, however, that the managers proceeded with caution, notwithstanding, for in the years from 1862 to 1867, the year of the final dissolution of the Russian-American Company, only 4,000 to 5,000 seals (gray pups) a year are said to have been taken. These figures are from the following table, which is copied from the report of the British Bering Sea commissioners (p. 214), those from 1865 being official:

Skins taken for shipment from Commander Islands, 1862–1867, by the Russian-American Company after the expiration of its third term.

Notes.	Year.	Number.
Only gray pups killed	1862	4,000
Do	1863	4,500
Do	1864	5,000
Do	1865	4,000
Do	1866	4,000
Do	1867	4,000
Total		*25,500

[1] Not only were females and pups killed, but the "bulls and young bulls" also, for in spite of their coarse hair the Chinese at Kiakhta paid high prices for them (Fur Seal Arb., VII, p. 165).

[2] Figures representing the catch during the Russian-American Company's terms are given in the final table of shipments by periods.

[3] In Nordenskiöld's "Voyage of the Vega," Am. ed., p. 609, there is a table of figures relating to the catch of seals on the Commander Islands involving several errors. Aside from the fact that it purports to give the catch on Bering Island only, while in reality the figures represent the catch on both Bering and Copper islands, it gives the catch for the year 1867 as 27,750 seals. Here is apparently a double error. Compared with the corrected figures given by Elliott (Monogr., p. 113), 27,500 is evidently meant to include the catch from 1862 to 1867, inclusive, in which case, however, the statement is 2,000 too high.

The table of the British commissioners in the note says "including Robben Island," but no skins were regularly taken there in those days.

During the so-called "interregnum"—that is, the years 1868–1870, inclusive—from the time the Russian-American Company abandoned the management of the islands until Hutchinson, Kohl, Philippeus & Co. assumed control, no restrictions, except such as the natives themselves might impose and enforce, were placed upon the slaughter, which in these three years averaged about 20,000 annually. The seals taken up to that time were exclusively gray pups, but during the interregnum at least one of the traders, viz, Mr. J. Malovanski, had become aware of the increased demand and higher prices for bachelor seals, and he consequently induced the natives to bring him skins of the latter. However, of the 60,000 killed a great many must have been young ones, but the proportion between the two classes will probably never be known. Three sets of figures are given for the catch in these three years, as follows:

Year.	Elliott (Monograph, p. 173).	Niebaum (Fur Seal Arbitration, III, p. 202).	British Bering Sea Commissioners (Rep., p. 214).
	Number.	Number.	Number.
1868	12,000	*15,000	12,000
1869	24,000	20,000	21,000
1870	24,000	30,000	27,500
Total	60,000	65,000	60,500

*About.

It is doubtful whether any of these figures are exact, but as they agree pretty well, and as the last set represents the official figures of the Russian administrator, they may be taken as authentic.[1]

Upon the arrival on the scene of the agents of Hutchinson, Kohl, Philippeus & Co., in 1871, it was found that the *indiscriminate* slaughter during these three years had again done sensible injury to the rookeries. Says Mr. C. F. Emil Krebs, who stayed on Copper Island from 1871 to 1881 (Fur Seal Arb., III, p. 195):

Upon my arrival at the island, in 1871, the native chief told me that the seals were not as plentiful as they had been formerly. I announced that we intended to secure 6,000 skins that year. They protested that it was too many, and begged that a smaller number be killed for one year at least. We, however, got the 6,000 skins, as proposed,[2] and an almost constantly increasing number in every subsequent year as long as I stayed on the islands, until in 1880 the rookeries had so developed that about 30,000 skins were taken, without in the least injuring them.

The history of the gradual increase of the yield of the rookeries during the following twenty years, and the subsequent decrease until the present day, is plainly shown in the following tables. It should be remarked that the lower figures of 1876, 1877, and 1883 are due not to a lack of seals on the rookeries, but to the fact that the company did not desire more (in 1883, in fact, not as many as they were obliged to take). The following comparison of the Commander Islands and Tiuleni catches with those of the Pribylof Islands demonstrates the correctness of this statement.

---

[1] I may here correct a mistake in the oft mentioned table presented by the British Bering Sea commissioners (Rep., p. 214). They run a line between the years 1869 and 1870 and mark it "Alaska Commercial Company's first term began." As a matter of fact the term (and *only* term) of Hutchinson, Kohl, Philippeus & Co., the term and company meant, did not begin until 1871, and the catch of 27,500 skins during 1870 is therefore to be credited to the merchants trading during the interregnum.

[2] Only 3,614 of that number were shipped in 1871, the remainder in 1872.

THE RUSSIAN FUR-SEAL ISLANDS.   99

Comparison of the catches at Commander Islands and Tiuleni with those at Pribylof Islands.

Year.	Commander Islands and Tiuleni.	Pribylof Islands.	Year.	Commander Islands and Tiuleni.	Pribylof Islands.
	Skins.	Skins.		Skins.	Skins.
1874	31,300	107,952	1880	48,504	100,634
1875	36,279	101,249	1881	43,522	101,734
1876	26,960	83,478	1882	44,620	101,736
1877	21,533	77,956	1883	24,609	77,063
1878	31,340	101,394	1884	53,263	101,013
1879	12,749	106,968			

There are a number of published statements referring to the seal catch on the Commander Islands since 1871, but none of them are complete, nor are the figures given for the separate islands. The figures also vary to some extent, for several reasons. In some cases the Tiuleni Island skins have been counted in with those of the Commander Islands. Thus, in Capt. G. Niebaum's statement (Fur Seal Arb., III, p. 204), by inadvertence the number of killed seals for 1890, 53,780, includes 1,456 skins from Tiuleni, the total for the Commander Islands being only 52,324. Many other discrepancies are explained by the fact that the various figures refer to various counts. Some may and do refer to skins shipped, others to seals killed. The almost unavoidable difference in the counting of such large quantities of skins is manifest when we remember that the skins are first counted at the salt-house and then again as they go over the ship's side into the hull. Upon these counts the official government statement is made up. The skins are then unloaded in Petropaulski, again loaded into the steamer, and again unloaded and counted in San Francisco. It is, therefore, not to be expected that lists made up from the various figures in the island count, the ship's count, and the custom-house count would agree exactly. The figures given in the following table are based chiefly upon the various station journals as well as the ships' logs, partly upon the figures already published, and partly upon a list showing the number of seals shipped between 1883 and 1891 from Bering and Copper islands separately, kindly furnished by Mr. Max Heilbronner, of the Alaska Commercial Company.

Number of fur-seal skins shipped from Commander Islands and Robben Island from 1871 to 1895, inclusive.

Year.	Bering Island.	Copper Island.	Robben Island.	Total.	Year.	Bering Island.	Copper Island.	Robben Island.	Total.
1871	0	3,658	0	3,658	1883	20,966	20,771	1,838	43,575
1872	14,392	14,964	0	29,356	1884	24,555	30,036	0	54,591
1873	13,044	14,661	2,694	30,399	1885	21,298	25,049	0	46,347
1874	13,406	15,489	2,414	31,309	1886	26,456	20,908	0	47,362
1875	12,712	20,440	3,127	36,279	1887	23,784	29,076	0	52,850
1876	10,358	15,074	1,528	26,960	1888	19,996	32,328	1,456	53,780
1877	7,192	11,392	2,949	21,533	1889	*17,881	†18,085	450	36,815
1878	8,130	20,070	3,140	31,340	1890	16,590	14,654	0	31,244
1879	13,572	25,166	4,002	42,740	1891	13,992	17,294	1,500	32,786
1880	15,190	30,014	3,339	48,504	1892	13,165	13,122	1,000	27,287
1881	16,078	23,237	4,207	43,522	1893	9,526	6,893	1,300	17,719
1882	18,512	22,002	4,106	44,620					
1883	13,480	13,170	2,049	28,699					
1884	21,384	28,060	3,819	53,263	Total	385,691	485,532	44,900	916,122

*Of these, Hutchinson, Kohl, Philippeus & Co. shipped 4,059; the Russian Seal Skin Co. shipped 13,825.
†Of these, Hutchinson, Kohl, Philippeus & Co. shipped 1,741; the Russian Seal Skin Co. shipped 16,324.

To this total should be added 416 skins taken from the schooner *J. H. Lewis*, seized in 1891, and 2,152 skins taken in 1892 from the seized schooners, which obtained them chiefly off Copper Island. The latter skins were sold by the Russian Government, part in Petropaulski (1,124), part in London, and were shipped in the company's steamer to San Francisco (see Fur Seal Arb., VII, pp. 375, 417). The total number of skins shipped from the Russian seal islands from 1871 to 1895, inclusive, is, therefore, 918,690.

That this list does not give an accurate idea of the number of seals killed in each particular year is clear from the fact that the fall catch of the year is not shipped until the following summer. In some years there was no fall catch at all, in others it was very considerable. Thus, for instance, in 1871, the first year of the lease of Hutchinson, Kohl, Philippens & Co., no less than 10,500 seals were killed on both islands, of which, however, only 3,658 were shipped from Copper Island (the island count, or 3,614 by the San Francisco count), while none at all were shipped from Bering Island. Full data of the actual number of seals killed in each year are not at hand, but the following table, based upon data furnished me by the late Mr. G. Chernick, then station-keeper on Bering Island, may serve as an indication of the difference between a list of seals killed and one of skins shipped.

Seals killed and skins shipped from Bering Island, 1871-1882.

Year.	Killed.			Shipped.	
	Total.	Summer.	Fall.	Skins.	Year.
1871	4,500	....	....	14,392	1872
1872	12,912	9,892	3,020	13,644	1873
1873	13,040	10,024	3,016	13,406	1874
1874	13,034	10,390	2,644	12,712	1875
1875	11,790	10,068	1,722	10,358	1876
1876	9,822	8,636	1,186	7,192	1877
1877	6,046	6,006	....	8,130	1878
1878	8,674	8,130	544	13,572	1879
1879	13,028	13,028	....	15,160	1880
1880	15,160	15,160	....	16,078	1881
1881	16,078	16,078	....	18,512	1882
1882	18,512	18,512	....		

It would have been interesting and instructive to have a list of skins taken from each rookery for a considerable length of time, but I have been unable to obtain the necessary data. The following table, however, furnishes this information for the years 1891 to 1895:

Fur-seals killed on the Commander Islands, 1891-1895.

Locality and season.	1891.	1892.	1893.	1894.	1895.
Bering Island:					
Summer—					
North Rookery	13,177	16,171	12,156	12,516	8,370
South Rookery	648	419	327	627	564
Fall.				592	
North Rookery	....	1,422	....	....	
South Rookery	....	87	22	....	
Copper Island:					
Summer	....	....	....	....	6,396
Karabelni	3,664	4,552	5,343	4,268	
Giluka	12,660	10,162	10,938	8,387	
Fall.				497	
Karabelni	....	451	86	....	
Giluka	....	502	381	....	
Total	30,149	33,766	29,253	26,887	15,330

Shipment of skins from the Commander Islands (exclusive of Robben Island), by periods.

1746 to 1760, 15 years (period of plenty of sea-otters, foxes, and sea-cows); annual average about 1,333..total about..	20,000
1761 to 1786, 16 years (other fur-bearing animals becoming scarce and sea-cow exterminated) annual average about 6,250................................total about..	100,000
1787 to 1798, 12 years (from discovery of Pribylof Islands to Russian-American Company), same annual average..............total in round figures about..	50,000
1799 to 1826, 28 years (from Russian-American Company to establishment of Atkha district), annual average about 476...total in round figures about..	15,000
1827 to 1841, 15 years (to expiration of Russian-American Company's second term), yearly average about 10,000 ....or total about..	150,000
1842 to 1861, 20 years (Russian-American Company's third term), yearly average 476...total about..	9,526
1862 to 1867, 6 years (hold-over of Russian-American Company), yearly average 4,250...total about..	25,500
1868 to 1870, 3 years (interregnum), yearly average 20,166 ....total about..	60,500
1871 to 1891, 20 years (lease of Hutchinson, Kohl, Philippeus & Co.), yearly average 36,791 ....total..	735,828
1891 to 1895, 5 years (lease of Russian Seal Skin Company to date), yearly average 27,077 ....total..	135,385
Skins seized within territorial waters, 1891 and 1892............................	2,568
Grand total...about..	1,304,307

As previously stated, some of these figures do not pretend to be more than guesses. Most of them are explained in the foregoing pages, but the figures for the years from 1787 to 1861 need some explanatory remarks as to how these guesses were made.

From 1787 to 1798, inclusive, 12 years, I have assumed the annual average to have equaled that of the foregoing 26 years, giving 46,152, or, in round figures, 50,000.

From 1799 to 1826, the period of 28 years during the lease of the Russian-American Company when the yield was not sufficient to induce the company to establish settlements on the islands, I have assumed that the annual average can not have exceeded the yield between 1842 and 1861, when the company still maintained the settlements, or, in round figures, 15,000.

For the 15 years from 1827 to 1841, inclusive, I have made the following guess: Assuming that Wrangell at the end of 1833 had 30,000 skins on hand, about 25,000 (Wrangell shipped, 1827–1833, 132,160 + assumed surplus on hand, 30,000=162,000 — Veniaminof's figures for killed seals on Pribylofs in years 1826–1832, 137,503=24,658) must have been taken on the Commander Islands from 1827 to 1832, inclusive. In 1840 the Russians had a demand for not over 30,000 skins annually (Simpson, Overl. Journ., p. 131). Probably they were nearly able to fill it, for Mr. E. Teichmann states (Fur Seal Arb., III, p. 579) that "up to the year 1853 about 20,000 skins were annually received in London" from the Russian-American Company. It is probably safe to assume, then, that 6,000 went to Kiakhta. Now, during the nine years from 1833 to 1841, inclusive, the Pribylof Islands yielded only 80,135. The assumed sale being 234,000 skins, and there being only 30,000 on hand and 80,000 killed on the Pribylofs, it follows that a yearly average of about 14,000 would have to be obtained on the Commander Islands, or about 125,000, to which should be added the 25,000 assumed to have been taken from 1827 to 1833, giving a total of 150,000.[1]

---

[1] Figures thus obtained do not pretend to any accuracy. How misleading the process may be is clearly illustrated in the table presented by the British Bering Sea commissioners (Rep., p. 132) and the explanation concerning the sources of information. They utilize the total given by Bancroft for 1842–1861, viz, 338,600 (the identical figures utilized above), and from this deduct the number of skins taken from 1842 to 1860, according to a different source, thus obtaining the number taken in 1861. Correcting an apparent error in the subtracter, the number for 1861 would be 19,689. October 14, 1861, the chief manager of the colonies, Furuhielm, writes home to the board of administration that "in the course of this year 47,940 seal skins have been taken from the islands of St. Paul and St. George." 19,689 calculated, but 47,940 taken! This is a sad commentary upon the probable accuracy of the calculated figures.

The only figures relating directly to the yield of the Commander Islands during this period are those by Tikhmenief, that there were exported from Bering Island, during the third term of the Russian-American Company, 9,526 fur-seal skins (Istor. Oboz. Obraz. Ross.-Amer. Komp., II, p. 296). These figures, from the connection, are meant to cover the whole export from the Commander Islands, as from the fact that the population of Copper Island at that time was but 90, all told, it seems probable that no fur-seals were taken on Copper Island at all.

ADMINISTRATION.

There remains to be said a few words concerning the Government administration of the Commander Islands.

Before the establishment of the Russian-American Company the islands were scarcely under any territorial jurisdiction, though in reality they were undoubtedly subject to the rule of the "commander" of Kamchatka, a naval officer residing in Petropaulski. With the advent of the Russian-American Company the direct control of these islands went out of the hands of the Russian Government, but it seems that the company took but slight interest in them until 1826, in which year they were incorporated into the Atkha District, with headquarters on Atkha Island. After the permanent location of a colony, a Russian "overseer" was stationed on Bering Island.

When, in 1868, the Russian-American Company's régime was at an end, the islands returned to the jurisdiction of the "ispravnik" in Petropaulski, while the remainder of the Atkha District became part of the United States by the cession of Alaska to the latter. Kamchatka being, since 1855, only a district of the so-called Coast Province (*Primorskaya Oblast*), the administration of the islands consequently rested with the governor at Khabarovka, subject to the authority of the governor-general of Eastern Siberia at Irkutsk.

Thus things remained until the growing importance of the seal business during the lease to Hutchinson, Kohl, Philippeus & Co. made it desirable to locate a higher official on the islands to represent the Government in its dealings with the company on the islands and to govern the natives. Mr. Nikolai Aleksandrovich Grebnitski was selected as the first "administrator," landing on Bering Island on August 21, 1877, and has continued as such up to the present time. His long retention in office, coupled with the fact that his salary has been raised repeatedly, that he has gradually risen in rank, until he now holds that of a colonel, and that he has been decorated several times, is ample proof that he has conducted the affairs of the Commander Islands to the full satisfaction of his Government.

As subordinates, two kossaks from Kamchatka were stationed, one on each island. Since 1890, however, another civil officer has been located on Copper Island, acting as Mr. Grebnitski's assistant there. Until last year, when he had to seek a milder climate, on account of broken health, this position was held by Mr. Nikolai Matveyevich Tielmann. His successor was on his way to the islands in the fall of 1895, on the bark *Bering*, but on account of the weather failed to make a landing and had to return to Vladivostok.

One of the first things attempted by Mr. Grebnitski, after putting the community affairs of the natives into shape, was to regulate the fur-seal business, i. e., the administrative portion of it as it related to the taking of seals on the rookeries, and the rules first framed were embodied in an order (*prikaz*) dated April 28, 1878 (o. s.), and the second chapter of a regulation (*predpisanie*) of the following May 1 (o. s.).

In the latter a form was provided which, when filled out and signed by the overseer and native chief, is returned to the office of the administrator. Printed blanks are now furnished, and to illustrate this useful document a sample is herewith appended, as follows:

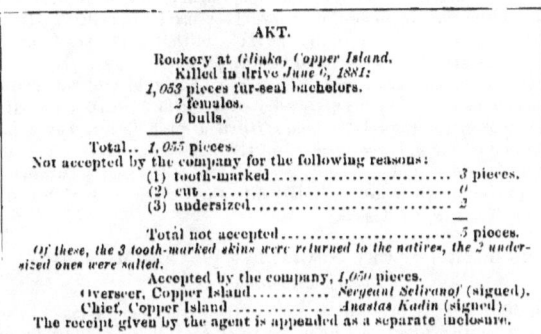

```
                              AKT.
                 Rookery at Glinka, Copper Island.
                     Killed in drive June 6, 1881:
                 1,053 pieces fur-seal bachelors.
                     2 females.
                     0 bulls.
          Total..  1,055 pieces.
          Not accepted by the company for the following reasons:
                 (1) tooth-marked........................  3 pieces.
                 (2) cut................................   0
                 (3) undersized.........................   2
                                          Total not accepted..................  5 pieces.
          (Of these, the 3 tooth-marked skins were returned to the natives, the 2 under-
          sized ones were salted.
                                Accepted by the company, 1,050 pieces.
          Overseer, Copper Island........... Sergeant Selivanof (signed).
          Chief, Copper Island ............. Anastas Kadin (signed).
          The receipt given by the agent is appended as a separate inclosure.
```

Gradually a set of elaborate regulations have been framed which govern the rookery business. Such as differ from those in vogue on the Pribylof Islands are here quoted from Lieut. Commander Z. L. Tanner's report for 1892 (Rept. U. S. Fish Com., 1892, p. 40), as follows:

None but natives are allowed to work on the rookeries.

A fine of 100 golden rubles is imposed by the Government upon anyone who kills a female fur-seal, and 10 rubles for killing a pup, and such additional fine shall be paid as shall be imposed by the natives themselves.

No person, native or otherwise, is allowed to wear boots with nails in them on the rookeries; rubber boots or tarbasi[1] must be used.

Chewing or smoking tobacco, expectorating, or attending to the requirements of nature are strictly prohibited on the rookeries.

Knives may be carried, but a stick with a metal ferule is not permitted.

No small boys or females are allowed on the rookeries, and dogs must be left half a mile from the rookeries during the breeding season.

Owing to the repeated raids on the rookeries, particularly those on Copper Island in the early eighties, by marauding schooners, which the natives in several cases had to drive off by means of powder and ball, an experiment was decided upon to station regular soldiers on the islands in order to protect them. In June, 1884, the Russian cruiser *Razboinik* brought one officer and twenty-three men for Copper Island and nine men for Bering Island. Five soldiers were stationed at the South Rookery of the latter island, where they did good service in driving off the schooner *Nakhalien* and capturing one of the crew. In a few years, however, the soldiers were withdrawn, and instead the watch force of the natives was organized in a military manner, one Kamchatkan kossak on each island and two conscript soldiers of the regulars, serving

---

[1] Native seal-skin moccasins.

their time, acting as officers, under the immediate command of the administrator and his assistant. Watchhouses are erected overlooking the rookeries, and the guards provided with good spyglasses and rapid-firing army rifles. Stands of arms and plenty of ammunition are kept in the Government building at the settlements.

The central authorities maintain the supervision of the local administration by occasionally sending out an inspector, or "revisor," as he is called. His duty is to ascertain the state of affairs generally, as well as the condition of the natives, to receive any complaints of the latter, and investigate their grievances.

A change has of late years been effected in the higher administration of the islands, inasmuch as they have been transferred from the Department of the Interior to the Department of the Imperial Domains, without prejudice, however, to the territorial jurisdiction of the governor-general of the Amur Provinces. The administrative status of the Commander Islands is therefore now exactly parallel to that of the Pribylof Islands in their double relation to the United States Treasury and the governor of the Territory of Alaska.

CONDITION OF THE COMMANDER ISLANDS ROOKERIES.

PRELIMINARY REMARKS.

When, in 1882, Prof. S. F. Baird sent me to the Commander Islands to study their natural history he also impressed upon me the desirability of obtaining some information in regard to the fur-seal and the sealing industry of the islands. Owing to my hurried departure—I had only 48 hours in which to prepare for the expedition destined to stay two years in the field—I failed to take a photographic outfit with me. In default of photographs, however, I made numerous sketches of the rookeries, and also undertook to construct maps of them by means of an azimuth compass and a pediometer. I submit some of the sketches with this report in exact facsimile of the originals; they have not been touched up in any manner (pls. 20, 41, 42, 43). For that reason they appear extremely crude, but it is thought that they will be accepted with more confidence in their present shape and carry with them more conviction than if they had been fixed up or "improved" in any way.

The only photographs of the rookeries in their palmy days were taken by the Russian Colonel Voloshinof, but with only a few exceptions they are not intended to portray the totality of seal life on the individual rookeries, and for that reason offer but scant material for comparison with my sketches of 1882-83, or my photographs of 1895, the more so since the points of view in all instances except one are different from mine. However, those that can be utilized in this connection I have reproduced.

When photographing the rookeries last summer I made a special effort to obtain views from the identical points from which I had made my sketches in 1882 and 1883. Taking into account the different focus of the eye and the photographic lens, I think a comparison between the sketches and the photographs will establish the general accuracy and truthfulness of the former.

When studying the rookeries in 1882-83, I did it with H. W. Elliott's Monograph of the Pribylof group in my hands. In the main I found that his observations in regard to seal life were applicable to the Commander Islands seals, and at the same time that the conditions of the sealing industry were also nearly the same on the two groups, so far as could be judged from descriptions alone. There were minor points in which I found, or thought I found, differences, but in the main I agreed, with one notable exception, however, viz. the estimation of the number of seals on the rookeries. Of course, his estimate related only to the Pribylof group, and as I knew the latter only from his description, I felt bound not to criticise him. But I became sure of this: His methods and results did not apply to the Commander Islands. Elliott's method was to ascertain the area of the rookeries in square feet and then multiply this with an average figure calculated from the number of seals, large and small, counted on a certain piece of ground. But I found insurmountable obstacles. In the first place, the method required not only a very detailed and accurate topographical survey on a large scale, of each rookery, but the calculation of the area presented an exceedingly difficult problem. No two pieces of ground are alike. In some the beach is smooth and the seals are lying close; others are covered with smaller or larger rocks and stones, where the seals lie scattered as a matter of necessity. In other places, again, there are open spaces or thin spaces. Then, again, the outlying rocks and reefs defy close calculation as to number and area. On Copper Island small herds of seals would be found in corners and coves, on ledges of cliffs, and under overhanging rocks, sometimes entirely out of sight and most times beyond computation. I found that every factor of the calculation would have to be estimated averages, and that these averages in their turn had to be founded upon estimated items; in short, that the whole calculation would have to be a product of guesses multiplied by guesses. As we have to deal with large figures, it is evident that a mistake in the estimated factors must result in disastrously great mistakes in the total number.

Suppose, for instance, that I had "estimated" the area covered by the seals on both islands to be 4,000,000 square feet. If I "estimated" the average ground covered by a seal (mother, pup, and bachelor) on the rookeries to be 2 square feet, I would obtain a total of 2,000,000 seals on the Commander Islands. But, on the other hand, if I guessed that on the average a seal, large and small, on the rookery occupies 5 square feet—and this would possibly have been more nearly correct—I would get only a total of 800,000 seals, large and small. According to this method, various persons might estimate the number of seals on North Rookery, Bering Island, from 20,000 to 120,000, and yet it might be impossible to convince any of them that they were mistaken.

A numeration of the seals being utterly valueless unless accurate, or at least approximately accurate, I naturally regarded such an estimate of the number of seals on the rookeries not only as useless, but as downright pernicious. Actual counting being impracticable, and an individual judgment of the number being about as valueless as the above method of calculation, unless acquired by a very long practice, I gave up all attempts at presenting figures.

When, after twelve years, I again visited these rookeries the same question confronted me. In one place, where I had an unusually good opportunity, I tried to make an estimate of the average area occupied by a seal on that particular rookery. On July 16, watching the seals before me on Kishotchnoye Rookery, Bering Island, I wrote in my notebook as follows:

Here is a harem right in front of me, 1 sikatch, 16 matki, and about as many pups. They are lying as close together as about the average, and they easily cover a piece of ground 20 by 20 feet, 400 square feet, or more than 11 square feet per animal, pups and all. Ten square feet per animal for this rookery is, therefore, I think, a fair estimate.

But when I came back to the North Rookery and tried to apply my estimate, I was entirely at sea. I could not make up my mind whether the seals on the average were lying as close as above, or closer. Of course, I could see places where they were thicker, and others where they were thinner, but I could not, to my own satisfaction, strike an average, if for no other reason, because there were great portions of the rookery of which I could get no general view. Under those circumstances I would have regarded it as the merest humbug to present any figures pretending that they meant anything. Consequently, I wasted no further time upon getting at the probable number of seals on the Commander Islands rookeries.

The only method which promises reliable results is the one adopted now on the Pribylof Islands by the experts of the United States Fish Commission, viz, to actually count the number of seals on several large tracts of rookery, each of the size of an acre or more. In this way an average per acre may be obtained, which, multiplied by the computed acreage of all the rookeries, will give an approximate number which may not be too far out of the way. But, unfortunately, this method is hardly applicable to the Commander Islands, for various reasons, chief of which is the impossibility of making an actual count over a sufficiently large area to insure a reliable average. The rookeries are so very different among themselves that it would be necessary to have a separate count of each of them.

COMPARISON BETWEEN THE CONDITION OF THE ROOKERIES IN 1882-83 AND 1895.

BERING ISLAND.

NORTH ROOKERY, 1882-83. (Plate 7.)

When I first visited the northern rookery, thirteen years ago, there were three distinct breeding areas, viz, the Reef and Sivutchi Kamen, counted as one; a smaller patch between Babin and the creek, and Kishotchnaya. The bachelors hauled out on many of the outlying rocks surrounding the reef, and also in the rear of it on the smooth, white parade-ground. A large patch of them occupied the space back of the breeding-ground at Babin, large numbers extending a considerable distance back on the grassy area later in the season. Between the creek and Kishotchnaya there were three patches of bachelors. The whole distance from Sivutchi Kamen to Blizhni Mys, therefore, was practically one continuous seal-ground. The breeding-grounds at Kishotchnaya were surrounded by a heavy fringe of bachelors, who also sported in great numbers on the smooth, gravelly space in the rear of the rookery. South of Kishotchnaya, between the latter and Maroshnik, were again two separate patches of bachelors. In 1883 for the first time bachelors were known to haul out regularly throughout the season on the beach called Kisikof, beyond Maroshnik. They used to haul out there—and even as far south as Fontanka—late in the season, but their permanent settling on the beach in question was then regarded as an indisputable proof that the rookeries were increasing. It was at this last-mentioned point that the *Otome*, an English schooner, with a Japanese crew, made a raid during a dark night in August, 1883, and killed 300 to 400 seals. The mate was captured by the natives and the schooner the next morning by Mr. Grebnitski, on board the steamer *Aleksander II*.

The rookeries were in excellent condition, both as to quantity and quality. All classes of seals were well represented, and only skins of standard size were taken. This was particularly the case in 1883, when the company's representatives had very strict orders not to accept a single skin under 8 pounds. During that year 50 per cent more skins could easily have been taken, but for business reasons the company wished to reduce the catch as much as possible, and it was only after some strong pressure was brought upon Captain Sandman by Mr. Grebnitski that he agreed to take as many as he did.

It is a fact well worth mentioning that even in those days females and pups got unavoidably mixed up in the drives. The percentage was not very great, but great enough to be a distinct feature of the drives on this island. However, as the drive progressed they were pretty successfully weeded out, and comparatively few reached the killing-grounds. Killable seals being plentiful, pods of females were allowed to escape along the route of the drive, even though they might include a few bachelors.

NORTH ROOKERY, 1895. (Plate s.)

Upon inspecting the North Rookery again last summer I found a great change in many respects. Before reaching the rookery itself the absence of fresh or decaying carcasses on the killing-grounds was in marked contrast to the noisome sight and smell which used to form the first impression of the visitor arriving at the village. Nowadays every carcass is utilized. The choice parts of the meat are salted down in the many boxes and barrels dotting the ground in the rear of the killing-grounds, while the rest, including the entrails, are put in holes in the ground for winter food for the sledge-dogs.

On the rookery itself the first change which struck me was the fact that the entire beach between Babin and Kishotchnaya was depleted of seals—not a single breeding seal between Babin and the creek, nor a bachelor—all the way to Kishotchnaya. Later on I found that the hauling-grounds south of the latter place were also deserted. Instead of the imposing series of breeding and hauling-grounds from Sivutchi Kamen to Kisikof, I found only two patches of breeding-grounds, now forming almost two distinct rookeries—the Reef and Kishotchnaya.

I was prepared for a diminution of the seals, and it caused me, consequently, no surprise. On the other hand, I was considerably surprised at finding (July 8-10 and July 15-20) the *breeding grounds* of the Reef outlined very much as I had seen them in 1883.[1] The bulk of the harems were located on the western side of the Reef, rounding the point of the "sands" and extending in a long, narrow horn south along the eastern edge of the latter. A narrow band obliquely across the "sands" formed a connection and separated off an oval bald spot of the white ground toward the northern extremity of the "sands." It is a noteworthy fact that this "bald spot" was an equally characteristic feature of the rookery in 1883 as in 1895. But what I did miss was another connecting band, viz, between the southeastern extremity of the breeding-seals toward the one alluded to above. While thus the distribution on the whole was the same as formerly, there was a perceptible shrinkage in the width of the areas covered by the seals, and it seems to me also in the density of the seals, though of this I can not be so sure. The rookery is looked at so much from the side that it is very difficult to judge correctly of the space between the seals.

[1] When I first saw the rookery on July 4 it had not quite filled out yet, and I thought the depletion very great indeed; there was then no sign of the oblique belt across the sands, and the seals at the southeast corner formed a small, isolated herd.

To show the changes from 1882 to 1895, I submit some illustrations and two maps, which need some words of explanation.[1]

The drawing submitted (pl. 20) is taken from a photograph of a pencil sketch made by me July 30, 1882. Mr. Grebnitski, in going to St. Petersburg in the autumn of 1882, was anxious to have it accompany his report, and upon his arrival at San Francisco had a photographic copy made, which he sent me, and which is here reproduced. Like most drawings, the vertical dimensions are exaggerated, but on the whole it gives a fairly accurate representation of the rookery. The inner edge of the breeding-grounds are obscured by an immense number of bachelors on the "parade" or "sands," but the sketch shows pretty conclusively that the salient features are yet maintained. The photograph by Voloshinof (pl. 27a), taken in 1885, unfortunately is not very clear, but there is enough in it to show that the breeding area, so far as it can be seen from the direction of the salt-house, has shrunk comparatively little. My photographs (pl. 21) were taken from practically the same standpoint as the sketch and Voloshinof's photograph, and they afford as good a comparison as can be expected from photographs taken at such a distance. Those taken from a somewhat different standpoint, viz, from the driveway (pl. 22), give perhaps a better idea of the rookery, small as they are.

The map representing the seal-grounds in 1883 (pl. 7) was sketched on August 21, and shows the distribution of the seals on that date—hence the lack of definiteness to the areas of red and the extension of the bachelor seals into the grass-covered area. The map showing the location of the seals in 1895 (pl. 8), however, represents the seals as they were located July 17 and 19.

At *Kishotchnaya* I found the same state of affairs as on the Reef, only that the patch had shrunk still more and the seals apparently covered the ground less densely than on the Reef. This last observation, however, is not to be relied upon, as the breeding-ground can be looked down upon from a much greater elevation (70 feet), though at a greater distance. Bachelor seals in small numbers hauled out on the outer rocks and in among the females in the rear of the rookery, but the center of the "parade" ground was deserted all summer, and never a seal entered the posterior third of the latter, now covered with a scanty growth of tufted grass.

It was at once apparent that there was a low percentage of *bulls* on both rookeries, though at the Reef I afterwards found that the condition was not quite so bad as I first was led to believe. Upon my third visit to the rookery, when the wind was favorable for approaching it from the west side, I discovered that there were a good many more bulls proportionately to the females on that side than on the eastern half, which is the one first reached and most commonly seen. The formation of the ground made it utterly impossible to make a reliable estimate of the average number of females to each bull by counting a sufficient number of harems. At Kishotchnaya, however, the opportunities were more favorable, and on July 16 I averaged at the south end of

---

[1] Dr. Slunin in his recent report (Promysl. Bog. Kam. Sakh. Komand. Ostr.) has been singularly unfortunate in misunderstanding an old map by Mr. Grebnitski with regard to the extent of the rookeries on Bering Island. In the legend on plate 7 the dotted areas are represented as being the "rookeries according to Grebnitski." I have the original map, the so-called "Sandman-Grebnitski" map, before me, and can assert positively that Grebnitski never meant to represent the rookeries by the dotted areas, which are nothing else but the reefs surrounding the island. Of course Grebnitski did not intend to convey the idea that more than 60 miles, or half the entire coast line of Bering Island, were occupied by the rookeries.

that rookery about 50 females to a bull, while at the northern end the harems appeared smaller, most of those counted containing 15 to 25 females. A great many females were in the water that day, however; so in all probability the whole rookery averaged no less than 40 females to the bull. This proportion did not seem to be the result of or to have caused any lack of vigor in the males, for there was quite a number of large *half-bulls* skirting the rookery or hauled out on the outlying rocks, looking longingly toward the breeding-grounds.

The greater falling off in this rookery was due to the decrease in the number of *bachelors*. But instead of affecting all classes this diminution was chiefly confined to the younger ones. Last summer all the skins were weighed individually on a spring balance as the killing went on, and an accurate tally kept. I submit below a table of weights of the skins taken in 13 drives between July 14 and September 13, 1895. From this it will be seen that no single skin under 7 pounds was taken, and of this weight only 235 skins; that in 4 drives not a skin under 8 pounds occurred; that in none of the drives was the average weight less than 9.7 pounds; that of 6,725 skins, 5,558 weighed 9 pounds and over; and that the average weight of these 6,725 skins was 10.3 pounds. This table is also very interesting, showing how uniform was the size of the animals driven during the whole period of two months. Its true significance, however, can only be appreciated when it is remembered that the rookeries were scraped absolutely clean, and that not a seal was allowed to escape that would have yielded an acceptable skin. It can be stated with almost absolute certainty that there was not a bachelor seal on North Rookery, Bering Island, of the class yielding 6-pound skins.

Weight of skins taken in 13 drives on North Rookery, Bering Island, 1895.

Date.	7 lbs.	8 lbs.	9 lbs.	10 lbs.	11 lbs.	12 lbs.	13 lbs.	14 lbs.	15 lbs.	Total.	Average.
1895.										No.	Pounds.
July 14	5	90	74	64	48	53	11	4	2	348	9.8
19	4	70	90	237	75	60	8	1	0	545	10
29	0	53	110	158	211	161	50	10	0	733	10.7
Aug. 2	0	42	54	140	150	140	90	0	0	616	10.9
4	9	35	40	27	31	50	20	5	0	217	10.3
6	0	56	107	194	211	114	193	60	0	875	10.6
8	0	10	30	60	48	11	20	10	0	189	10.6
12	25	100	100	80	90	36	40	61	0	532	10.3
22	4	85	139	215	203	179	28	52	0	905	10.6
24	15	40	35	28	46	38	14	16	0	232	10.4
31	104	211	171	62	103	120	100	9	0	880	9.7
Sept. 10	50	93	80	66	85	40	35	10	0	459	9.8
13	19	47	34	20	29	18	17	12	0	194	9.8
Total	235	932	1,064	1,328	1,360	1,018	536	250	2	6,725	10.3

Though not literally absent, the *yearlings* were practically so. From the next table, which shows the number of each class of seals contained in the same 13 drives, it will be seen that out of 29,112 seals driven to the killing-grounds only 540 were yearlings, or 1.86 per cent. It was a constant source of wonder on Bering Island, in 1895, what had become of the yearlings. From time to time it was confidently predicted that they would turn up "later," but they did not come at all. There was a slight proportionate increase after the middle of August, but too trifling to amount to anything. And again I must emphasize the fact that the rookery was scraped clean in search of seals. This fact is startlingly disclosed by the following table, and because of its great importance it requires a full explanation.

Details of 13 drives on North Rookery, Bering Island, 1895, showing sex and age of seals driven.

Date.	Killed.	Escaping.				Total driven.	Remarks.
		Females.	Yearlings.	Pups.	Bulls.		
1895.							
July 14	348	1,305	0	13	11	1,677	
19	545	1,090	11	60	9	1,734	
29	723	1,738	23	35	13	2,542	
Aug. 2	616	1,436	14	67	8	2,141	
4	217	779	9	35	7	1,047	
6	875	2,014	5	150	11	3,064	
8	189	1,134	5	63	4	1,395	
13	502	2,077	74	104	5	2,792	
22	805	2,928	173	295	8	4,300	
24	232	1,295	58	51	4	1,600	
31	880	2,250	55	108	5	3,307	
Sept. 10	459	1,718	38	69	8	2,292	14 stagy.
15	194	825	77	115	3	1,214	51 stagy.
Total	6,725	20,568	540	1,183	96	29,112	
Percentage of total driven	23.10	70.65	1.86	4.06	0.33	100.00	

Upon my arrival, in 1895, I impressed upon Mr. Grebnitski the desirability of having such a census prepared, and suggested that Selivanof, the kossak in charge of the rookery, be ordered to undertake the work. Mr. Grebnitski, fully aware of the great importance of knowing exactly what classes were represented in each drive, at once took up the suggestion and ordered Selivanof to make a detailed tally of each drive according to the scheme I furnished. The drive on July 19 I counted myself conjointly with Selivanof, and the tally sheet is here produced to show how the work was done and how much reliability can be placed upon it. The seals killed and those escaping from each pod, as it was called and slaughtered, were separately counted, Feoktist Ivanof Korsakovski counting the dead ones, Selivanof and I those allowed to escape.

Tally of drive taken July 19, 1895, North Rookery, Bering Island.

Pod No.	Killed.	Escaping.				Pod No.	Killed.	Escaping.			
		Females.	Yearlings.	Pups.	Bulls.			Females.	Yearlings.	Pups.	Bulls.
1	8	15	2			22	20	21		4	
2	9	35		1		23	10	30	1	1	
3	7	38		1		24	26	10	1	2	
4	13	28				25	11	21			
5	16	34	1	2		26	12	10			1
6	11	32				27	18	29		2	2
7	18	22				28	23	16		9	
8	11	28	1			29	28	43		6	
9	7	23		2		30	12	35		3	
10	9	25				31	22	42		1	
11	12	9	1	4		32	20	51		9	
12	11	26				33	11	12			
13	6	20				34	7	21			
14	9	26		1		35	15	40		6	1
15	21	28		4		36	12	25		2	
16	5	34				37	10	29		2	
17	16	34			1	38	11	35		2	
18	9	26				39	30	51		1	2
19	13	35		2							
20	20	27	2	3		Total	538	1,090	11	69	9
21	11	28									

The accuracy of the above tally is attested by the fact that the number of skins taken in this drive was 545. Sometimes the killed ones of the previous pod were lying so close to those being counted that it was difficult to ascertain the exact number, in which case the smaller figure was noted. And so with the escaping ones. Selivanof and I counted separately; if we differed, and a recount was not practicable, we took the lowest figure. The percentages are, therefore, very nearly correct. If there is any error, it is in understating the number of females, but I am sure that the possible error does not exceed 1 per cent.

The figures of the 13 drives in the table previously given were ascertained in the same manner, and I have no doubt that they are essentially correct. No tally was kept previous to the drive on July 14, and I failed to obtain the details of the drive on July 24, but there is no reason to believe that the percentage of the classes was different in these drives, except that I was informed that there were no females or pups in the first drive, June 13. In order to complete the record of this rookery for 1895, I submit the following table of the skins taken in each drive during the summer season:

Total number of skins taken on North Rookery, Bering Island, during the summer season of 1895.

Date of drive.	Skins.	Date of drive.	Skins.
June 13	110	Aug. 6	875
June 25	187	Aug. 8	189
July 6	262	Aug. 12	532
July 14	348	Aug. 22	905
July 19	545	Aug. 24	232
July 24	1,057	Aug. 31	880
July 29	733	Sept. 10	459
Aug. 2	616	Sept. 13	191
Aug. 4	217		
		Total	8,341

Looking again at the table of the classes in the 13 drives, we note that it was necessary to drive off over 29,000 seals in order to obtain 6,725 skins, and that of those 29,000 no less than 20,568 were females. As already stated, there is no reason to suppose that the percentage of females differed materially in the other 4 drives, except one. If, therefore, we calculate the corresponding figures for a total of 8,231 (8,341−110) skins, we find that in order to obtain 8,341 skins, the total catch for the season, it was necessary to drive off to the killing-grounds 35,741 seals, of all ages, of which *the astounding number of 25,174 were females.* In this count are not included such females as were allowed to escape along the road of the drive, although the number of females thus culled was comparatively few, as the men were afraid of letting a single killable bachelor escape.

Nothing could better illustrate the straits to which this rookery has come. On the other hand, nothing could better demonstrate how little the driving disturbs the seals. Here is a rookery where the females have been driven probably as long as seals have been taken, though not in the same proportion as now. Yet, the females return to be driven over and over again, and the *breeding-ground* is the part of the rookery least affected in the general decrease.

A great amount of mortality due to starvation was observed among the pups, but is here only alluded to, as I have treated of that question in another connection (p. 78).

SOUTH ROOKERY, 1882. (Plate 9.)

This rookery, although probably the remnant of the innumerable multitudes which Steller speaks of, has not been of much account of recent years. After the interregnum, 1869–1871, it was so insignificant that no regular catch seems to have been made until 1880, although occasionally, i. e., before and after the season closed on North Rookery, a few seals were killed at Poludionnoye in order to get fresh meat for the main village, Nikolski. Thus, in 1878, 50 were killed in June and 30 on November 5.

The result was that the rookery was gradually increasing. Finally, in 1880, it was deemed sufficiently large to station a small force of men under Mr. Volokitin at the place, and in that year 787 skins were taken. It seems, however, that the capacity of the rookery was underestimated and not enough salt was landed, so that no more could be taken care of. In 1881, in spite of the complaint that although there are "many sikatchi on both rookeries" there are "but few holustiaki, mostly in the water," the South Rookery yielded 1,150 skins. The following year (1882) the catch was 1,410.

When I visited this rookery on August 21, 1882, I found the entire beach between the first and second cape west of the waterfall covered with seals, the breeding seals occupying the portion nearest to the water, the bachelors patches at both ends and in the rear up to the inner grass-covered belt.

SOUTH ROOKERY, 1895. (Plate 10.)

How different when I approached the same ground again August 17, 1895, thirteen years later almost to the date! Only a handful of female seals were left at the extreme western end of the rookery.

I am very fortunate in being able to present copies of two photographs taken by the late Colonel Voloshinof in 1885, which, as they are taken from almost the same standpoint as one of my own (pl. 29), afford excellent comparison between the conditions of Poludionnoye Rookery then and now. In the right-side half of his double picture (pl. 31a) a series of smaller rocks in the water extends from the beach to the outer end of the west reef. This series of rocks will be recognized toward the lower left-hand corner in my photograph (pl. 29), and will serve to orient the reader. It will then be seen that the entire beach, which, in my picture of 1895 is absolutely bare of seals, is covered with thousands in Voloshinof's picture of 1885, and that the compact body of seals then extended even a good distance beyond. To complete the comparison I add another photograph of mine (pl. 28) looking in the opposite direction (toward the waterfall), which shows the utter desolation of the entire beach beyond the little black patch.

As for the proportions of the various classes of seals on this rookery I found the conditions to be similar to those on the North Rookery. It was reported in Nikolski that there had been only 1 bull on the rookery in 1895, but upon inquiry at the rookery I was informed by Nikanor Grigorief, the native in charge, that the actual number of sikatchi had been 5. This number may be considered exact, and the number of females to each bull was, therefore, probably nearly 100. There were plenty of pups when I visited the rookery, and no barrenness of the females was suggested.

By dint of hard scraping no less than 564 skins were secured in 1895, 159 of them, however, between August 17 and September 9.

COPPER ISLAND.

KARABELNOVE ROOKERY, 1882-83. (Plate 11.)

The distribution of seals on this rookery, as I found it during the week July 3-10, 1883, is shown on the map (pl. 11). Every available space under the cliffs was occupied by breeding females. Even the ledges at the foot of them and the lower portion of the steep ravines were full of them. The bachelors were obliged to be satisfied with the outlying reefs and rocks, with the beach on the east side of Karabelni Stolp, and the rocky beaches at Vodopad and beyond. The rookery was in excellent condition, all classes of seals being well represented. In fact, there was unquestionable proof that the rookery was increasing.

Curiously enough this fact was brought home to the natives located at Karabelni by the circumstance that they were unable to obtain in good season the number of skins required from this rookery. When I arrived at Karabelni in the beginning of July the natives were deeply concerned because of their failure to obtain the last 1,000 skins. As the families are paid for each skin brought to the salt-house, this meant a serious loss to those stationed at this point. They finally decided to go to Gilinka, where the season was already over, and there got all the skins they wanted. In answer to my inquiry as to the cause of their failure to obtain the skins at Karabelni I was told that it was because the rookery was increasing. Self-contradictory as this statement appeared, it was nevertheless easily explained. The main hauling-ground of the bachelors, i. e., the one yielding most skins and from which the seals could be driven, was the Karabelni Stolp. Looking at the map (pl. 11) it will be seen that at the base of the neck there was a large breeding-ground. The breeding seals were increasing here to such an extent as to occupy the whole space along the beach and actually shutting off the hauling-ground, thus making it impossible to drive any seals from that place. The men were therefore obliged to take the skins at Vodopad and Krepkaya Pad, which meant that they had to carry every skin on their backs across the island. When it is considered that the population, even under ordinary circumstances, was rather insufficient for the work, it may easily be understood what a hardship this increase of the rookery involved. But not only the breeding seals were increasing, the bachelors were also extending their territory. The result was that skins were taken in Maluka Bukhta for the first time. At this place the women did the skinning and carrying, for even here the skins had to be carried, while the men were engaged at Krepkaya Pad.

In addition to the map I have submitted three original field sketches of the rookery as I found it on July 3, 1883 (pls. 41-43). While making no claim for artistic merit I do claim for them sufficient accuracy for an intelligent comparison with my photographs of 1895, which were taken from the identical standpoints. The sketches have not been touched since I left the rookery in 1883 and are here reproduced in facsimile so as to eliminate the possibility of even unintentional alterations.

KARABELNOYE ROOKERY, 1895. (Plate 12).

On July 31, 1895, Mr. Grebnitski and I landed in Stolbovaya Bukhta and pitched our tent on the beach just west of the killing-ground. It was very foggy and the water high, so that we could not pass the point into Martishina Bukhta. Next morning, at 4.30 a. m., the fog still prevailed, but the water was low and we made our way along the beach to the rookery. We passed on to the Stolp without meeting a seal, where in 1883 thousands of breeding seals blocked the way of the drives. Only a small solid patch, leaning on the south base of the cliff, remained, an isolated outpost at this end of the rookery. At the Stolp itself we found a couple of small harems only at the northern end, and towards the southern extremity a small patch of bachelors, hardly more than a dozen. In the distance I could discern through the fog faint outlines only of the breeding-grounds.

After breakfast the fog lifted and I ascended the bluffs, which rise 300 feet above the breeding-grounds. The photographs which are herewith appended (pls. 38-40) were taken from the various stations at the edge of these bluffs, marked on the maps, care being taken to select the same points from which I had made my sketches twelve years previously.

I found that while on the whole the breeding grounds had retained their former shape—necessarily, because of the natural conditions of the beach—there was a great thinning out of the ranks of the *females*. At the same time a large area at the northwestern end had become nearly depopulated. At first I credited the thinness of the breeding herds to the bright weather, but another visit to the heights the next morning showed no improvement.

That day I saw no *bachelors*, except the little patch at the Stolp; none at Vodopad and Krepkaya Pad. At Malinka Bukhta, I was informed, they had ceased to haul up several years ago. The next day we saw a few more bachelors—a somewhat larger patch—at the Stolp, and two other patches, of possibly a hundred seals each, one on each side of the Vodopadski Nepropusk.

But one feature that struck me with surprise was the great number of *bulls* and *half-bulls*. This abundance of old males was particularly interesting, coming, as I did, directly from Bering Island, where this element was so scarce.

Pups were present in good proportion.

The decrease in the yield of this rookery has been considerable. While as far back as 1881 6,500 skins were secured without trouble, it was impossible for the men, in 1895, try as hard as they might, to secure more than 2,000. They were given full swing and encouraged to take as many as possible, though they needed no special encouragement, for the decrease in skins meant a corresponding decrease in food and comfort during the following winter. Moreover, the season was extended to the first week of September, and yet with no better results. Between August 12 and September 10 they could scrape together only 188 skins.

GLINKA ROOKERIES, 1882-83. (Plate 13).

The capacity of Glinka used to be more than double that of Karabelni, having in good years yielded over 20,000 skins. The best hauling-grounds were Palata, Zapadni, and Pestshanaya, but bachelors then hauled out as far as Babinskaya Bukhta in the south and Gorelaya Bukhta in the north. These distant grounds were only drawn upon occasionally, and the grounds between Urili Kamen and Palata Mys furnished the bulk of the skins. Of these Pestshani hauling ground was the most prolific and the handiest, although the driving was very severe before the new salt-house was built, and single drives yielding more than 4,000 skins from this place were no exceptions.[1]

The principal breeding-grounds occupied the inaccessible beach between the Stolbi in Gavarushkaya Bukhta to Palata Mys, comprising Sikatchinskaya and Zapalata, the gully and basin north of Palata, and, finally, the family grounds designated as Zapadni or Zapadni Mys. Palata, to the looker-on coming over the mountains, was probably the most impressive rookery view in the whole Commander Islands group. The solid blackening masses of breeding seals, filling the gully to overflowing and extending under the bluffs and along the beach on both sides, was a sight never to be forgotten. My original sketch, made in 1883 from a prominent point 800 feet above, is unfortunately lost or mislaid, and I am therefore obliged to substitute an elaboration of it (pl. 52) made shortly after my return, probably in January or February, 1884. I know it to be a pretty faithful rendering of the sketch, but of course the latter would have been more authentic.

Zapalata and Sikatchinskaya were the mainstay of the rookery, however. There the breeding seals were absolutely safe against all possible interruptions from the land

---

[1] Dr. Slunin reports that in 1887 a drive yielding 6,000 took place from this hauling-ground.

side, while the bays themselves are wonderfully sheltered by reefs and outlying rocks, thus affording admirable places of safety for the growing pups, features which will be fully appreciated by an inspection of plates 55 and 56.

To illustrate the condition of these rookeries during the palmy days of the business I am fortunate enough to be able to copy a couple of Voloshinof's photographs (pls. 53 and 57a) made in 1885, to which I shall refer more in detail later on.

GLINKA ROOKERIES, 1895. (Plate 14.)

On the 2d of August I approached the Glinka rookeries in a boat from the north and proceeded along their entire front from Lebiazhi Mys to Babinskaya Bukhta, where we camped. I saw breeding seals in most of the places where I formerly saw them, but in vastly reduced numbers. Bachelors were also seen, but they were few and far between. At Pestshani hauling-ground, the place which once supplied many thousands, and which even as late as 1893 furnished 3,137 skins, there was not a single bachelor. True, a drive had been made from that place only a few days earlier, which had resulted in 700 skins, but these 700 skins were all that this famous hauling-ground yielded in 1895.

However, the location of nearly all the former hauling-grounds was marked, not so much by little bunches of a dozen bachelors or so, but, curiously enough, by a line of black half-bulls. They had hauled up and occupied the beaches with regular intervals, much as do the old bulls in spring before the arrival of the females; in fact they were in a measure playing sikatch! These lonesome, patiently waiting polusikatchi were first seen at the old hauling grounds on both sides of Lebiazhi Mys, and then on the west side of Peresheyek and of Pestshani Mys, and finally at the eastern end of Babinskaya Bukhta. At these places they had hauled out by themselves. But, in addition, hundreds of these nearly mature young bulls (or probably mature, though not strong enough to fight the older ones) skirted the breeding-grounds, hauling out on outlying rocks and paying attention to the females coming out for a swim or a trip to the distant feeding-grounds. On the breeding-grounds dark-haired, vigorous-looking bulls abounded.

This superabundance of vigorous, mature males was a strongly marked feature of the rookery. This is the more remarkable, if we remember that it was already late in the season when I visited Glinka and that, although I stayed until August 11, I saw no diminution of it. The natives also informed me that on account of the still greater number of bulls earlier in the season the fighting had been violent and incessant on the rookeries. This abundance of bulls I have been told has been noticed for several years.

In strong contrast to this exuberance of virility was the thinness of the *female* ranks. They spread over nearly the same territory as formerly, but the lines had shrunk and in many places there were large bare gaps. The magnificent Palata showed many of the characteristic features that I knew so well, and yet it was only the shadow of the old rookery. The line running backward up the gully was there, but it was very thin and narrow and broken in places. A comparison of my old sketch (pl. 52), taken at high water, with my recent photograph from the identical standpoint, low water (pl. 54), will give some idea of the difference I saw. Although taken from a point somewhat different from mine, Colonel Voloshinof's photograph of Palata as it looked in 1885 (pl. 53a) fully bears out my sketch, when it is remembered that he was standing several hundred feet lower to the right and that consequently the solid belt of seals at the base of Palata must look so much narrower on his picture than on mine. My other photographs (pls. 48, 49), looking toward Palata and Sabatcha Dira from the outlying rocks off the former, serve to more fully illustrate the disconnected and thin character of the breeding-grounds in 1895.

And as with Palata, so with Zapalata. The change was less striking, though by no means less radical. On the contrary, Zapalata, in proportion, was even more deserted. It is a source of great satisfaction to me that in photographing this rookery I happened to place my camera on the exact spot where Colonel Voloshinof ten years previously had exposed a plate, and although it evidently met with some mishap, so that this picture is one of the less satisfactory ones, I have reproduced the two (pls. 56 and 57a). On the whole light beach my photograph shows nothing but stones, while the same area in Voloshinof's is teeming with thousands of breeding seals. By turning my camera in the opposite direction I obtained the other picture (pl. 55) showing the same depleted condition.

To complete the series of photographs illustrating the condition of the various parts of the rookery, I finally reproduce one by Mr. Grebnitski, taken from the rocks in Sikatchinskaya Bukhta August 3, as I had no opportunity to photograph it myself. It tells the same story (57b).

The total number of skins shipped from Glinka in 1895 was 4,809 (including a few hundreds of the autumn catch of 1894), a trifle more than one-half the catch of the previous year.

In view of the great number of half-bulls and bulls it is interesting to note that the skins both from Karabelni and from Glinka were unusually small. No regular tally of the weight of the entire catch was kept on Copper Island, but upon our arrival there was a great complaint of the lightness of the skins. During my stay at Glinka, from August 2 to 11, the natives were unable to take more than one small drive, in spite of their anxiety to make more money and to obtain more fresh meat. The skins of this drive were weighed according to Mr. Grebnitski's directions, who himself kept tally. The weight of the skins was noted to the half pound, but to simplify the list and make it easily comparable with the corresponding ones upon Bering Island I only recorded whole pounds; a skin weighing 7½ pounds, for instance, I counted as 8 pounds, while 7¼ pounds was recorded as 7. Mr. Grebnitski's tally and my tally will differ to that extent, but the average will undoubtedly be very nearly the same. This average, it will be seen, is scarcely 7¾ pounds. When I visited Copper Island in 1883 the company refused every skin under 8 pounds.

Weight of skins brought to the salt-house at Glinka, Copper Island, August 8, 1895.

Weight.	Number.
Under 6½ pounds (4½ to 6¼)	35
7 pounds	108
8 pounds	40
9 pounds	17
10 pounds	11
11 pounds	6
12 pounds	5
13 pounds	2
14 pounds	3
15 pounds	1
Total number of skins	228
Average weight of skins..........pounds..	7.6

COMPARATIVE CONDITION OF THE BERING ISLAND AND COPPER ISLAND ROOKERIES, 1895.

In what little there has been said and written about the seal industry on the Commander Islands it has always been assumed that the conditions, aside from the difference in the physical aspect of the rookeries, were the same on both islands constituting the group. And this was actually the case not very long ago, at least in 1882–83, and, so far as I could ascertain, up to 1890. In that year, it is said, the bachelors were becoming somewhat scarce on Copper Island and some active work had to be done in order to secure the desired quantity, but inasmuch as this quantity appears to have been the largest ever shipped from Copper Island, the falling off can not have been excessive, though it may have been apparent on the hauling-grounds.

In 1892, however, the decrease in the number of females on Copper Island became serious enough to cause public comment, while on Bering Island difficulty was experienced in obtaining the requisite, though now limited, number of bachelors.

Whatever the cause of the recent disturbance of the equilibrium of the rookeries on the Commander Islands, each island has been affected differently, and the conditions to-day of the rookeries on Copper Island deviate radically from those of Bering Island. It may be useful to compare them point for point.

In Bering Island the number of females in proportion to the mature males is very much greater than on Copper Island. This results in an apparent deficiency in bulls on Bering Island and a corresponding superabundance of them on Copper Island.

In Bering Island the killable males are of great size, as proven by the weight of the skins, which in 1895 averaged over 10 pounds. The greatest deficiency was consequently in the younger seals, while yearlings were almost entirely absent. The proportion between the ages of the killables was quite reversed on Copper Island, where a lack of the older bachelors was seriously felt, while the great bulk of the skins taken were from the younger classes, the skins averaging probably less than 8 pounds.

As for the pups, it may be stated that they were abundant in proportion to the females on both islands, and no difference could be discovered in that respect. On Bering Island I found a considerable mortality due to starvation among the pups. On Copper Island no such thing was observed, but this negative result must not be taken as a proof or even an indication that no such mortality took place. It must be remembered that most of the breeding-grounds on Copper Island are inaccessible, and that it is almost an impossibility to distinguish the dead bodies of the pups from such a distance as it is necessary to watch them on Copper Island.

It was by the merest accident that I myself discovered the sad state of affairs on Bering Island, for if I had not gone over the rookery after the wholesale raid of the breeding-ground I should have remained in ignorance of the fact. The natives themselves were either concealing it, out of fear that they would be blamed, or, more likely, they were ignorant of the extent of the calamity. After the season is over the natives keep aloof from the rookeries, as they are strictly enjoined from disturbing the breeding-grounds without necessity. The simple fact, therefore, that I can report no unusual mortality on the Glinka or Karabelui rookeries proves nothing one way or the other.

RAIDING OF COMMANDER ISLANDS ROOKERIES.

The rookeries of Bering and Copper islands have always been a sore temptation to marauding schooners, especially those of the latter island, where, in addition to the fur-seals, there was a fair chance of obtaining a number of the costly sea otters, a few of which would go a long way to pay for the expenses and risks of such an expedition. The material is not at hand for an exhaustive list of all the attempted and accomplished raids on the Commander Islands rookeries, but I shall give a sufficiently detailed account to show that considerable damage has been done by the pirates.

Leaving out of consideration the possible raids during the flourishing times of the whale fishery in the forties, and coming down to recent days, we find that at first the raiders were attracted to Copper Island by their knowledge of the plentiful occurrence of the sea-otter on that island, a knowledge gained by many of them during their visits to the islands during the "interregnum." We thus find the American schooner *Three Sisters*, Captain Herendeen, caught on July 22, 1879, at anchor off the Northwest Cape of Copper Island, the mate and sailors camping ashore near the sea otter rookery. Twenty-nine skins of grown sea-otters and 16 sea-otter pups were taken from her, but also 123 fur-seals, which it was claimed, however, were taken at sea. Instead of seizing the vessel, the authorities let her go with a warning. The seal skins found on her proved that sea-otter was not the only game looked for, and in the same year, on August 10, an unknown schooner, off Glinka, attempted to land three boats, but the natives frightened them off.

The year 1880 saw an increased activity on the part of the poachers, who were much emboldened by their successes in the Okhotsk Sea and the Kuril Islands. As early as July 7 the *Three Sisters*, of San Francisco, Captain Beckwith, was seen at anchor off Glinka Rookeries, killing seals; the crew was driven off by the natives shooting at them. Mr. E. P. Miner (Brit. Counter Case, App., p. 113; Fur-Seal Arb., VIII, p. 700) gives the following graphic account of this raid:

She was chartered by H. Liebes & Co., and was supposed to be going out on a sea-otter and fur-seal hunting expedition, but as a matter of fact all of us who shipped as hunters knew that the vessel had been fitted out for a raid on the rookeries on the Commander Islands. Early in July we started from the Alaskan coast for the Commander Islands, and about the middle of the month landed on the west side of Copper Island. We landed in the day time in a fog. There were three boats. We had killed about 800 seals before we were seen, but had taken none of them on board the vessel. A baidarka with natives in it came along then, and we knew that warning would be given to the people on the island, and we began skinning the seals. In about an hour what appeared to be fifty men came across the island to where we were, and began firing at us with blank cartridges. We started off at once, but when some distance from land began killing seals in the kelp. Then they fired on us with bullets, and we went on the schooner. All the skins we got of the seals we killed was 153. Before we made the raid on the seal rookery we had anchored at the north end of Copper Island, where sea-otters are plentiful, and while there a baidarka full of natives came out to us and served a warning on the captain, telling him that he must not hunt within 5 miles of the islands—the miles were, I suppose, meant for Russian miles. We went from Copper Island to the Kurile Islands to look for sea-otter, and after getting one sailed on the 4th August for San Francisco.

On July 13, 1880, a schooner was reported at anchor close to the beach of North Rookery, Bering Island, and being discovered had probably but poor success. Not so, however, with the schooner that raided the Glinka rookeries about two weeks later, killing "a number of seals, say about 400." This can hardly have been the *Otsego*, Captain Isaackson, flying the Dutch flag, which was boarded on August 6 by the steamer

Aleksander II at Glinka, but was found to have "4 to 5 fur-seals only." On the next day Mr. Grebnitski boarded the schooner *Alexander*, Captain Littlejohn. The latter swore that he had shot the 53 seals found on board, denying that he had been near a rookery, and was warned off. Captain Sandman on August 12 confiscated 4 sea-otters from the schooner *Flying Mist*, Captain Bradford, which was found at anchor "around the Northwest Cape (Copper Island) close inshore about 8′ SE. from rocks," but with "apparently no seals."

On September 1 the kossak and a watchman boarded the schooner *Serenty Six*, Captain Potts, off the Southeast Cape, Copper Island, finding only one man on board, the rest being on shore. The watchmen went after them, but the schooner's crew made directly for the vessel as soon as they saw them coming, and got away. "On shore the watchman found about 40 seal carcasses which the schooner's people had killed and skinned, all bulls."

The raiders did not confine themselves to Copper Island by any means, for on September 10 an unknown schooner visited the South Rookery on Bering Island, killing about 25 seals, and two days later a schooner, possibly the same, was reported "on the north side shooting seals at sea," but left on the approach of the steamer *Aleksander II*. After the departure of the latter, the schooner came in again on September 13, but the whaleboat which was sent ashore was driven away, by the natives firing at the crew, before any seals were killed.

Captain Littlejohn, in the schooner *Alexander*, evidently took no heed of the warning given him, for on October 16 he was on the Glinka Rookeries and took "some seals again," an exploit which he repeated on the moonlight night of the 18th, when he secured "a number of seals (mostly cows) before morning."

Although the record for 1881 is not quite so black, it is in some respects fully as interesting.

On Bering Island two schooners appeared at the North Rookery on October 8 and landed 6 whaleboats, killing many seals, mostly females and young ones. Mr. Grebnitski himself went to the rookery, but the schooner had already left. Exactly a week later two schooners again arrived off the North Rookery, possibly the same, landing 5 whaleboats early in the morning of October 16. This time, however, the natives were prepared, and 40 of them, well armed with rifles, met the raiders. The latter now opened negotiations, the captain offering a gold watch to the chief, money to the men, and whisky to all for the privilege of taking 300 fur-seals. The natives refused, and the raiders, after having examined some of the Berdan breech loading rifles and having received an affirmative answer to their question whether the natives would shoot if they should attempt to kill any seals, withdrew. "Seeing that they could do nothing, they put to sea."

It is probably to a raid in 1881 that Mr. S. L. Beckwith's testimony relates (Fur Seal Arb., VIII, p. 810), in which he states that as "a mate on the vessel *Alexander*, belonging to Hermann Liebes, of which Captain Carlson was master," "in 1880, or thereabouts," he "went ashore and raided Copper Island, and got about 100 seals, and we would have got a great many more, for we had about 1,200 killed when we were fired upon. A Japanese vessel was there the day before raiding and several of the raiders were shot." This last information seems to tally with the following record from Bering Island: "October 11. A schooner has been at Staraya Gavan. Buried one Japanese."

The fact was that the natives, incensed by the numerous raids, were using their guns freely during 1881. Thus, earlier in the season the *Annie Cashman*, of San Francisco, went to Copper Island, and Mr. E. P. Miner states (Fur Seal Arb., VIII, p. 701):

We landed there one clear day, and in 1½ hours took 250 seals, and had them all on board before the natives came to where we were. We went away then, but came back the next night. We were fired on by the natives, and did not land.

It went particularly hard with the British schooner *Diana*, sailing from Yokohama earlier in the season. She had been raiding various rookeries on the Kuril Islands and finally went to Copper Island, where she came to grief. She anchored off Zapalata and a boat was immediately sent ashore. They did not reach it, however, for behind the rocks a large band of natives, under command of the kossak, Selivanof, were lying in wait. When the boat was well within range, the kossak gave the signal and a complete rain of bullets struck the unfortunate boat. One man was killed, one severely wounded, and the boat, nearly sinking, made the schooner with the greatest difficulty. It is said that fully 300 shots were fired by the natives. The *Diana*, now severely crippled, sought safety in flight, but on the way to Petropaulski unfortunately fell in with a Russian man-of-war—the *Strelok*, if I remember rightly. The suspicion of the commander was aroused, an investigation made, which resulted in the imprisonment of the crew and the confiscation of the vessel, in spite of the plea of the captain that no raid was intended and that the boat was sent ashore only to take water, of which the schooner was short.

The case was made the subject of diplomatic correspondence between Great Britain and Russia, and the latter power sent a revisor to Copper Island in 1882 to investigate the matter. His report was favorable to the natives, no doubt, for the Russian Government, in recognition of their meritorious conduct, invested the native chief of Copper Island with a silver-laced kaftan, while Selivanof was promoted to be a sergeant and a beautiful Toledo blade was presented to him upon which was engraved a suitable inscription commemorative of the occasion.

It was plain that something would have to be done to check this growing evil, which had already been assuming alarming proportions, but the authorities were puzzled how to proceed effectively. One or two large war vessels were already patrolling the region, but their service was very ineffective, as they did not take the risk of going close under the foggy and dangerous coasts of the islands. It was thought, however, that strict regulations for the whole traffic of trading and hunting in Russian waters, which would leave the schooners no excuses or technical loop holes, would deter the marauders, especially in view of the past experience, and seeing that the Russian Government was in earnest in backing up the natives in their defense of the rookeries. A proclamation was therefore prepared and issued, first by the Russian consul at Yokohama and afterwards also by the Russian consul in San Francisco, the publication being specifically authorized by the Imperial Russian Ministry of Foreign Affairs. The consular warning was as follows:

NOTICE.

At the request of the local authorities of Bering and other islands, the undersigned hereby notifies that the Russian Imperial Government publishes, for general knowledge, the following:

1. Without a special permit or license from the Governor-General of Eastern Siberia, foreign vessels are not allowed to carry on trading, hunting, fishing, etc., on the Russian coast or islands in the Okhotsk and Bering Seas or on the northeastern coast of Asia, or within their sea boundary line.

2. For such permits or licenses foreign vessels should apply to Vladivostok, exclusively.

3. In the port of Petropaulovsk, though being the only port of entry in Kamtchatka, such permits or licenses shall not be issued.

4. No permits or licenses whatever shall be issued for hunting, fishing, or trading at or on the Commodore or Robben Islands.

5. Foreign vessels found trading, fishing, hunting, etc., in Russian waters without a license or permit from the Governor-General, and also those possessing a license or permit who may infringe the existing by-laws on hunting, shall be confiscated, both vessels and cargoes, for the benefit of the Government. This enactment shall be enforced henceforth, commencing with A. D. 1882.

6. The enforcement of the above will be intrusted to Russian men-of-war, and also to Russian merchant vessels, which for that purpose will carry military detachments and be provided with proper instructions.

(Signed) A. PELIKAN,
His Imperial Russian Majesty's Consul.

YOKOHAMA, *November 15, 1881.*

This proclamation was distributed to all outgoing vessels, and evidently had some effect, as the raids during the years following fell off very considerably. A few skippers, more desperate than the others, however, were still taking chances. Thus, on August 12, 1882, the schooner *Otome*, of Yokohama, with a Japanese crew, but European officers, raided the North Rookery on Bering Island, though with disastrous results. After having tried the watchfulness of the natives during dark and foggy nights for more than two weeks, three boats were sent ashore from the *Otome* on the 12th of August after dark. At Kisikof, the southern extremity of the rookery, about 350 bachelor seals were clubbed, and the skinning was already far advanced when the natives crept up to the pirates and captured the mate; the next morning the schooner was seized by Mr. Grebnitski on board the steamer *Aleksander II*. The *Otome* was finally taken to Vladivostok and condemned. The captain was charged with piracy, but Mr. Snow, who had passage in the schooner, was allowed to go, as there was no proof of his connection with the affair as owner or supercargo.

The fact that the proclamation did not entirely stop the raiding, induced the Russian authorities in 1884 to station a detachment of soldiers on the islands for their protection, as related elsewhere in this report, and the schooner *Sakhalien*, raiding the South Rookery on Bering Island, fell the first victim to the regulars.

The captains of the schooners were becoming wary, and, to avoid being captured within the 3-mile limit of the territorial waters, adopted the tactics of keeping some distance at sea, only sending their boats or canoes to kill the seals on or off the rookeries, as the case might be.

The first schooner caught in this practice seems to have been the British vessel *Araunah*, Captain Siewerd, which was seized off Copper Island on July 1, 1888, by Grebuitski, in the *Aleksander II*. The significant point was that while the schooner itself was not nearer than 6 miles, two of its canoes were hunting seals within half a mile of the shore, and, in spite of the diplomatic remonstrances by Great Britain, Mr. Grebuitski was fully sustained by Mr. Giers, the Russian minister for foreign affairs, in his letter of August 16, 1889. However, although caught as a raider, the *Araunah* was in reality a regular pelagic sealer from British Columbia, with Indian hunters and Indian canoes.

PELAGIC SEALING AT COMMANDER ISLANDS.

The tactics described in the closing paragraphs of the chapter relating to the raiding of the rookeries, of sending the canoes in among the breeding seals off the rookeries, to kill them in the water while the schooner remained at sea, were the forerunner of pelagic sealing around the Commander Islands. It was claimed by the crew of the *C. G. White*, Captain Hagman, who gave themselves up (in 1890) to the authorities on Copper Island, that they were blown ashore after having lost their vessel; but the natives evidently thought differently, for they fired upon three of the boats as they attempted to land, killing one man and wounding two, while seven bullets went through the boats. However, as the schooner was not captured, the men were sent back to San Francisco in the company's steamer. While it is true that the *James Hamilton Lewis* (formerly the *Ada*) was caught right under the South Rookery of Bering Island in 1891, by the Russian war vessel *Aleut*, it is certain that many of the 416 skins (90 per cent of which it has been stated were females) confiscated were killed at sea.

When but few seals were left on Robben Island and the Kurils to raid, the schooners fitting out in Japan turned their attention to following up the Commander Islands herd on its northward migrations along the outer side of the Kuril chain, adopting the regular methods of pelagic sealing. Owing to the necessity of having heavier and stronger vessels on that coast, because of the much more severe weather and the consequent greater risk, the pelagic sealing developed much slower on the Asiatic side than on the American, and played a comparatively unimportant rôle up to 1892.[1]

The latter year saw the total prohibition of sealing in the eastern, or American, part of Bering Sea, according to the *modus vivendi* between Great Britain and the United States pending the fur-seal arbitration by the Paris tribunal. The sealing fleet was already on their way when they were informed of the closing of Bering Sea, the result being that quite a number of the vessels, rather than return home, made straight for the Commander Islands to try their luck there. No less than 32 Canadian vessels crossed over to the Russian side after having completed their coast catch. In addition, there seems to have been 5 British schooners sailing from Japan, consequently altogether 37 British vessels. To these must be added a few American schooners, of which I have no detailed account at hand. Capt. Charles Lutjens, in the *Kate and Anna*, caught about 150 seals "between from 40 to 100 miles south of the Commander Islands, and these were seized and confiscated" (Fur Seal Arb., VIII, p. 714). The *Henry Dennis* obtained 189 seals, as detailed elsewhere in this report.

These facts are shown in more detail in the following table, which is extracted from the record of the entire British Columbia sealing fleet, as given in the Twenty-fifth Annual Report of the Canadian Department of Marine and Fisheries (pt. II, pp. 60–61).

---

[1] The British Bering Sea commissioners, writing in June, 1892, could therefore state as a "fact that pelagic sealing, as understood on the coast of America, is there [Asiatic coast] practically unknown." It is probable, however, that the real beginning was made already in 1891, though on a small scale. Capt. Chas. Lutjens, of San Francisco, owner of the schooner *Kate and Anna*, states (Fur Seal Arb., VIII, p. 715) that on going into Bering Sea on June 6, 1891, he was warned out, and went directly to the Russian side, where he got 450 seals. The *Penelope*, Capt. J. W. Todd, of Victoria, was also there that year; also *Beatrice*, Capt M. Keefe, who got 500 seals there; *Umbrina*, Capt. J. Matthews, 30 seals; *Maud S.*, Capt. A. McKeil, and probably several others.

Report of British Columbia sealing fleet sealing in "Asiatic" waters in the season of 1892.

Schooner	Lower coast catch.	Upper coast catch	Asiatic catch.	Total.	Schooner.	Lower coast catch	Upper coast catch.	Asiatic catch.	Total.
Annie E. Paint	166	412	421	1,019	Mary Ellen	35	507	304	846
Annie C. Moore	64	379	447	990	Mermaid		164	238	402
Arietis		418	738	1,156	Mountain Chief			(seized.)	
Agnes McDonald		591	373	964	Ocean Belle	128	687	646	1,461
Brenda		409	512	921					(seized.)
Carlotta G. Cox	436	1,695	636	2,737	Oscar and Hattie	25	186	261	472
C. H. Tupper	308	967	542	1,817	Penelope	345		1,362	1,707
Carmolite	174	705	(seized.)	879	Rosie Olsen			(seized.)	
C. D. Rand	28		(seized.)	28	Sea Lion	472	629	833	1,934
Dora Siewerd		224	673	897	Sadie Turpe		454	244	695
E. B. Marvin	183	1,434	436	2,045	Teresa	85	306	175	564
Enterprise			507	507	Thistle (str.)	79		4	83
Favourite		450	202	652	Triumph		284	257	541
Geneva	270	420	600	1,290	Umbrina	143	707	623	1,473
Henrietta	44	108	(seized.)	152	Victoria	23		558	581
Maria			(seized.)		W. P. Sayward	180		909	1,089
Mascot	107	220	119	446	Walter A. Earle	100	1,226	541	1,866
Maud S	185	769	748	1,502	Walter L. Rich		182	204	386
May Belle	149	145	230	524	W. P. Hall			416	416

The total catch by the Canadians alone amounted to about 17,000 skins.¹ Out of this number probably no less than 14,000 were skins of female seals. Adding to this the number of seals killed, but lost, those captured by the United States schooners, and those shot during the northward migration during the spring of that year, it is easy to conceive how enormous and irreparable must have been the blow inflicted upon the *breeding* seals of the Commander Islands during the year 1892.

With over 40 vessels scouring the seas around the islands, their boats and canoes following the female seals as they went to and from the feeding-grounds, no wonder that the latter were discovered by the sealers, and in these places undoubtedly most of the damage was done.

But not all the schooners were satisfied with taking the seals outside of the territorial waters of Russia; they adopted the tactics of sending the boats inshore to hunt off the rookeries, and as a consequence many of them had to feel the claws of the bear. The Russian authorities, evidently in anticipation of what would happen, had several cruisers patrolling her seas, and no less than seven schooners, one hailing from the United States and the other six owing allegiance to Great Britain, were captured by the commanders of the cruisers *Zabiaka*, Captain de Livron, and *Vitiaz*, Captain Zarine, and by Mr. Grebnitski on board the company's steamer *Kotik*. The schooners were taken to Vladivostok, condemned, and sold, except the *Rosie Olsen*, which was rechristened the *Prize* and given to Capt. W. Copp, of the *Vancouver Belle*, on condition that he take 37 of the captured sailors to British Columbia. The other sailors were sent home in the American ship *Majestic*, except the men of the schooners *Marie* and *Carmolite*, who were taken to Vladivostok and then shipped to Japan.

The schooners, whose capture created a great excitement in Canadian sealing circles, were as follows:

(1) *C. H. White*, of San Francisco, seized by the *Zabiaka* July 16, between Copper Island and Bering Island.

¹ Total of the "Asiatic catch" in the above table 14,804
  Seized by Russian war vessels 2,418

  Total... 17,222
Some of the skins seized by the Russians were taken on the Northwest coast.

(2) *Willie Metiowan*, of Shelburne, N. S., seized by the *Zabiaka* July 18,[1] about 18 miles[2] southwest of Palata, Copper Island.

(3) *Rosie Olsen*, of Victoria, B. C., seized by Mr. Grebnitski, July 26, in 55° 23′ north latitude and 165° 27′ east longitude, or about 10 miles northwest of Zapadni Mys, Bering Island.

(4) *Ariel*, of Victoria, B. C., seized by the *Zabiaka*, on July 28, apparently about 10 miles southwest of the Copper Island rookeries.[3]

(5) *Vancouver Belle*, of Vancouver, seized by the *Zabiaka*, on August 12, about 17 miles south of the southern extremity of Copper Island.

(6) *Marie*, of Maitland, N. S., seized by Mr. Grebnitski, August 21, in 54° 36′ north latitude and 168° 24′ east longitude, or about 9[4] miles northeast from the south end of Copper Island, the nearest land.

(7) *Carmolite*, of Vancouver, seized by the *Vitiaz* (with Admiral S. O. Makarof on board), August 29, in 54° 29′ north latitude and 168° 2′ east longitude, about 6 miles[5] southeast of the isthmus (Peresheyek) of Copper Island.

In addition, (1) one boat and crew belonging to the schooner *Marvin* were seized by the natives on one of the Copper Island rookeries for killing seals. (2) Three boats and crews having clubbed seals on the rookeries were captured by the *Zabiaka* on July 24, 9 miles from the southern extremity of Copper Island; they belonged to the schooner *Sayward*. (3) Two boats and 6 sailors from the *Annie C. Moore* were caught on one of the rookeries by the natives.

The number of skins taken from the British schooners was as follows:

Name of vessel.	No. of skins.
Marie	622
Rosie Olsen	379
Carmolite	608
Vancouver Belle	594
W. Metiowan	76
Ariel	139
Total	2,418

The confiscated skins were sold by auction, part in Petropaulski, part in London.

The prize moneys from the sale of the schooners and outfits were distributed among the captors.

It will be seen that all of the British schooners were captured outside of the 3-mile limit, and diplomatic remonstrances and claims for damages were at once made by Great Britain. The Russian Government appointed a special commission to investigate the seizures, and found that the *Marie*, *Rosie Olsen*, *Carmolite*, and *Vancouver Belle* were properly seized, as their boats had been sealing in territorial waters, while

---

[1] By some mistake the date is given as June 6 in the report of the Russian commission as rendered in the 26 Ann. Rep. Canad. Dept. Fish., p. CLIX. July 6, old style, is probably intended.

[2] In the same report the distance from the coast is given as 21 miles, although the position is said to have been 54° 24′ north latitude and 167° 43′ east longitude, which is a trifle more than 18 miles from the nearest point of Copper Island.

[3] The positions and distances in the report quoted above are so contradictory that it is hard to tell which is meant to be correct. Thus, in the present case, it is stated (p. CLIX) that "The schooner *Ariel* was seized by the cruiser *Zabiaka* on the 16th July (old style) at 3.30 a. m., in 54° 31′ north latitude and 167° 40′ east longitude. At the time of the seizure she was making away from the coast under easy sail, and was 21 miles from Copper Island." Of course both statements can not be correct.

[4] Seven in the report above referred to.

[5] Eight miles according to the above report.

the proof that the *Willie McGowan* and *Ariel*, or their boats, had been sealing inside the 3-mile limit was considered insufficient. The findings of the commission are rendered in detail in the Twenty-sixth Annual Report of the Canadian Department of Fisheries.

The experience of 1892 was conclusive proof that it was feasible for the schooners to stay 20 miles away from the islands and yet send in their boats to the rookeries to prey upon the breeding seals going to and fro. It was also made plain that there would be very little chance of stopping the traffic by means of large cruisers patrolling the sea. The Russian authorities, therefore, were very anxious to establish a prohibitive zone around the islands wide enough to make it impossible for the boats to raid the rookeries independently, the mere presence of the schooner inside of this limit being evidence of illegal sealing. Negotiations were progressing during the winter of 1892 and 1893 between the two governments, and finally, in May, 1893, a provisional agreement was entered into between Russia and Great Britain establishing a protective zone of 30 miles around the Commander Islands and Robben Island. It is evident that the Russian authorities at that time were unaware of the fact that the great bulk of the skins taken by the British Columbia sealing fleet were obtained on the feeding-grounds of the breeding females, and were also ignorant of the exact location of these grounds, or they would not have rested satisfied with the zone of 30 miles, which has been of but very little protective value to the seals. In view of the role which the Russian acceptance of this 30-mile zone played in the establishment of the 60-mile zone around the Pribylof Islands, it is important to remember that in accepting the *30-mile zone* the Russians had a much more limited *object* in view, viz, *to make it impossible for the pelagic sealers to raid the rookeries.*

THE PROVISIONAL AGREEMENT OF MAY, 1893.

The provisional arrangement, which was to be entirely without retroactive force as regards the British vessels seized in 1892, is as follows:

I. During the year ending December, 1893, the English Government will prohibit their subjects from killing or hunting seal within a zone of 10 marine miles on all the Russian coasts of Behring Sea and the North Pacific Ocean, as well as within a zone of 30 marine miles around the Komandorsky Islands and Tuléneu (Robben Island).

II. British vessels engaged in hunting seals within the aforesaid zones, beyond Russian territorial waters, may be seized by Russian cruisers, to be handed over to British cruisers or to the nearest British authorities. In case of impediment or difficulty, the commander of the Russian cruiser may confine himself to seizing the papers of the aforementioned vessels, in order to deliver them to a British cruiser or to transmit them to the nearest British authorities on the first opportunity.

III. Her Majesty's Government engage to bring to trial before the ordinary tribunals, offering all necessary guaranties, the British vessels which may be seized as having been engaged in sealing within the prohibited zones beyond Russian territorial waters.

IV. The Imperial Russian Government will limit to 30,000 the number of seals which may be killed during the year 1893 on the coasts of the islands of Komandorsky and Tulenew (Robben Island).

V. An agent of the British Government may visit the aforementioned islands (Komandorsky and Tulenew) in order to obtain from the local authorities all necessary information on the working and results of the agreement arrived at, but care should be taken to give previous information to these authorities of the place and time of his visit, which should not be prolonged beyond a few weeks.

VI. The present arrangement has no retroactive force as regards British vessels captured previously by the cruisers of the Imperial Russian Marine.

The British Parliament enacted the necessary legislation (Seal Fishery, North Pacific, Act 1893), an "order in council" was passed July 4, 1893, and the agreement went into effect. The Russian war vessels the *Zabiaka* and the *Yakut*, the latter a small transport, as well as two British cruisers, kept up a constant patrol of the 30-mile zone.

The success of 1892 and the continued closure of the American side of Bering Sea during 1893 drove the great majority of the sealing fleet over to the Asiatic side early in the season, and the Commander Islands herd was, therefore, preyed upon to a previously unknown extent along the Japan coast during the migration, in addition to the slaughter of the females on the feeding grounds. No less than 35 schooners from Victoria, B. C., were sealing off the Commander Islands, mostly outside the 30-mile limit, and made a haul of 12,013 skins, while 22 schooners had hunted off the Japan coast, obtaining a total of 29,270 skins. It is stated that, in addition to the above figures relating to the Canadian fleet, the number of skins landed at Hakodate, Japan, by American vessels was 18,587, and by Hawaiian vessels 3,212, a total of 21,799 skins. A small percentage of these was undoubtedly contributed by the Kuril herd and Robben Island seals, but it is safe to say that the pelagic sealing of 1893 yielded about 60,000 Commander Island skins, the majority females. How many more were wastefully killed and lost it is impossible to say.

I append a list of the Canadian vessels sealing on the Asiatic side in 1893, extracted from the Twenty-sixth Annual Report of the Canadian Department of Fisheries (pp. CLXVI–CLXVII), as follows:

Report of vessels of British Columbia sealing fleet sealing on the "Russian side," season 1893.

Vessels.	Tons.	Crews.			Boats.	Canoes.	Masters.	Catch.	
		White.	Indian.					Japan coast.	Russian side.
Victoria, B. C.:									
Triumph	98	7	28		4	14	C. N. Cox		623
Sapphire	108	8	26		12	3	Wm. Cox		341
E. B. Marvin	117	27			8		J. Gould		517
Mascot	40	7	14		2	7	H. F. Sieward		327
Dora Sieweard	94	24			7		R. O. Lavender		431
Minnie	46	5	20		2	10	J. Mohrhousn		20
Annie E. Paint	82	23			8		A. Bissett		401
Diana	50	19			6		A. Nelson		294
Mermaid	75	23			8		W. H. Whiteley	940	315
Fawn	59	3	21		2	10	L. Magneson		77
Ocean Belle	83	25			8		T. O Leary		547
Arietis	86	23			7		A. Douglass	920	161
Aimoka	75	5	14		1	7	G. Heater		46
Katharine	82	6	19		2	9	W. D. McDougall		363
Enterprise	69	24			7		J. W. Todd	1,027	274
Agnes McDonald	107	25			7		M. F. Cutler	2,333	433
Viva	92	23			6		J. W. Anderson	1,441	30
Umbrina	98	24			7		C. Campbell	1,827	625
Vera	60	19			5		W. Shields	1,910	99
Otto	86	8	24		2	12	M. Keefe		397
Mary Taylor	42	18			5		E. Shields		240
Brenda	100	26			8		C. E. Locke		408
Libbie	93	23			7		F. Hackett	1,242	389
City of San Diego	46	14			5		M. Pike	942	101
Geneva	92	26			8		W. O'Leary	1,612	454
Casco	63	19			6		O. Buckley	1,473	190
Carlotta G. Cox	76	24			7		W. D. Byers	2,386	376
Oscar and Hattie	81	21			7		W. E. Baker	1,178	1,020
Teresa	65	20			6		E. Lorenz	677	147
Sadie Turpie	56	21			7		C. Le Blanc	927	475
Maud S	97	24			7		R. E. McKeil	989	58
Mary Ellen	63	23			7		W. O. Hughes	1,573	406
Walter L. Rich	76	24			7		S. Balcom		517
Annie C. Moore	113	26			8		J. Daley	822	333
Walter P. Hall	98	23			7		J. B. Brown	708	263

Wise by experience, the sealing fleet kept pretty well outside the 30-mile zone, though the following seizures of British vessels were made:

(1) *Minnie*, of Victoria, British Columbia, seized by the *Yakut*, July 17, 21 miles southeast of Copper Island.

(2) *Ainoko*, of Victoria, British Columbia, seized by the *Yakut*, July 22, 16 miles south of Copper Island.

(3) *Maud S.*, of Victoria, British Columbia, seized by the *Yakut*, August 29, 22 miles southwest of Copper Island.

(4) *Arctic*, of Shanghai, seized by the *Zabiaka* within the 30-mile zone.

Of these, only the *Minnie* was afterwards condemned.

The provisional agreement as given above was renewed in 1894 and 1895 for those years. Owing to the threatening political aspects, as a consequence of the Japanese-Chinese war, the Russian Government had only one ship patrolling the 30-mile limit in 1895. The British cruiser *Caroline* did patrol duty early in the season, and was relieved by the *Porpoise*, Captain Francis R. Pelly, commanding. No seizures were made in that year.

As schooners flying the flag of the United States were also among the fleet preying upon the Commander Islands herd, it was found necessary to establish a *modus vivendi* with the United States similar to the provisional agreement with Great Britain. An arrangement, differing only in a few verbal changes from the latter, was drawn up by the Imperial Minister for Foreign Affairs, Mr. Giers, and signed in Washington by the representatives of the respective governments on May 4, 1894. The exact text of this arrangement, which "shall only be in force until further orders," is found in Executive Document No. 67, Senate, Fifty-third Congress, third session, being the President's Message regarding the Enforcement of Regulations respecting Fur Seals, p. 82.

The Twenty-seventh Annual Report of the Canadian Department of Fisheries contains an account of the Canadian pelagic sealing operations on the Asiatic side during 1894, by Mr. R. N. Venning, from which we quote the following abstracts:

> The vessels this year operating in the vicinity of the Russian Seal Islands are reported to have kept well outside the protective zone, principally working about 100 miles southeast of Copper Island. As a consequence, the present year's operations are marked by an almost total absence of interference with the Canadian fleet by Russian authorities.
>
> The only instance reported is that of a sealing boat of the schooner *May Belle*, of Victoria, B. C., manned by Joseph Morrell, Charles K. Leclaire, and James Costin, which lost the vessel in a fog, and after remaining out all night and failing to find the schooner on the following morning, the occupants, fearing a storm which was threatening, made for the shore of Copper Island for shelter. They were discovered and arrested before landing.
>
> The boat and her equipment were retained at Copper Island and the three men were taken to Petropaulovski, on the mainland of Kamchatka, where, after a detention of 32 days, they were handed over to Her Majesty's ship *Daphne*, taken to Yokohama, Japan, and delivered to Her Majesty's consul at that port.
>
> They were imprisoned, but released some four hours later, and informed by the consul that the charge against them was not sufficient for their detention. They were accordingly sent by Her Majesty's consul to Victoria, B. C., by Canadian Pacific Railway steamship, where they arrived on the 26th November, 1894.
>
> Claims for damages have been filed by the parties and by the owners of the sealing boat, and representations have been made to Her Majesty's government on the subject.

Report of vessels of British Columbia sealing fleet in the vicinity of Copper Island, season 1895.
[From 27 Ann. Rep. Canada Dept. Fish.]

Vessels.	Tons.	Crews.		Boats.	Canoes.	Masters.	Catch.	
		White.	Indian.				Japan coast.	Vicinity Copper Island.
Victoria:								
Enterprise	69	22		8		O. Scarf	1,254	314
Rosie Olsen	39	6	16	2	8	A. B. Whidden	1,043	
Umbrina	99	25		8		C. Campbell	2,588	153
Oscar and Hattie	81	24		7		A. Folger	1,733	176
Diana	58	19		6		A. Nelson	1,961	433
Brenda	100	26		8		C. E. Locke	2,583	343
Arietis	86	25		8		A. Douglass	1,197	
Casco	61	22		6		O. Bucholz	1,926	
Dora Sieward	94	26		8		F. Cole	2,584	
Walter A. Earle	68	8	20	2	10	L. Magnesen	1,471	
Fawn	59	6	18	1	9	M. Keefe	911	
Agnes McDonald	107	26		8		M. Cutler	1,707	471
W. P. Hall	99	24		7		J. B. Brown	710	
Mermaid	73	25		8		W. H. Whiteley	1,603	505
City of San Diego	46	16		5		M. Pike	1,304	250
Mary Taylor	43	19		5		E. Robins	874	250
Libbie	93	22		7		F. Hackett	1,016	200
May Belle	58	14		6		E. Shields	925	197
Mary Ellen	63	23		7		W. O. Hughes	1,909	86
Viva	92	26		7		J. Anderson	1,437	
W. P. Sayward	66	20		6		G. Percy	606	35
Penelope	70	20		7		L. McGrath	1,506	296
Vera	60	19		6		W. S. Shields	1,076	
Carlotta G. Cox	76	24		7		W. Byers	1,947	
Otto	86	25		8		J. McLeod	1,014	623
E. B. Marvin	96	23		7		C. J. Harris	2,118	
Annie E. Paint	82	26		9		A. Bassett	1,497	531
Geneva	92	27		8		W. O'Leary	1,092	558
Teresa	63	25		7		F. Gilbert	1,102	130
Ocean Belle	83	22		6		T. O'Leary	830	274
Sadie Turpie	56	22		8		C. Leblanc	1,783	171
Maud S	97	24		8		R. McKiel	1,343	86
Aurora	41	18		5		H. J. Lund	603	21
Florence M. Smith	99	27		8		J. Allen	96	81
Mascot	40	4	16	1	7	H. F. Sieward	558	
Pioneer	66	24		6		W. E. Baker		1,263
Vancouver:								
Beatrice	49	21		6			1,703	
United States:								
Louis Olsen							435	
Anna Matilda							7	
Josephine							48	
Total							49,489	7,427

The pelagic sealing seasons of 1894 and 1895 are most notable for the excessive number of skins taken during the migration and for the falling off in the catch on the Copper Island feeding-grounds, indicating the approaching exhaustion of this locality. But, in addition, the latter year is notable for being the first year in which pelagic sealers have to any extent attacked the feeding-grounds of the Bering Island rookeries.

It has been long known that seals occurred in summer in the waters northwest of Bering Island, from Cape Kamchatka to Karaginski Island; but it seems as if in 1895 the sealers repaired there systematically and with success. I am indebted to Mr. C. H. Townsend for this information and for the following abstracts of the logs of the schooners *Ida Etta*, sealing off Cape Nagikinski, and *Jane Grey*, sealing off Cape Afrika.

Schooner Jane Grey.

Date.	Location.	Seals.
1895.		
Aug. 16	56° 44′ N. 164° 25′ E	28
Aug. 17	56° 09′ N. 164° 10′ E	8
Aug. 18	56° 09′ N. 164° 10′ E	2
Aug. 19	56° 09′ N. 164° 10′ E	1
Aug. 20	56° 09′ N. 164° 10′ E	13
Aug. 21	56° 09′ N. 164° 10′ E	13
Total		65

Schooner Ida Ella.

Date.	Location.	Seals.
1895.		
Aug. 20	Cape Nagikinski, SW. 30 miles	37
21	Cape Nagikinski, SW. 20 miles	35
24	Cape Nagikinski, SW. 20 miles	28
26	Cape Nagikinski, SW. 20 miles	28
27	Cape Nagikinski, W. 30 miles	10
31	Cape Nagikinski, W. 30 miles	3
Sept. 1	Cape Nagikinski, WSW. 25 miles	25
2	Cape Nagikinski, SW. 20 miles	6
3	Cape Nagikinski, SW. 30 miles	4
4	Cape Nagikinski, SW. 25 miles	4
	Total	180

I am also indebted to Mr. Townsend for figures relating to the catch of 1894, and for the information that the total Japan coast catch for 1895 amounted to 31,048 skins, and total catch of the pelagic sealers in Russian waters 7,684 skins; together, 38,732 skins. The Commander Islands herd, therefore, lost in 1895 no less than 35,000 seals, the majority females, besides the unknown number killed without being captured.[1]

During the five years 1891 to 1895, inclusive, the "Asiatic catch" by pelagic sealers may be summed up as follows:

Year.	Nationality of vessels.	Japan catch.	Russian catch.	Totals.	Grand totals.
1891					5,847
1892	Canada	(?)	17,222		26,752
	United States	(?)	1,224		
1893	Canada	29,270	12,013	41,283	63,082
	United States and Hawaii			21,799	
1894	Canada	49,483	7,437	56,920	90,067
	United States	31,376	1,771	33,147	
1895	Canada	18,686	6,605	25,291	38,732
	United States	12,362	1,079	13,441	

* From the report of Hon. Charles S. Hamlin, Assistant Secretary, U. S. Treasury (Doc 137, Senate, Fifty-fourth Cong., 1st sess., pt. I, p. 6). During that year 18,000 skins are recorded from "undetermined localities," some of which are probably "Asiatic" in their origin.
† This total is derived from Mr. Hamlin's report (l. c.). The "Japan catch" of 1892 was therefore over 8,300.

It will be seen that the known pelagic "Asiatic catch" from 1892–95 was over 218,000 skins. Allowing the 8,000 skins for the Kurils and Tiuleni, the *known* loss in that period to the Commander Islands herd was about 210,000 seals, apart from the loss of wounded ones, etc. The number of seals killed on the islands in the same period was 105,236. The pelagic *catch* was therefore twice as large as that on the islands, while the loss to the herd from that cause was much greater. It is certainly no exaggeration to say that *the actual loss to the herd in those four years has averaged 100,000 a year, one-half of which were probably females, while even in the palmiest days of exclusive land sealing the loss only averaged 50,000 seals a year, all males.*

To illustrate and complete this chapter on pelagic sealing I have had plotted on map 1 the position of 11 schooners off the Commander Islands during the sealing season. The positions for each noon are connected by straight lines and the figures represent the number of seals taken during the preceding 24 hours. Extracts from the log books are appended herewith. The logs are given *in extenso* in the Fur Seal Arbitration case, except that of the *Henry Dennis*, for which I am indebted to Mr. Townsend.

[1] Mr. Townsend has since informed me that the loss to the Commander Island herd is to be increased by at least 10,000 seals, as shown by reports from consuls, etc., recently received.

Catch of seal skins on board of British schooner Umbrina, 1892.

Date.	Latitude.	Longitude.	Remarks.	Daily catch.	Totals.
1892.					
July 20	53 50 N.	167 30 E.	Killed from schooner	2	855
22	53 50 N.	167 30 E.	......do......	1	856
23	53 40 N.	167 10 E.	......do......	1	857
24	53 40 N.	166 10 E.	Boats out all day	17	874
25	53 50 N.	167 00 E.		12	886
26	53 40 N.	166 50 E.		65	951
27	53 30 N.	166 25 E.		68	1,019
28	53 40 N.	166 50 E.		27	1,046
Aug. 1	53 30 N.	166 50 E.		3	1,049
2	53 40 N.	166 55 E.		10	1,059
3	53 34 N.	166 40 E.		8	1,067
4	53 40 N.	165 30 E.		65	1,132
5	53 45 N.	165 10 E.		72	1,204
6	53 55 N.	165 10 E.		56	1,260
7	54 10 N.	165 30 E.		10	1,270
10	54 40 N.	166 30 E.	Killed from schooner	1	1,271
11	53 47 N.	166 40 E.		5	1,276
12	53 40 N.	166 50 E.	Killed from schooner	1	1,277
16	53 55 N.	167 00 E.		8	1,285
17	55 55 N.	166 50 E.		21	1,306
18	53 30 N.	166 45 E.		25	1,331
19	53 40 N.	168 40 E.	Killed from schooner	1	1,332
21	53 35 N.	166 35 E.		15	1,347
22	53 35 N.	166 45 E.		55	1,402
23	53 50 N.	166 35 E.	Killed from schooner	2	1,404
24	54 00 N.	166 35 E.		62	1,466
25	53 50 N.	166 30 E.	Killed from schooner	1	1,467
26	54 00 N.	166 35 E.	......do......	1	1,468
30	53 35 N.	166 30 E.	......do......	2	1,470
31	53 30 N.	166 40 E.	......do......	3	1,473
				620	

Extract of return showing the dates on which seals were taken, the number taken each day, and the noon position on each such dates, of the schooner Maud S. on her sealing voyage for the season 1892.

Date.	No. of seals taken.	Latitude.	Longitude.
1892.			
July 14	11	53 10 N.	166 10 E.
15	10	53 33 N.	166 55 E.
21	10	53 33 N.	165 20 E.
22	12	53 12 N.	165 40 E.
23	7	52 40 N.	167 22 E.
26	1	53 24 N.	166 30 E.
27	57	53 24 N.	166 04 E.
28	99	53 21 N.	168 08 E.
29	14	53 33 N.	168 00 E.
Aug. 2	3	54 10 N.	167 11 E.
3	8	53 55 N.	166 45 E.
4	12	53 50 N.	166 59 E.
5	40	53 44 N.	167 04 E.
6	41	53 35 N.	166 01 E.
7	71	53 30 N.	165 51 F.
8	3	53 35 N.	165 49 E.
10	24	54 11 N.	167 00 E.
11	12	53 04 N.	166 40 E.
13	5	53 50 N.	165 14 E.
14	2	54 45 N.	164 58 E.
17	15	56 48 N.	166 15 E.
18	8	56 35 N.	167 25 E.
19	2	55 39 N.	167 57 E.
21	1	53 48 N.	169 10 E.
22	7	53 22 N.	168 02 E.
23	114	52 51 N.	167 45 E.
25	10	52 40 N.	167 36 E.
26	16	52 44 N.	167 58 E.
27	7	52 55 N.	167 34 E.
31	31	52 52 N.	167 58 E.
Sept. 4	12	53 15 N.	167 20 E.
5	30	53 14 N.	167 38 E.
6	1	53 01 N.	167 08 E.
7	34	53 06 N.	167 08 E.
10	9	52 51 N.	167 19 E.
	745		

THE RUSSIAN FUR-SEAL ISLANDS.

Extract of return showing the dates on which seals were taken, the number taken each day, and the noon position on each such dates, of the schooner Vancouver Belle on her sealing voyage for the season 1892.

Date.	No. of seals taken.	Latitude.	Longitude.
1892.		° ′	° ′
July 4	3	54 11 N.	168 52 E.
5	2	54 05 N.	167 15 E.
8	1	54 04 N.	167 00 E.
9	14	54 12 N.	169 03 E.
10	2	54 16 N.	169 32 E.
13	5	54 13 N.	169 30 E.
14	22	54 10 N.	168 30 E.
16	1	55 25 N.	167 20 E.
17	1	55 40 N.	166 10 E.
20	1	55 16 N.	166 24 E.
25	8	55 28 N.	170 24 E.
26	2	55 03 N.	169 08 E.
27	8	53 56 N.	166 08 E.
28	103	54 05 N.	167 35 E.
29	11	54 05 N.	167 35 E.
30	1	54 07 N.	167 00 E.
31	1	54 15 N.	167 00 E.
Aug. 1	13	54 04 N.	167 10 E.
2	1	54 10 N.	167 10 E.
3	13	54 20 N.	167 33 E.
4	5	54 12 N.	167 26 E.
5	14	53 54 N.	167 35 E.
6	24	54 10 N.	167 38 E.
7	31	54 13 N.	167 20 E.
8	1	54 20 N.	167 01 E.
10	3	54 20 N.	166 06 E.
11	3	54 15 N.	166 30 E.
	296		

Extract of return showing the dates on which seals were taken, the number taken each day, and the noon position on each such dates, of the schooner Beatrice (Vancouver) on her sealing voyage for the season 1892.

Date.	No. of seals taken.	Latitude.	Longitude.	Total seals to date.
1892.		° ′	° ′	
July 24	1	51 54 N.	168 56 E.	
25	3	53 17 N.	167 48 E.	
26	64	54 17 N.	167 40 E.	
27	112	53 54 N.	167 56 E.	
28	10	53 38 N.	167 30 E.	907
Aug. 1	4	53 28 N.	167 01 E.	
2	15	53 20 N.	168 15 E.	
3	28	53 50 N.	167 18 E.	
4	28	53 23 N.	168 15 E.	
5	47	53 36 N.	167 34 E.	
6	75	53 26 N.	167 36 E.	
7	8	53 22 N.	166 07 E.	
9	12	53 45 N.	166 20 E.	
10	5	53 24 N.	165 52 E.	
11	7	54 07 N.	165 51 E.	
16	12	53 21 N.	166 37 E.	
17	15	53 18 N.	167 04 E.	
18	14	53 10 N.	167 21 E.	
21	9	53 36 N.	169 29 E.	
22	27	53 19 N.	169 00 E.	
23	5	53 20 N.	169 04 E.	
24	21	54 06 N.	168 17 E.	
25	1	53 32 N.	168 12 E.	
	536			

Extract of return showing the dates on which seals were taken, the number taken each day, and the noon position on each such dates, of the schooner Arietis on her sealing voyage for the season 1892.

Date.	No. of seals taken.	Latitude.	Longitude.	Total seals to date.
1892.		° ′	° ′	
July 21	1	54 08 N.	169 00 E.	480
22	25	53 48 N.	169 30 E.	505
25	21	53 30 N.	169 00 E.	526
26	16	53 00 N.	168 45 E.	542
27	160	53 20 N.	169 00 E.	702
28	17	54 00 N.	168 45 E.	719
29	1	54 00 N.	168 55 E.	720
31	5	54 10 N.	168 30 E.	725
Aug. 1	3	54 00 N.	169 00 E.	728
2	5	53 45 N.	168 45 E.	733
3	13	53 40 N.	168 30 E.	746
4	118	53 20 N.	168 15 E.	864
5	154	53 20 N.	168 20 E.	1,038
7	16	53 40 N.	168 45 E.	1,054
8	3	54 00 N.	168 00 E.	1,057
9	4	54 00 N.	168 30 E.	1,061
10	3	53 45 N.	168 00 E.	1,064
18	14	53 00 N.	169 00 E.	1,078
22	25	52 30 N.	167 40 E.	1,103
24	40	53 00 N.	168 00 E.	1,143
29	6	53 00 N.	169 00 E.	1,149
	650			

Extract of return showing the dates on which seals were taken, the number taken each day, and the noon position on each such dates, of the schooner Agnes McDonald on her sealing voyage for the season 1892.

Date.	No. of seals taken.	Latitude.	Longitude.	Total seals to date.
1892.		° ′	° ′	
July 26	18	52 38 N.	168 02 E.	608
27	97	52 48 N.	168 08 E.	705
28	26	52 40 N.	168 00 E.	731
Aug. 1	12	53 30 N.	167 35 E.	743
2	54	53 52 N.	167 05 E.	797
3	17	53 40 N.	167 02 E.	814
4	24	54 03 N.	166 17 E.	838
5	6	54 07 N.	165 05 E.	844
6	4	54 18 N.	165 45 E.	848
7	4	54 05 N.	166 35 E.	852
9	5	54 07 N.	167 15 E.	857
10	3	54 02 N.	167 42 E.	860
11	11	53 42 N.	165 37 E.	871
17	11	53 43 N.	168 02 E.	882
18	18	53 12 N.	165 25 E.	900
20	3	53 05 N.	166 10 E.	903
21	8	52 45 N.	166 58 E.	911
22	52	53 30 N.	167 42 E.	963
25	1	52 28 N.	168 44 E.	964
	374			

Extract of return showing the dates on which seals were taken, the number taken each day, and the noon position on each such dates, of the schooner Henry Dennis on her sealing voyage for the season 1892.

Date.	No. of seals taken.	Latitude.	Longitude.
1892.		° ′	° ′
Aug. 1	1	56 37 N.	168 30 E.
3	13	56 40 N.	168 38 E.
4	40	56 27 N.	168 13 E.
5	108	56 20 N.	168 07 E.
6	26	56 37 N.	168 10 E.
7	1	56 43 N.	167 50 E.
	189		

THE RUSSIAN FUR-SEAL ISLANDS.

Extract of return showing the dates on which seals were taken, the number taken each day, and the noon position on each such dates, of the schooner Annie E. Paint on her sealing voyage for the season 1892..

Date.	No. of seals taken.	Latitude.	Longitude.	Total seals to date.
1892.				
Aug. 3	5	52 55 N.	166 40 E.	569
4	3	52 32 N.	166 01 E.	572
5	24	53 04 N.	165 21 E.	596
6	46	52 30 N.	165 30 E.	642
8	53	52 47 N.	165 37 E.	695
12	15	53 00 N.	166 40 E.	710
17	8	53 02 N.	166 46 E.	718
19	33	52 59 N.	166 31 E.	751
21	8	52 48 N.	166 12 E.	759
22	26	52 58 N.	166 14 E.	784
23	48	52 59 N.	166 25 E.	832
27	32	52 58 N.	166 35 E.	864
31	13	52 51 N.	167 00 E.	878
Sept. 5	16	53 00 N.	167 30 E.	894
12	28	53 00 N.	165 58 E.	922
13	19	52 50 N.	165 40 E.	941
20	44	52 00 N.	169 11 E.	985
	421			

Extract of return showing the dates on which seals were taken, the number taken each day, and the noon position on each such dates, of the schooner W. P. Hall on her sealing voyage for the season 1892.

Date.	No. of seals taken.	Latitude.	Longitude.
1892.			
July 21	6	54 25 N.	170 00 E.
24	5	54 35 N.	169 10 E.
27	50	54 30 N.	168 50 E.
Aug. 2	19	54 29 N.	168 40 E.
3	15	54 03 N.	168 55 E.
4	40	53 35 N.	168 40 E.
5	49	53 30 N.	169 00 E.
6	36	54 05 N.	168 30 E.
8	20	54 35 N.	168 55 E.
9	40	54 25 N.	169 00 E.
10	10	54 05 N.	168 35 E.
11	27	54 10 N.	168 55 E.
21	6	53 00 N.	169 35 E.
22	30	52 55 N.	169 00 E.
27	2	52 20 N.	168 30 E.
	366		

V.—CONCLUSIONS.

SUMMARY.

To gain a clear understanding of the fur-seal question, in so far as it relates to the Russian Seal Islands, it may be well to sum up the essential points as follows:

The topographical character of the rookeries on Bering Island and on Copper Island are essentially different. On the former the grounds are low and accessible, and the drives are unusually easy, involving but little hardship on the seals, even compared with the rookeries on St. Paul Island, Pribylof group. On Copper Island, however, the rookeries are situated at the base of high precipices, very difficult of access, and the drives, from the mountainous nature of the island, are as harsh and trying as it is possible to imagine.

Notwithstanding this difference in the topography, the conditions of seal life on the rookeries were practically alike on both islands previous to, during, and some time after my first visit to the islands in 1882–83. It is an indisputable fact that the seals were increasing markedly in number during that period on both islands.

Of late years the seals have been rapidly decreasing on both islands, the decrease corresponding to the same phenomenon on the Pribylof Islands, but taking place proportionately about five years later on an average.

When I again visited the islands, in 1895, I found the conditions of seal life on the rookeries had so changed as to radically differ on the two islands. On Bering Island, in addition to a marked decrease in killables, there was a notable scarcity of old bulls, while the decrease in breeding females was less apparent. On Copper Island, while the number of killables was small, sexually mature male seals were, on the contrary, plentiful, and at the same time the number of females had decreased enormously.

Prior to 1892 the Commander Islands seals had suffered but little from pelagic sealing in general and practically nothing from preying upon the feeding-grounds of the female seals, at the very time when the Pribylof Island sealing-grounds were being rapidly exhausted.

Since 1892 the whole body of the pelagic sealing fleet has preyed, during the most precarious season of seal life, largely upon the female seals visiting the feeding-grounds off Copper Island.

An unusual mortality of starving seal pups has not been observed until last year on Bering Island, but the natural conditions of the Copper Island rookeries are such as to make it easy to overlook such a fact.

The 30-mile zone stipulated in the Russian-British arrangement of 1893 has only put a stop to the raiding of the rookeries, but has been found utterly valueless as a protective measure against pelagic sealing.

The rookeries of the Commander Islands will become exhausted within a few years if the present conditions are allowed to continue much longer.

CAUSES OF THE DECREASE.

Three different causes, either of them alone, or in combination with the others, have been generally regarded as responsible for the undeniable decline of seal life on the seal islands of the Bering Sea and North Pacific Ocean, viz, excessive driving of the male seals, raids on the rookeries, and pelagic sealing. It may be well to inquire how each of these alleged causes applies to the conditions prevailing on the Russian islands.

It has been claimed that the *driving* of the male seals results in sapping their vitality and impairing their procreative powers, thus causing a double decline by shortening the life of the individual and causing a smaller number of pups to be born. I have elsewhere in this report discussed this question. Here it will suffice to simply inquire, How do the facts observed on the Commander Islands agree with this theory? I have already summarized the facts, but they will bear a brief repetition. On Bering Island the driving is so easy that even the black pups driven in flocks with the adults are uninjured; yet there was quite a deficiency in bulls, virile and otherwise. On Copper Island the drives are beyond comparison the hardest known anywhere; yet there was a surplus of exceedingly virile bulls; and still, if we may be allowed a comparison with the Pribylof Islands, we may add that the decrease in killables on Copper Island is of a much later date than the corresponding decrease on the Pribylofs. Now, if the driving had had the slightest influence upon the numbers of the seals, how did it happen that the seals were increasing while it is a fact that the drives have never been easier, but if anything rather harsher? Nothing seems more clear and logical than this proposition, viz, that if the driving is the cause of the decline, we should expect the falling off in bulls to have taken place on Copper Island, and not on Bering Island; but the reverse is just the case. I am, therefore, compelled to absolve the driving of the responsibility for the decrease on the Commander Islands.

The contention that the occasional *raids* practiced on the rookeries by marauding schooners are materially to blame for the decrease has found but slight support, and the experience on the Commander Islands does not substantiate it. I have shown that the Commander Islands seals were increasing in spite of the numerous raids in the early eighties; I have also shown how the little rock of Robben Island has continued to yield killable seals in spite of an unparalleled history of raids. It is safe to say that the annual catch of the raiders of the latter island greatly exceeded that of the legitimate killing on shore, and yet the falling off in the yield is not greater than that of the other islands.

There remains the *pelagic sealing*. Up to 1892 there was no startling decrease of the female seals on the Commander Islands rookeries, while there had been for a couple of years some difficulty in getting the former number of killables. In 1892 the sudden invasion of the whole body of the pelagic sealing fleet upon the unprotected feeding-grounds of the Copper Island female seals took place, followed by similar inroads in 1893 and 1894. The melancholy decimation of the female seals on the Copper Island rookeries as witnessed by me in 1895 can be directly traced to this preying upon the herd off Copper Island. The extension of the hunt to the Bering Island feeding grounds in 1895 explains easily the presence in great numbers of pups starved to death on the Bering Island Rookery. The somewhat earlier falling off in killables is attributable to the increase in the winter and spring catch off Japan.

The simultaneous or sequential occurrence of the above facts and phenomena is evidently more than a mere coincidence. As cause and result, they fit like a hand in a glove, and *I have been unable to resist the force of the logic which places the blame for the decrease of the Commander Islands seals upon pelagic sealing, and upon pelagic sealing alone.*

FUTURE PROSPECTS ON THE COMMANDER ISLANDS.

The Commander Islands seal herd, originally and at its best only half the numerical strength of the Pribylof herd, is being killed off so rapidly that in a season or two it must become utterly unprofitable to hunt them in the open sea. If the destruction is allowed to go on much further it is feared that it will take a very long time before the rookeries can be to any degree restored, even under the most effective protection.

If, on the other hand, really protective measures could at once be instituted, I am of the opinion that it will be possible to repair the damage within a reasonable time. It may not be possible to bring back the palmy days of 50,000 skins a year, but it might yet be feasible to render the business profitable to the natives, the Government, and the fur trade.

This may to many appear as a rather optimistic view, but I base my opinion on the well-established fact of the quick recovery and rapid replenishing of the rookeries during the beginning of the lease of Hutchinson, Kohl, Philippeus & Co., as well as upon the wonderfully recuperative powers of the herds as demonstrated in the history of Robben Island. A graphic demonstration of an estimated increase would bear out this opinion, but as being chiefly speculatory, and therefore outside the limits which I have endeavored to keep in this report, is here left out of consideration.

RECOMMENDATIONS.

The Commander Islands being outside the boundaries of our own country, recommendations by the present writer as to the protection and management of the fur-seal business may seem to be out of place. Perhaps, therefore, I ought to have called the following paragraphs suggestions rather than recommendations. The friendly cooperation shown by the Russian authorities, however, has led me to give these, my personal opinions, a more definite form.

In the first place, any protection to be effective must be established by international agreement between all the powers directly interested, viz, Russia, Japan, Great Britain, and the United States. Separate action is apt to be disastrous. It has thus far not only resulted in protective regulations which do not protect, but the English-American *modus vivendi* of 1892 was unquestionably the beginning of the ruin of the Commander Islands rookeries.

As to the measures to be recommended, it may at once be stated that only radical and total prohibition can be effective. A short period of complete stoppage of sealing will produce more good than three times as long a period of partial protection. The recent history of fur-seal protection has shown the utter failure of halfway measures.

The special recommendations which I should be inclined to make are as follows:

(1) Total and absolute prohibition of pelagic sealing in the North Pacific Ocean and Bering Sea at all seasons for at least six years.

(2) After that time total prohibition at all seasons in Bering Sea and Pacific Ocean west of 175° east longitude and north of 52° north latitude, or, if preferable, within a zone of 150 nautical miles from the islands.

(3) Total prohibition of killing on land for one year.

(4) After that time bachelor seals to be taken on land not later than August 1.

The total prohibition of pelagic sealing for six years is thought to be sufficient to restock the rookeries with females to the extent that at least an equilibrium of the herd may be attained.

One year's total prohibition on land is thought sufficient to furnish enough males to start with for the increasing number of females. It is also supposed that there will be enough males left every year from those not hauling out until August 1. The reason why I do not advocate a longer prohibition of killing on land than one year is that I regard a large surplus of mature males on the rookeries beyond the actually indispensable number for the impregnation of every female as a check to the increase of the herd. The herds on the Commander Islands, as well as on the Pribylof Islands, must have been practically at equilibrium at the time of their discovery by man, and I attribute this solely to the fact that there must have been a superabundance of males sufficient to prevent an increase. The killing off of the superfluous number of males must inevitably result in a rapid increase of the herd. Similar conditions exist among other polygamous animals, which have been known to increase rapidly by the killing off of a great number of the males.

The natives would have to be supported for one year, but that undertaking ought not to be so expensive on the Commander Islands as it might appear at first glance. The first thing to be done would be to exterminate the sledge-dogs on Bering Island. They eat more seal meat and fish than the natives, and are a general nuisance. A few Kamchatka horses would do much better service than all the dogs, and, supplemented with a few more good boats on the island, would suffice for transportation and travel. The Bering Islanders, having nothing else to do during the whole year of the prohibition, could easily put up an extra quantity of dried salmon at Sarauna, which, with the quantity saved from the dogs, would go a long ways toward the feeding of the Copper Islanders. The latter, having still the sea-otters, could well afford to pay the Bering Islanders something for the fish. Besides, it might be so arranged as to have fox hunts on both islands during the year of the "zapuska," or prohibition.

———

There seems to be no good reason why the Governments in question should not be able to agree upon some such scheme of protection, which appears to be both equitable and effective. However, should both reason and self-interest prove unavailing, and it should be found impossible to effect a satisfactory protection, the question naturally arises, What is to be done with the remaining seals?

There would certainly be no reason for limiting the number of male seals to be taken on land. The restriction placed upon the killing on the islands under the present conditions results in nothing but a one-sided attempt at preservation of the rookeries for the benefit of the pelagic sealers.

As for a total extermination of the herd, simply to prevent the pelagic sealers from getting any more seals, it may well be remarked that the measure seems well-nigh superfluous, as there will soon be no seals for the pelagic sealers to kill. A perusal of the chapter on Robben Island might raise the question whether it would be effective.

However, the issue is not an actual one in the present case; for, so far as I know, the Russian authorities are not publicly discussing the possibilities of such a step. At the same time it should not be forgotten that Russia's position is more advantageous than that of the United States in this respect, as it is bound by no such moral obligations, much less legal ones, as would have confronted her had she ever submitted the main points in the case to international arbitration.

LIST OF ILLUSTRATIONS.

(The maps and photographs are by the author unless otherwise stated.)

Plate
No.
1.—Map of western portion of Bering Sea. Solid red line is 30 miles from shore of Commander Islands; broken red line 150 miles from same. Figures in red indicate the noon positions of 11 schooners and the number of seals taken during the preceding 24 hours.
2.—Isotherms of the surface of the sea for August 16. (From Makarof's "Vitiaz i Tikhi Okean," pl. VII, with the permission of the author.) This map also serves as a general map of the region, showing the relative position of the islands mentioned in this report.
3.—Temperatures and specific gravity of the water in Bering Sea between Kamchatka and the Commander Islands, July 29 to August 2, 1888. (From Makarof's "Vitiaz i Tikhi Okean," pl. VIII, by permission of the author.) Vitiaz station No. 107, July 29, 4 p. m.; 108, July 29, 6.40 p. m.; 109, July 30, 9 a. m.; 110, July 30, 8.15 p. m.; 111, July 31, 8.37 p. m.; 113, August 2, 4.30 p. m. Temperatures in centigrades; depths in meters.
4.—Map of Bering Island. From surveys by the author in 1882-83 and 1895.
5.—Maps of Copper Island. From surveys by the author in 1882-83 and 1895.
6.—Map of straits between Robben Island and Cape Patience, Sakhalin. From a plan by Lieutenant Schultz, I. R. N., 1885.
Plan of Robben Island (Tiuleni Island). From a plan by Lieutenant Shamof, I. R. N., 1884.
7.—Map of North Rookery, Bering Island. Distribution of seals, 1882.
8.—Map of North Rookery, Bering Island. Distribution of seals, July, 1895.
9.—Sketch map of Poludionnoye Rookery, Bering Island. Distribution of seals, 1882.
10.—Sketch map of Poludionnoye Rookery, Bering Island. Distribution of seals, 1895.
11.—Map of Karabelnoye Rookery, Copper Island. Distribution of seals, July 3-10, 1883.
12.—Map of Karabelnoye Rookery, Copper Island. Distribution of seals, August 1-2, 1895.
13.—Map of Glinka Rookeries, Copper Island. Distribution of seals, July 13-16, 1883.
14.—Map of Glinka Rookeries, Copper Island. Distribution of seals, August 2-7, 1895.
15a.—*Heracleum lanatum*, North Rookery, Bering Island, August 23, to show the luxuriant growth of vegetation.
15b.—Yurt or sod-hut, Nikolski, Bering Island, August 20, 1895.
16a.—Wooden frame of yurt, North Rookery village, Bering Island, 1895.
16b.—Kamchatkan cattle, Nikolski, Bering Island, 1895.
17a.—Nikolski village, Bering Island, from bluff back of schoolhouse, July 11, 1895. In the background to the left the three Saranna Lotka Mountains.
17b.—New schoolhouse (left) and governor's office (right), Nikolski village, Bering Island.
18a.—Company's house, Nikolski, Bering Island. Mr. Grebnitski inside of fence; Mr. Kluge outside.
18b.—Company's store, Nikolski, Bering Island, 1895. Beyond, Mr. Grebnitski's residence.
19a.—Reef and Sivutchi Kamen, North Rookery, Bering Island, from sledge road. Killing-grounds with barrels for salted seal meat in middle foreground. July 15, 1895.
19b.—Reef and Sivutchi Kamen, North Rookery, Bering Island, from driveway at lower end of killing-grounds, July 9, 1895, 6.30 p. m.
20.—Reef and Sivutchi Kamen, North Rookery, Bering Island. Pencil sketch by the author, July 30, 1882, to show distribution of seals.
21a.—Reef and Sivutchi Kamen, west half, North Rookery, Bering Island, July 15, 1895, 5 p. m., to show distribution of seals as compared with pl. 20.
21b.—The same, east half.
22a.—Reef, North Rookery, Bering Island, from driveway, July 15, 1895, 5.30 p. m., showing plenty of seals in the water; west half.
22b.—The same; east half.
23.—Kishotchnaya, North Rookery, Bering Island. July 16, 1895, 9.45 a. m., low water.

Plate
No.
24.—Salt-house with skin chute, North Rookery, Bering Island. Natives making ready to carry the bundled seal skins to the boats for shipping. August 13, 1895.
25a.—Beach at North Rookery, Bering Island. Group of natives with seal skins at the landing-place waiting for the boats from the steamer. Salt-house in the background to the left.
25b.—Village at North Rookery, Bering Island. To the left the company's house; in the center the kossak's house; in the background the yurts, or sod huts, of the natives (the new village). From salt-house, August 13, 1895.
26a.—Reef, North Rookery, Bering Island, July 4, 1895, about 2 p. m. Reduced copy of photographs by C. H. Townsend. Breeding seals in three disconnected patches to the left of picture.
26b.—Same. July 9, 1895, about 5 p. m. Photograph by N. Grebnitski, showing the breeding seals occupying a continuous area; also the "band" across the "sands."
27a.—Reef and Sivutchi Kamen, North Rookery, Bering Island. Photograph by Colonel Voloshinof, 1885. From nearly same point as pl. 22, with which it should be compared for distribution of seals on breeding-ground.
27b.—Steller's Arch, near South Rookery, Bering Island, August 17, 1895.
28.—South Rookery, Bering Island, from the west (photographic station No. 3, see map, pl. 10) toward the waterfall. August 17, 1895, 2 p. m.
29.—South Rookery, Bering Island, looking west from photographic station No. 1. August 17, 1895, noon.
30.—South Rookery, Bering Island. Females and pups. From photographic station No. 2. August 17, 1895, noon.
31a.—South Rookery, Bering Island. Copy of photograph by Colonel Voloshinof to show distribution of seals in 1885. Western half.
31b.—Same. Eastern half. Both from nearly same standpoint as my pl. 29.
32a.—Salt-house, South Rookery, Bering Island. Nikanor Grigorief, the native overseer. September 9, 1895.
32b.—Waterfall at South Rookery, Bering Island.
33.—Preobrazhenskoye village, Copper Island, looking west. In the background, Pestshani Mys, the tops being hidden in the fog, and the company's steamer, Kotik, at anchor. The nearest light-painted house is the schoolhouse; the one farther back is the dwelling and office of the assistant administrator; the dark houses to the right of it are the company's store, magazines, and dwelling-house. July 28, 1895.
34a.—Karabelni village, Copper Island, from the beach at mouth of river. August 12, 1895.
34b.—Glinka village, Copper Island, from the hill behind it. August 7, 1895.
35.—Glinka village, Copper Island, from the beach. In the middle ground the salt-houses to the left, the government's house to the right. August 11, 1895.
36a.—Interior of salt-house, Glinka, Copper Island. Seal skins in salt.
36b.—Same. Seal skins bundled, ready for shipment.
37.—Beach at Glinka village, Copper Island. Natives getting ready to leave for the main village after having finished the sealing.
38a.—Karabelui Stolp, Copper Island, from photographic station No. 4 (see map, pl. 12). August 1, 1895, noon.
38b.—Karabelui Stolp, Karabelnoye Rookery, Copper Island. From bluff, photographic station No. 1. August 2, 1895, 9.15 a. m.
39.—Karabelnoye Rookery, Copper Island, looking west toward Karabelui Stolp, from photographic station No. 3. August 1, 1895, 11 a. m.
40.—Karabelnoye Rookery, Copper Island, looking east toward Vodopadski Mys, from photographic station No. 2. August 1, 1895, 10 a. m.
41.—Karabelui Stolp, Copper Island. Pencil sketch by the author, July 3, 1883, from photographic station No. 1, to show distribution of seals as compared with my photograph of 1895, from same standpoint, pl. 38b.
42.—Karabelnoye Rookery, Copper Island, looking west. Pencil sketch by the author, July 3, 1883, from photographic station No. 3, to show distribution of breeding seals as compared with my photograph of 1895, from same standpoint, pl. 39.
43.—Karabelnoye Rookery, Copper Island, looking east. Pencil sketch by the author, July 3, 1883, from photographic station No. 2, to show distribution of breeding seals as compared with my photograph of 1895, from same standpoint, pl. 40.
44a.—Bolshaya Bukhta, Karabelnoye Rookery, Copper Island. From reef at extreme end of Karabelni Stolp. The snow patch at the beach is the same as the one seen near the lower left-hand corner in pl. 40. From a photograph by Mr. Grebnitski, August 1, 1895, 9.45 a. m.
44b.—Drive steps, Stolbovaya Bukhta, Karabelnoye Rookery, Copper Island. August 1, 1895. From photographic station No. 5.
45.—Drive steps and waterfall, Vodopad, Karabelnoye Rookery, Copper Island, August 2, 1895.
46.—Palata, Copper Island, seen from Zapadni, to show character of beach. Photograph by Mr. Grebnitski, August 7, 1895.
47.—Palata beach, Glinka, Copper Island, showing the character of the beach. Photograph by Mr. N. B. Miller, of the U. S. Fish Commission S. S. Albatross, June 4, 1892.
48.—Palata Rookery, Copper Island, from a rock off the rookery. Looking up the gully to the right, Palata; mountains in the background hidden in the fog. August 2, 1895, 2.30 p. m.
49.—Palata Rookery, Copper Island, from the same point as pl. 48, looking toward Sabatcha Dira. Top of mountains hidden in the fog. August 2, 1895, 2.30 p. m.

Plate
No.
50.—Palata Rookery, Copper Island, from nearly the same point as pl. 55, looking down the gully toward Karabelni. In lower left-hand corner, slope of Palata; in upper right-hand corner, Zapadni and Pestshani Mys. August 7, 1895, 12.30 p. m.
51.—Palata Rookery, Glinka, Copper Island, August 7, 1895, 9.40 a. m. From hill north of Palata, on map (pl. 14) marked 806 feet.
52.—Palata Rookery, Glinka, Copper Island. From a sketch by the author, July 16, 1883. Standpoint same as my photograph of 1895 (pl. 51) to show distribution of seals.
53a.— Palata Rookery, Glinka, Copper Island. Photograph by Colonel Voloshinof, 1885. Standpoint a little farther to the right and lower down than my sketch of 1883 (pl. 52) and my photograph of 1895 (pl. 51).
53b.—Zapadni Rookery, Glinka, Copper Island. Photograph by Colonel Voloshinof, 1885. For comparison with pl. 54a as regards distribution of breeding seals.
54a.—Zapadni Rookery, Glinka, Copper Island. From same point as pl. 51 (hill on map 14 marked 806 feet) looking west. The extreme promontory in the background to the left is Vodopadski Mys, then follow Lebiazhi Mys and Pestshani Mys. August 7, 1895.
54b.—Urili Kamen Rookery, Glinka, Copper Island. Looking from Peresheyek toward Pestshani Mys, which is hidden in the fog. Breeding seals among the stones in the foreground. August 3, 1895, 10 a. m.
55.—Zapalata Rookery, Glinka, Copper Island. From base of crest of Palata (just beyond watchhouse), looking toward Stolbi. August 7, 1895, noon.
56.—Zapalata Rookery, Glinka, Copper Island. From base of crest of Palata (same standpoint as pl. 55), looking toward the extreme end of Palata. August 7, 1895, noon.
57a.—Zapalata Rookery, Glinka, Copper Island. From a photograph by Colonel Voloshinof, 1885. Standpoint exactly the same as my photograph of 1895, pl. 56, with which it should be compared for distribution of the seals.
57b.—Sikatchinskaya Bukhta, Glinka, Copper Island, seen from the rocks off the rookery. Photograph by Mr. Grebnitski, August 2, 1895.
58a.—Driveway from Zapadni Rookery, Glinka, Copper Island. Rainy morning. August 8, 1895, 7.30 a. m.
58b.—Driveway up from Pestshani hauling-grounds, Glinka, Copper Island. August 2, 1895.
58c.—Pestshani salt-house, near Glinka village, Copper Island. August 4, 1895.
59a.—Hutchinson, Kohl, Philippens & Co.'s steamer *Alexander II*. From a photograph by H. W. Domes, Oakland, Cal.
59b.—Schooner *Bobrik*, Capt. D. Greenberg, in the harbor of Petropaulski. The guard-ship of Robben Island, belonging to the Russian Seal-Skin Company. August 27, 1895.
59c.—Reduced copy of Choris's picture of fur-seals on the rookery at St. Paul, Pribylof Islands. Voy. Pitt. aut. Monde, pl. XV.
60.—Salmon weir, "Zaporr," across the river at Saranna, Bering Island. July 20, 1895. The weir is full of silver salmon.
61a.—Saranna village, west half, Bering Island. The salmon weir in the foreground. July 20, 1895.
61b.—Saranna village, east half, Bering Island. In foreground scaffolding with salmon hung up to dry. July 20, 1895.
62a.—Native dragging along a seal which is too tired to move. Drive from Zapadni, Glinka, Copper Island. August 8, 1895, 8.45 a. m. Drizzling rain.
62b.—Baby skin-carrier. Same drive.
63a.—Salt-house at Popoěski, near Karabelni village, Copper Island. August 12, 1895.
63b.—Seals sliding down the last embankment, Glinka village, Copper Island. Drive, August 8, 1895.
64.—Dead seal pups in wind rows, Reef, North Rookery, Bering Island. September 16, 1895, 8.15 a. m.
65a.—Petropaulski harbor, Kamchatka, from hill behind the town. In the background, on the south side of Avatcha Bay, the volcano Velutchinskaya Sopka. The men-of-war, the British cruiser *Porpoise* (white) and the Russian transport *Yakut* (black), off the Russian Seal Skin Company's wharf. August 26, 1895.
65b.—Petropaulski, Kamchatka, from the Russian Seal Skin Company's wharf. In the background the volcano Koriatskaya Sopka. The vessel anchored in the stream is the Russian transport *Yakut*. September 2, 1895.
66a.—The Russian Seal Skin Company's wharf, magazines, and steamer *Kotik*, Capt. C. E. Lindquist, at Petropaulski, Kamchatka. September 1, 1895.
66b.—Headquarters of the Russian Seal Skin Company, Petropaulski, Kamchatka. September 2, 1895.

INDEX.

	Page.
Abandonment of the Commander Islands	89
Abundance of bulls on Copper Island	114, 115, 117, 135
Acanthinula harpa	24
Acarids of Commander Islands	23
Acknowledgments	5
Aconitum	25
Ada, schooner	122
Adèle, schooner	55, 57
Administration, Commander Islands	102
Robben Island	53
Ages, proportionate number	63
Agnes McDonald, schooner	132
Agreement between Russia and Great Britain	125
United States	127
International	136
Agriculture	33
Agriolimax hyperboreus	23
Agrotiphila alaskæ	22
Ainoko, schooner	127
Alaska Commercial Co	6, 29, 91
Albatross, Fish Commission steamship	4, 10, 11
Aleksander II, steamer	54, 55, 59, 92, 93, 106, 119, 121
Aleut, gunboat	58, 122
Aleuts	26, 28
Alexander, schooner	119
Algæ around Bering Island	26
Alleged changes of habits	82, 83
lateness of season in recent years	84
Almquist, Dr. E	19, 25
Alopecurus stejnegeri	24
Altitude of pass at Karabelni	47
between Pagani and Glinka	50
Palata and Glinka	50
Zapadni and Glinka	50
Preobrashenskaya Sopka, Copper Island	43
Analysis of peat	34
Andreanovski natives	26
Anemone narcissiflora	25
Anisotoma abbreviata	22
Annie Cashman, schooner	56, 120
Annie C. Moore, schooner	124
Annie E. Paint, schooner	133
Arannah, schooner	121
Archangelica	25
Arctic fox	21; 30, 95
Arctic, schooner	58, 59, 127
Ariel, schooner	124, 125
Arietis, schooner	132
Ari Kamen	36, 38
Arrival of bulls on Bering Island rookeries	64, 66
Copper Island	61
killables in 1895, late	84
seals on Robben Island	53

	Page.
Artemisia tilesii	25
Asiatic catch, 1891-1895	129
1892	123
1893	126
Atkha district	26, 89, 90
Attu islanders	26
Aurivillius	23, 24
Aurora borealis, Bering Island	17
Babin, Bering Island	40, 106
Babin, Glinka rookeries	50
Babinskaya bukhta, Copper Island	50, 114, 115
Pad, Copper Island	48
Babinski Kamen, Bering Island	40
Bachelors, Do all haul out?	67
Badaef, Abraham	76
Baidara mountains	37
Baird, Prof. S. F	104
"Bald spot" breeding-ground, North Rookery, Bering Island	107
Barometer, mean monthly, on Bering Island	13
Bassof	29, 95
Bats on Bering Island	21
Bathymetric observations	8, 9
Bdella villosa	23
Bean, Dr. T. H	22
Beatrice, schooner	122, 124
Beckwith, Captain	118
Beckwith, S. L., mate	119
Benedict, J. E	23
Becardina bairdii	21
Berckhan, artist	60
Berghaus's Chart of the World	10
Bering, bark	102
Bering Island	36
Bering Island drives easy	76
Bering Islanders compared with Copper Islanders	28
Bering Sea, hydrography	8, 11
Bering, Vitus	7
Betula ovresmanni	25
Birch wood	33
Birds on Commander Islands	21
Births on Commander Islands	28
Blair, Capt. J. G	52, 53, 54, 55, 57
Blank forms for drives	103
Blizhni Mys, Bering Island	41
Blizhnoye lezhbistche	41
Blue fox	21, 30, 95
Bobrovaya Bay, Copper Islands	43
Bobrovi Kamoni	43, 44
Bobrovi Valley	43
Bobrik, schooner	53
Bodies of dead pups	80, 81
Boilman	23

141

	Page.
Bolshaya Bukhta, Copper Island	46
Bradford, Captain	119
Branchipus paludosus	23
Brandt, Captain	58
Bravery of bulls	67
Brunner, Lieutenant	53
British Bering Sea Commissioners	55
	57, 60, 86, 96, 97, 98, 101, 122
Bryant	61, 69, 82
Bryanthus	26
Büchner, Dr. E	60
Bulls, virility of	66, 76
Butterfly	22
Buyan	37, 38
Calculation of number of seals	105
Callotaria ursina	29, 60, 66
Canadian sealing fleet in Asiatic waters, 1892	123
1893	126
1894	128
Cape Afrika, sealing off	87, 128
Manati	37
Matveya	44
Nagtkinaki, sealing off	87, 129
Patience	52, 56
Waxell	37
Yushin	40
Carcasses on rookeries	107
Carex raritiora	24
Carlson, Captain	119
Caronolite, schooner	123, 124
Caroline, cruiser	127
Carpmael, C	52
Cassiope lycopodoides	26
occyoccoides	24
Cattle	31
Cause of decrease	134
Census of drives on Bering Island	110
Cerithiopsis stejnegeri	24
Chætopoda	24
Changes of habits	82, 83
Characteristics of natives	36
Chernick, G	12, 92, 100
Choris, artist	61
C. G. White, schooner	122, 123
Classes of seals	60
Clear days, Bering Island	15
Climate of Commander Islands	12
Climate of Robben Island	52
Close season on Commander Islands	89
Cloudiness, expressed in percentages	16
Cloudy days, Bering Island	15
Codfish as seal food	70
Coleoptera	22
Colonization of Commander Islands	26
Commander Islands	7
abandonment	89
discovery	7
Commission, Russian, to investigate seizures	124
Communism on Bering Island	35
Community fund	35
Comparison between Commander Islands and Pribylof Islands catches	98, 99
condition of rookeries in 1882-83 and 1895	106
condition of rookeries on Bering and Copper islands, 1895	171
number of seals killed and skins shipped	100

	Page.
Comparison of weather on Commander Islands and on Pribylof Islands	13
Compensation for sealing	35
Conclusions	134
Condition of Commander Islands rookeries	87, 94, 104
natives	29
Robben Island rookeries	53
Consular warning	56, 129
Contract of Hutchinson, Kohl, Philippeus & Co	93
Russian Seal Skin Company	93, 94
Conulus fulvus var	23
Copp, Capt. W	123
Copper Island	43
drives severe	76
Islanders compared with Bering Islanders	28
Cormorant, Pallas's	22
Counting number of seals on rookeries	105, 106
Crabs of Commander Islands	23
Creophilus villosus	22
Crowley, J. B	4, 6
Criminal offences	28
Cruelty in driving	74
Crustaceans of Commander Islands	23
Dall. W. H	19, 23, 24
Dalnaya Bukhta	46
Daphne, cruiser	127
Daphnia longispina	23
Dead pups in windrows	80, 81
Deaths on Commander Islands	28
Decrease, cause of	134
of seals on Karabelnoye Rookery	114
rookeries	134
Deficiency of bulls on Bering Island	108, 117, 135
Department of imperial domains	104
Description of Bering Island	36
Copper Island	43
Robben Island	52
Details of drives on Bering Island, 1895	110, 111
Dewey, Dr. Fred. P	34
Diana, schooner	59, 120
Diaptomus ambiguus	23
Difficulty of distinguishing sexes on rookery	65
Diptera	22
Disappearance of carcasses	81
Discovery of Commander Islands	7
Pribylof Islands	84, 88, 95
Robben Island Rookery	54
Discrepancies in counts of skins shipped	99
Disintegration of carcasses	81
Distribution of the seals on North Rookery, Bering Island	63
Districts of fox hunting	30
Doctor	36
Does the female seal nurse her own pups only?	77
Dogs	32, 137
Drake, F. J	5, 6
Dress of natives	35
Drift ice, Bering Island	17
Driftwood	33
Drive from Pestshani hauling-grounds, Glinka	72
Zapadni	73
Drive on North Rookery, Bering Island	74, 79
Polavina Rookery, St. Paul Island	71
Bering Island easy	135
Bering Island, first	85
Commander Islands	72
Copper Island hard	135
Drive steps, Stolbovaya Bukhta, Karabelni	46, 47

THE RUSSIAN FUR-SEAL ISLANDS. 143

	Page.
Drive steps, Vodopad, Karabelni	47
Driveway, Karabelni	46, 47
North Rookery, Bering Island	41
South Rookery, Bering Island	43
Driving, effect of	70
not responsible for depletion of rookeries	77, 135
Druzhinin	20, 95
Ducks, tame	33
Dybovski, B	19, 24, 27, 39, 89
Earth slides on rookeries	45
Earthworms on Commander Islands	24
Effect of driving	70
Egerman, Lieutenant	52
Elliott, H. W	61, 82, 83, 96, 97, 104
Elymus mollis	40
Empetrum nigrum	26
Entomostraca of Bering Island	23
Enumeration of seals	105
Esperia lingua var. arctica	24
Estimate of number of seals	105
Etholin, Chief Manager	89
Eumetopias stelleri	20
Eupagurus gilli	23
hirsutiusculus	23
middendorfii	23
nudosus	23
Eurycercus glacialis	23
Eurynorhynchus pygmæus	21
Excrements on the rookeries	69
Expiration of lease of Hutchinson, Kohl, Philippeus & Co	93
Explanation of alleged lateness of phenomena	86
Extermination of Pallas's cormorant	22
sea cow	20, 40, 95
Extirpation of seals	137
Exuberance of virility on Copper Island	115
Fair days, Bering Island	15
Fauna of Commander Islands	19
Fecal matter on rookeries	70
Fedoskia	33, 37, 39
Fedoskia Lake	37
Feeding-grounds of Bering Island seals	87, 128
Commander Islands seals	87
Copper Island seals	87
Robben Island seals	53
Fekshptoff Island	59
Felix, schooner	57
Females driven on Bering Island	76, 107, 110, 111
in drives	63
Female seals nursing their own pups	77, 78
Field-mouse, red, on Bering Island	21
First arrivals of seals on rookeries	86
First drives on Bering Island	65
Fishes of Commander Islands	22
Flattening of dead pups	81
Flora of Commander Islands	19, 24, 25
Flying Mist, schooner	119
Foggy days, Bering Island	16
Folger, Capt. A. C	55, 56
Fontoaka, Bering Island	106
Food of seals at the islands	69
Foxes, Arctic or Blue	21, 30, 95
Fox hunting	30
Fritillaria camtschatcensis	25
Fuel	33
Fur-seal, northern	60
Furuhielm, Chief Manager	101

	Page.
Futility of concluding from habits of other animals as to those of the seals	78
Future prospects on Commander Islands	136
Gamasus arcticus	23
Gardens	33
Gavanskaya Reshka	38
Gavarushkaya, Glinka	48, 50
Gavanskoye Ozero	38
Gavia alba	21
Geometridæ	22
Geranium erianthum	25
Giers, Russian minister of foreign affairs	124, 127
Gladkovskaya, Bering Island	36, 37
Gladkovski Kamen, Copper Island	44
Gladkovskoye Ozero, Copper Island	44
Glavnoye-Glinkovskoye lezhbishtche	50
Glinka rookeries	48, 100, 114, 115
1882-83	114
1895	115
Glinka village	45
Glinkovskoye lezhbishtche	48
Goats	33
Golder, Captain	57
Gorelaya bukhta, Glinka	49
Copper Island	48, 114
Governor-General of Amur Provinces	104
Gray, Prof. Asa	24
Great Shantar	59
Grebnitski Harbor	36
Grebnitski, N. A	5, 19, 22, 32, 38, 64, 67, 69, 70, 102, 106, 107, 108, 110, 116, 119, 121, 123, 124
Grebnitskoye Seleni	38
Grigorief, Nikanor	64, 112
Grunberg, D	5, 6, 53, 54, 58
Habits, alleged changes of	82, 83
Habits of seals	61, 82
Hagman, Captain	122
Hair-seals, Commander Islands	21
Hamlin, Charles S	129
Hapalogaster grebnitskii	23
mandtii	23
Hardships in driving	74
Harems, size of	64, 76
Hauling-grounds in Kamchatka	63
Herendeen, Captain	118
Heilbronner, Max	99
Helene, schooner	57
Hemiptera	22
Henry Dennis, schooner	87, 122, 126, 132
Hens	33
Heracleum lanatum	25
Hermann, William	59
History of the Russian sealing industry	88
History of Robben Island	54
Holustiaki	60
Horses	32
House-mouse on Bering Island	21
Houses	35, 99
Humidity, relative, Bering Island	16
Hundred-and-fifty-mile zone	130
Hundred-fathom line	9, 10
Hutchinson, Kohl & Co	91
Hutchinson, Kohl, Philippeus & Co	53, 54, 57, 91, 92, 94, 98, 101, 102
Hyalina radiatula	23
Hydrodamalis gigas	20
Hydrographic notes	6

	Page
Hymenoptera	22
Ice Company	90, 91
Ida Etta, schooner	87, 128, 129
Illustrations of fur-seals	60, 61
Increase of Karabelnoye Rookery	113
Insects of Commander Islands	22
Instruments, meteorological, used at Bering Island	12
Intermarriage	27
International agreement	136
Interregnum	90, 98, 111, 118
Intoxicating liquors	29
Introduction	3
Ioann Pretercha, sloop	95
Isaackson, Captain	118
Itinerary	4
Ivory gull	21
Ixodes borealis	23
fimbriatus	23
Jane Grey, schooner	87, 128
J. H. Lewis, schooner	90, 122
Johnson, Captain	56
Kadiak islanders	26
Kamchatka coast charted too far east	10
rookeries	58, 83
Kamchatka, steamer	56
Kamennaya	37
Kantor, A	6, 92
Karabelui stolp	44, 45, 114
village	45
Karabelnoyo lezhbishtche	45
Rookery	45, 100, 112, 113
1882-83	112
1895	113
Kate and Anna, schooner	122
Keefe, Capt. M	122
Killer at Commander Islands	21
Killing-grounds, Glinka	50, 51
North Rookery, Bering Island	41
South Rookery, Bering Island	43
Kishotchnaya	41, 77, 106, 107, 108
Kishotchnoye lezhbiatbche	41
Kishotchnaya, proportion between sexes	64
Kisikof	41, 106, 107
Kisutch	31
Kite, black-eared	22
Kjellman, Dr.	10, 24
Kluge, E	6, 31, 53, 54, 55, 63, 92
Koenigia islandica	24
Komandor	8, 38
Komandorski Ostrova	7
Korabelai, etc. (See Karabelni.)	
Kostromitinof, Alexander	92
Kotik, steamer	123
Kotiki	60
Krasheninikof	53, 88
Krasnaya riba	31
Krebs, C. F. Emil	92, 98
Krepkaya Pad	46
Krusenstern, Captain	58
Kulomakh	50
Kuril Island Aleuts	26
Kuril Islands	59
ceded to Japan	7
colonized	26
Lacunella reflexa	24
Ladiginsk	38

	Page
Ladiginskaya River	38
Lagopus ridgwayi	31
Larus glaucescens	81
Latax lutris	20
Late arrival of seals	84
Lateness of stagiocss	85
Lathyrus maritimus	25
Lato sealing	84
Latitude in the phenomena of seal life	62
Lease of Hutchinson, Kohl, Philippeus & Co	93
Russian Seal Skin Company	93, 94
Lobiazhaya bukhta	49
Lebiazbi Mys	48, 49, 115
Leon, schooner	53, 55, 56, 57
Lepidoptera	22
Lichens of Bering Island	25
Ligusticum scoticum	25
Lilljeborg, W	23
Limachevski, Captain	54
Limax hyperboreus	23
Limit of skins to be taken on Commander Islands	125
Limnaea humilis	24
ovata	24
Lindquist, C. E	5, 6
Lindquist, Julius	92
Linnell, M	22
Linotaenia chlonophila	23
Lissoukovaya Bay	38, 39
Lithobius stejnegeri	23
sulcipes	23
Littlejohn, Captain	119
Livron, Captain de	123
Location of rookeries when first discovered	30
Log of schooner Agnes McDonald	132
Annie E. Paint	133
Arietis	132
Beatrice	131
Henry Dennis	132
Ida Etta	129
Jane Grey	128
Maud S	130
Umbrina	130
Vancouver Belle	131
W. P. Hall	133
Logs plotted	120
Loiseleuria procumbens	26
Loss to Commander Islands herd	129
Lotka mountains	37
Lucas, F. A	22
Lütke, Admiral	89
Lugebil, Joseph	92
Lutjens, Capt. Chas	122
McKeil, Capt. A	122
Majestic, ship	123
Makarof, S. O	8, 53, 124
Maliuka Bukhta, Copper Island	46, 114
Malovanski, John	6, 98
Mammals of Commander Islands	20
Management of sealing business in 1882	92
Manati, Cape	37
Map of Glinka rookeries	51
Karabelnoye Rookery	47
North Rookery, Bering Island	42, 107
Rubben Island	52
South Rookery, Bering Island	43
Marie, schooner	123, 124

THE RUSSIAN FUR-SEAL ISLANDS. 145

	Page.
Maroshishnik	41, 106
Martishina Bukhta	45, 112
Marvin, schooner	124
Marx, Dr	23
Matinée, schooner	56
Matki	60
Matthews, Capt. J	122
Maud S, schooner	87, 122, 127, 130
Mauna Loa, schooner	55
May Belle, schooner	127
Maximum temperature Bering Island	14
Measurements of seals	66
Mertensia maritima	25
Mesophelon stejnegeri	21
Meteorology of Commander Islands	12
Robben Island	52
Methods of calculating number of seals	105
Microlepidoptera	22
Migration of Commander Islands seals	62
Military organization of natives for protection of rookeries	103
Military guard for rookeries	103, 121
Microtus rutilus	21
Milvus melanotis	22
Miner, Capt. E. P	56, 57, 118, 120
Minimum temperature Bering Island	14
Minnie, schooner	127
Modus vivendi between Great Britain and United States	122, 136
Modus vivendi between Russia and United States	127
Mollusks of Commander Islands	23
Moral decline of natives	29
Morgan, Thomas F	6
Mortality of pups	78, 79, 81, 111, 117, 134
Mosquitoes	22
Mount Steller	37
Mud huts	35, 42
Municipal institutions	35
Mus musculus	21
Myriapods of Commander Islands	23
Mya Terpenia	52
Mystery, schooner	58
National Museum, United States	8, 19
Native population of Commander Islands	26, 27
Natural history of fur-seal	62
Naval guard for Robben Island	57
Nepropusk, Karabelui, Copper Island	46
Nerpitcha Bukhta, Copper Island	46
Nesava arctica	23
Nicbauın, Capt. G	53, 54, 55, 99
Nikolski	38
meteorological station	12
peninsula, Kamchatka	92
Noctuidæ	22
Nordenskiöld	31
Nordenskiöld's Vega Expedition	19, 97
Nordquist, O	19
North American Commercial Co	6
North Rookery, Bering Island	49, 100
1882–83	106
1895	107
North Star, schooner	55, 57
Notice to poachers by Russian consul	120
Number of bulls on South Rookery, 1895	112
dead pups on North Rookery, Bering Island	80, 81
females driven in 1895	111

	Page.
Number of foxes killed	30
seals killed on Commander Islands	95, 96, 97, 99
each rookery	100
Pribylof Islands, 1786–1833	96
on rookeries	105
sea-otters killed	30
skins taken on North Rookery, 1895	111
Robben Island	58
Nursing of pups by their mothers	77, 78
Octopods as seal food	69, 70
Okhotsk Sea rookeries	58
Olsen, Prof. Julius	8
Oncorhynchus kisutch	31
nerka	31
Optimistic view	136
Orca gladiator	21
Origin of fauna and flora of Commander Islands	19
Osernaja Reshka	34
Ostrof Miodui	43
Otome, schooner	56, 57, 106, 121
Otsego, schooner	55, 118
Outline of rookeries	63
Oxypoda opaca	22
Paetz, Waldemar	92
Pagani	48, 49, 51
Paluta	48, 49, 50, 114
Palatinski Mys	49
Palatinskoye lezhbishtche	48
Panof	95
Patula ruderata var. pauper	23
Peat	33, 34
beds	33
Pelagic flora at Bering Island	26
sealing at Commander Islands	122
cause of decrease	135
off Japan	62
Pelikan, A., Russian consul	121
Pelly, Francis R	5, 6, 79
Pencil sketches by author offered in evidence	104, 108, 113
Penelope, schooner	57, 122
Perosheyck, Copper Island	43
Glinka, Copper Island	48, 49, 115
Peresheyckski kamen, Glinka rookeries	49
Pestshanaya bukhta, Glinka rookeries	43, 49
Pestshani hauling-grounds, Glinka rookeries	49, 72, 114 115
salt-house, Glinka	51, 73
Pestshani Mys, Glinka rookeries	48, 49
Pestshanoye, Glinka rookeries	48
Lake	44
Petersen, Captain	59
Petropaulski	92
meteorological station	12
Pfluger, Vice-Consul	90
Phalacrocorax perspicillatus	22
Phanerogams of Commander Islands	24
Philippeus	56, 91
Phoca fasciata	21
fœtida	21
groenlandica	21
largha	21
ursina	60
Photographs of rookeries	63, 104, 108, 112, 113, 115, 116
Physeter macrocephalus	21
Pieris japonica	25
Pine, Captain	59
Pisidium equilaterale	24
Plants of Commander Islands	24

F. C. B. 1896—10

	Page
Plateaus on Bering Island	37
Pleurotoma beringi	24
Plotting of sealing logs	129
Podutiosnaya	37
Polavina Rookery, St. Paul Island	71
Polavine	36, 37, 38
Poluliounoye lezhbishtche	42
Rookery	39, 42
Polusikatchi	60
Popof	95
Popofski, Karabelni	47
Population of Commander Islands	26
Porpoise, cruiser	79
Position of Bering Island	36
Commander Islands	7, 11
Copper Island	43
Robben Island	52
Potamilla neglecta	24
Potatoes	33
Potts, Captain	119
Powers, Captain	59
Precipitation, Bering Island	16
St. Paul Island	18
Preobrazhenskaya Sopka	43
Preobrazhenskoye village	44
Prevailing winds, Bering Island	17
Pribylof	84
Pribylof Islands ceded to United States	7
weather compared with that of Commander Islands	18
Price of sea-otter skins	29
Prize, schooner	123
Prohibition of killing on land	136
pelagic sealing	136, 137
Proportionate number of sexes and ages on rookeries	63
Prospects, future, on Commander Islands	136
Protassof	84, 95
Provisional agreement of May, 1893	125
Ptarmigans	31
Pupilla arctica	24
decora	24
Pups driven on Bering Island	76, 107, 110, 111
Pups, mortality of	78, 79, 81
Pyrus	25
Raids not cause of decrease	135
of Commander Islands rookeries	118
Robben Island	54, 55, 56, 57, 58
Rain gauge	13
Rangifer tarandus	21
Ranunculus hyperboreus	24
Rathbun, R	4
Razboinik, cruiser	56, 57, 103
Recolonization of Commander Islands	89
Recommendations	136
Record of soundings in Bering Sea	11
Redfish	31
Roof	106, 107
Reef rookery, Bering Island	40
Reefs	38
Regulations for fox hunting	30, 31
hunting sea otters on Copper Island	21, 29
governing the business on the rookeries	103
Reindeer on Bering Island	21, 33
Relation of Commander Islands fauna and flora	19
Relative humidity, Bering Island	16, 18
Relics of Bering's expedition	8
Religion	36

	Page
Rental paid by Hutchinson, Kohl, Philippeus & Co	93
Russian Seal Skin Company	91
Report of British Columbia sealing fleet 1892	123
1893	126
1894	124
Report on Canadian pelagic sealing on the Asiatic side, 1894	127
peat from Bering Island	34
Revisors	104, 120
Rhododendron chrysanthum	25, 26
kamtschaticum	25
Rifovoye lezhbishtche	40
Robben Island	52
Robbin Island	52
Robin Island	52
Rocky Point, St. Paul Island	71
Rookery, Robben Island	53
Rose, J. N	24
Rosie Olsen, schooner	123, 124
Rosset, Lieutenant	51
Rubus chamæmorus	26
Rules governing sealing business	102
Russian-American agreement of May, 1894	127
company	54, 89, 95, 97, 101, 102
Russian-British agreement of May, 1893	125
modus vivendi	87
Russian commission to investigate seizures	124
notice to poachers	120
sealing industry	88
Seal Skin Company	6, 54, 57, 59, 93, 101
Russkoye Tovarishtchestvo Kotikovikh Promislof	92
Rytina gigas	20, 95
stelleri	20
Sabatcha Dira	46
Sahlberg, J	22
Saipan, schooner	4
Sakhalin Island	52
Sakhalin, schooner	103, 121
Salix	25
Salmon as seal food	70
fishery on Bering Island	31
Salt-house, North Rookery, Bering Island	41
Karabelni	47
Pestshani	51
Popofski	47
South Rookery, Bering Island	43
Salt-houses, Glinka	51
Sandman, Capt. J	52, 55, 59, 92, 107, 119
"Sandman-Grebnitski" map	108
Saranna Lake, Bering Island	37, 38
Saranna River, Bering Island	70
Saranna village and river	31, 37, 39
Saranna settlement, Bering Island	60
Saranskie Lotki	37
Sayward, schooner	124
Scammon, Captain	54, 61
Schools	36
Scope of the work	3
Sea-cow	20
Sea-lion	20
Sea Lion Rock, Bering Island	40
Seal rookeries, Bering Island	39
Copper Island	45
Seal life on Commander Islands	60
rookeries	135
Seals hurt while driven	75
Sea-otter	20, 21, 29, 95

THE RUSSIAN FUR-SEAL ISLANDS.

	Page.
Sea-otter rocks, Copper Island	43
Seebär	60
Seizures of schooners	123, 124, 127
Selivanof, Kussak	80, 110, 129
Seniavin, corvette	89
Serodka	46
Seventy-six, schooner	119
Severnie Lotki	37
Severni Mys	40
Severnoye	39
Severnoye lezhbishtche	40
Sexes, proportionate number	63, 64
Shalfcef	23
Shanof, Lieutenant	52, 56
Shantar Islands	59
Shantarski Islands	59
Sheep-raising recommended	31, 32
Shelikof, G. I	84, 88, 95
Shipment of skins from Commander Islands	101
Siewerd, Captain	121
Signal Service, United States	12
Sikatchi	60
Sikatchinskaya, Glinka	48, 50, 114
Silphidæ	22
Silver salmon	31
Siphonaptera	22
Sivutchi Kamen, Bering Island	40, 106
Copper Island	44
Robben Island	52
Sketches of Karabelnoye Rookery	104, 108, 113
Sketch of Palata Rookery, 1883	114
Skins taken on Robben Island	58
Skins seized, 1892	123
shipped from Commander Islands, by periods	101
Sledge-dogs	32, 137
Slunin, Dr	21, 53, 65, 108, 114
Snow, Bering Island	16, 17
Snow, Mr	59
Sod huts	35, 39
Soldiers to guard the rookeries	103, 121
Soundings	9, 10, 11
South Rookery	39, 42, 100, 111, 112
1882	111
1895	112
Bering Island, number of bulls	64
Sperm-whale at Commander Islands	21
Spiders of Commander Islands	23
Spiræa kamtschatica	25
Sponges at Commander Islands	24
Spoon-bill sandpiper	21
Sredni Island	59
Staginess of skins	85, 86
Staggy skins on Pribylofs	86
Stairway for driving seals	46, 47
Stanley-Brown, J	4, 6, 71, 76
Staphylinidæ	22
Staraya Gavan	33, 37, 38, 39
Staritchkovaya Bukhta, Copper Island	46
Starvation, cause of death of pups	80, 82
Starving pups	78
Statistics	95
Steller, G. W	6, 19, 20, 24, 39, 60
St. Iona Island	58, 59
Stolbi, Zapalata	50
Stolbovaya Bukhta, Copper Island	46
Stolp, Karabelni	44, 45, 114

	Page.
Stotchnoi Mys	37
Strelok, cruiser	120
Strombella callorhina var. stejnegeri	24
Stuxberg, Dr	19
Styela arctica	22
Suggestions	136
Summary	134
Support of natives during "Zapuska"	137
Snabkof, Sergei	65
Sv. Joann Rylskoi, sloop	93
Swan Bay	49
Tables of population	27
Tables, meteorological	13, 14, 15, 16, 17
Tally of drive on North Rookery	110
skins weighed at Glinka, 1895	116
Tanner, Z. L., Lieut. Commander	103
Tarbassi	35
Teichmann, E	101
Telmessus cheiragonus	23
Temperature at Cape Patience	52
mean, Bering Island	13
of Robben Island	52
water	8, 9
water at Robben Island	52
Terpenia Mys	52
Ternees on Bering Island	37
Thirty-mile zone	87, 125, 134
Thomas, Dr. Lloyd	70, 80
Three Sisters, schooner	118
Thunderstorms, Bering Island	17
Tielmann, N. M	102
Tikhmenief	90, 102
Tiuleni Island (see Robben Island)	63, 99
Tiuleni Ostrof	52
Todd, Capt. J. W	122
Tolstykh	20, 95
Tonkoi Mys, east	37
Topographical character of rookeries	134
Toporkof Island	36, 38
Townsend, C. H	5, 6, 62, 129
Trapeznikof	20, 95
True, F. W	4, 69, 71, 72, 76
Tunicates of Commander Islands	22
Tulénow	125
Turnips	33
Tuscarora, soundings	10
Umbrina, schooner	122, 130
Upson, W. F	55
Urili kamen, Glinka Bay	49
Glinka rookeries	48, 49, 114
Karabelni	47, 49
Vanessa urticæ	22
Vasey, Dr. G	24
Vancouver Belle, schooner	87, 123, 124, 131
Vega expedition	19, 22, 23
Vegetables	33
Velocity, maximum of winds, Bering Island	17
Voniaminof, Ivan	60, 82, 96, 101
Venning, R. N	127
Veratrum album	25
Vespertilio	21
Village, North Rookery, Bering Island	41, 42
of the Transfiguration	14
Viola biflora	25
Virility of bulls	66, 76
Visit to place of Bering's shipwreck	8

	Page.
Vitiaz, corvette	123, 124
Vitiaz i Tikhi Okean	8
Vitiaz, soundings	11
Vitrina exilis	23
Vkhodni Point	38
Vladimir, schooner	55
Vladimir, sloop	95
Vodopad, Karabelnoye Rookery	46, 114
Vodopadski Mys	46
Voice of females, variation in	78
Volokitin, F	36, 92, 112
Voloshinof, Col. N	57, 104, 108, 112, 115, 116
Voluntary extirpation of seal herd	137
Vorobief	95
Vosnessenski	19
Vulpes lagopus	21
Walter L. Rich, schooner	59
Warning to poachers by Russian consul	120
Watch houses on rookeries	104
Weather of Commander Islands compared with that of Pribylof Islands	18
Webster, D	5, 55
Weight of skins	65, 106, 109, 116
Westerlund	23

	Page.
Whales at Commander Islands	21
Wiemuth, Dr	24
Williams, C. A	6
Willie McGowan, schooner	124, 125
Winds, maximum velocity, Bering Islands	17
Winds, prevailing, Bering Island	17
Worms on Commander Islands	24
W. P. Hall, schooner	133
Wrangell, Admiral von	60, 96, 101
Yakut, transport	58, 126, 127
Yugof	95
Yurt	35, 42
Yushin's Valley	38
Zaikof, Aleksander	65
Zabiaka, cruiser	123, 124, 126, 127
Zapadni, Glinka rookeries	46, 114
Zapalata	48, 50, 114
Zapuska	137
Zarine, Captain	123
Zhirovaya Bukhta	44
Zholti Cape natives	27
Ziphius grebnitskii	21
Zone of 150 miles	136
Zone of 30 miles	125

1

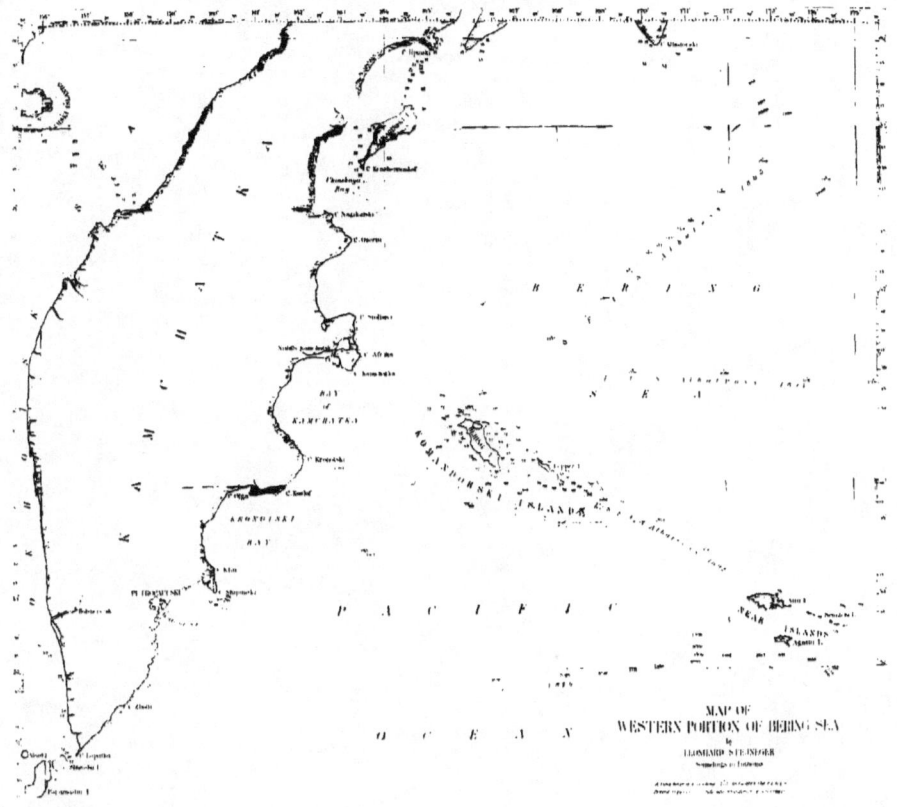

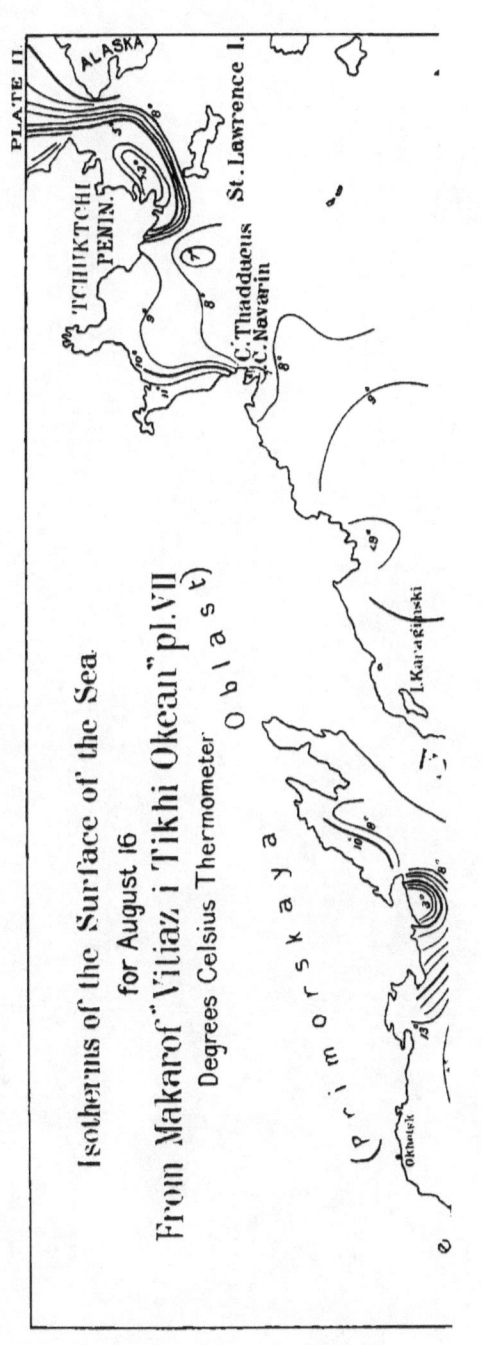

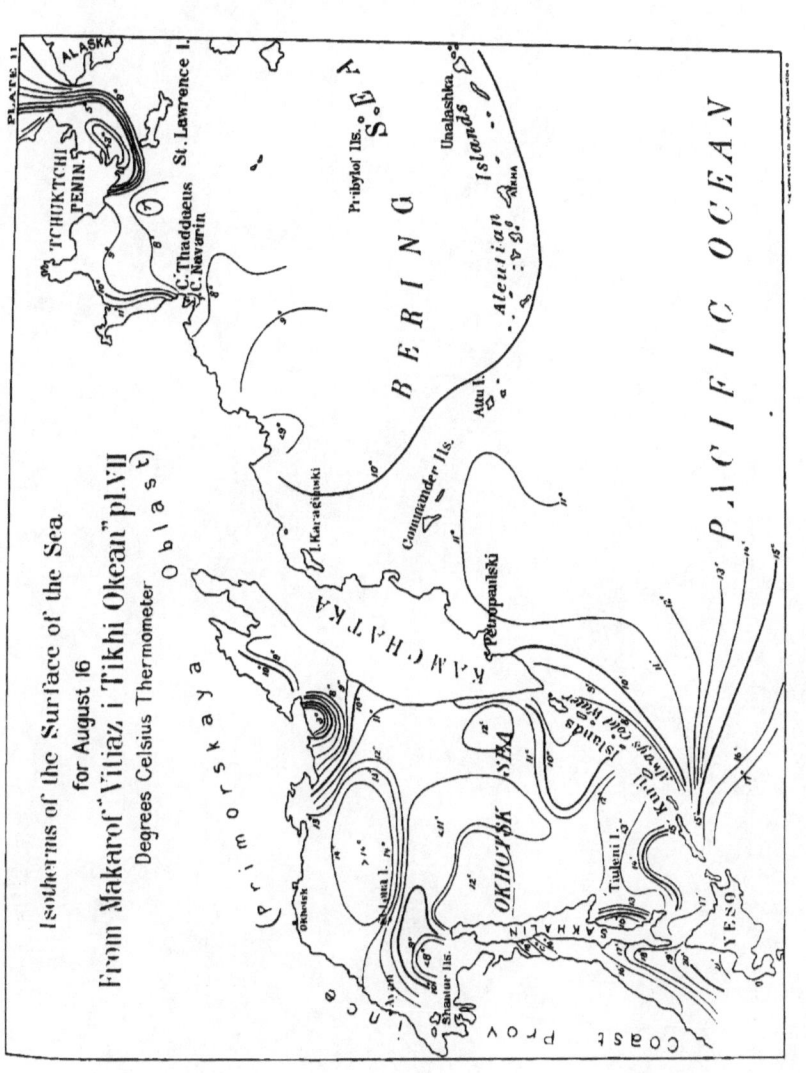

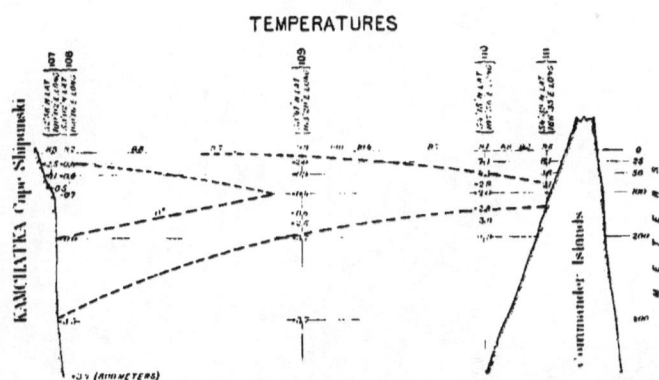

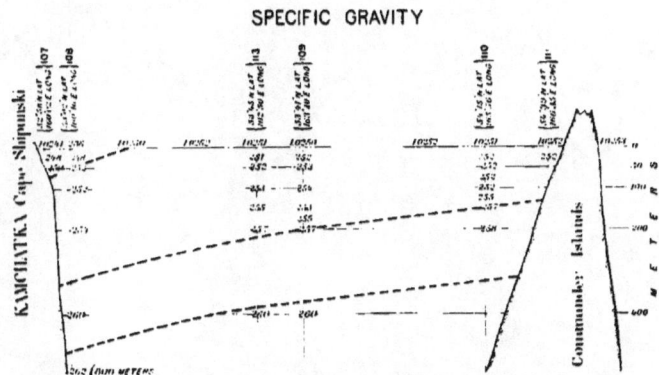

TEMPERATURES AND SPECIFIC GRAVITY OF THE WATER IN BERING SEA BETWEEN KAMCHATKA AND THE COMMANDER ISLANDS, JULY 29 TO AUGUST 2, 1888.

(From Makarof's "Vitiaz i Tikhi Okean," Pl. VIII, by permission of the author.)
"Vitiaz" Station No. 107, July 29, 4 p. m.; 108, July 29, 10 p. m.; 109, July 30, 9 a. m.; 110, July 30, 8.45 p. m.; 111, July 31, 8.37 p. m.; 113, August 2, 1.30 p. m.
Temperatures in centigrades; depths in meters.

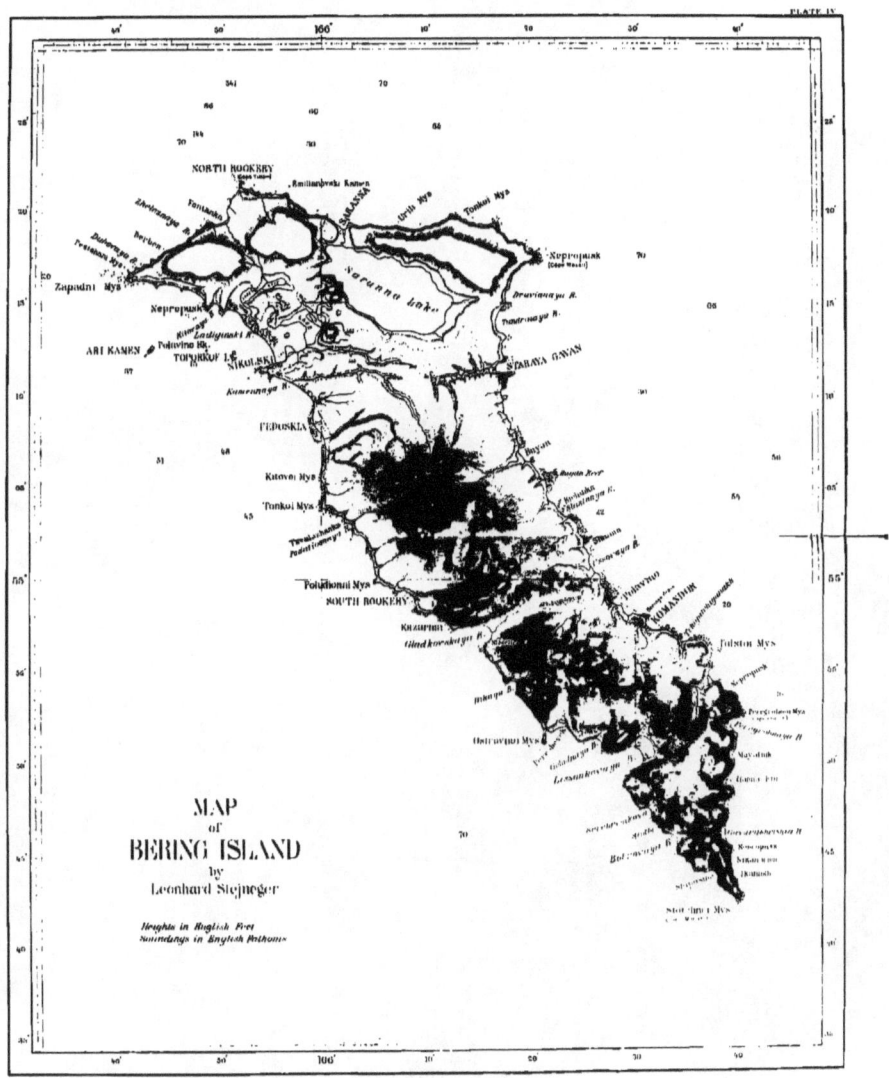

5

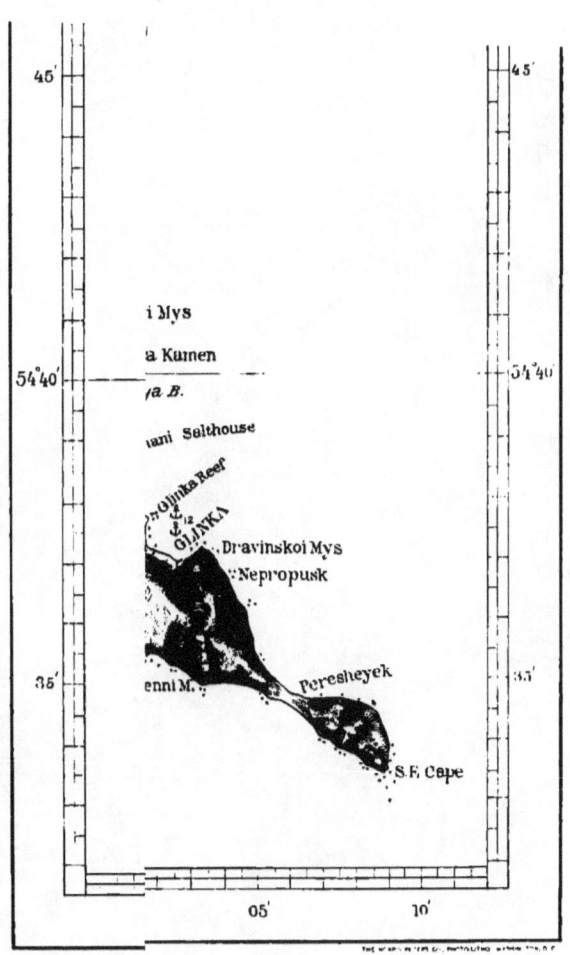

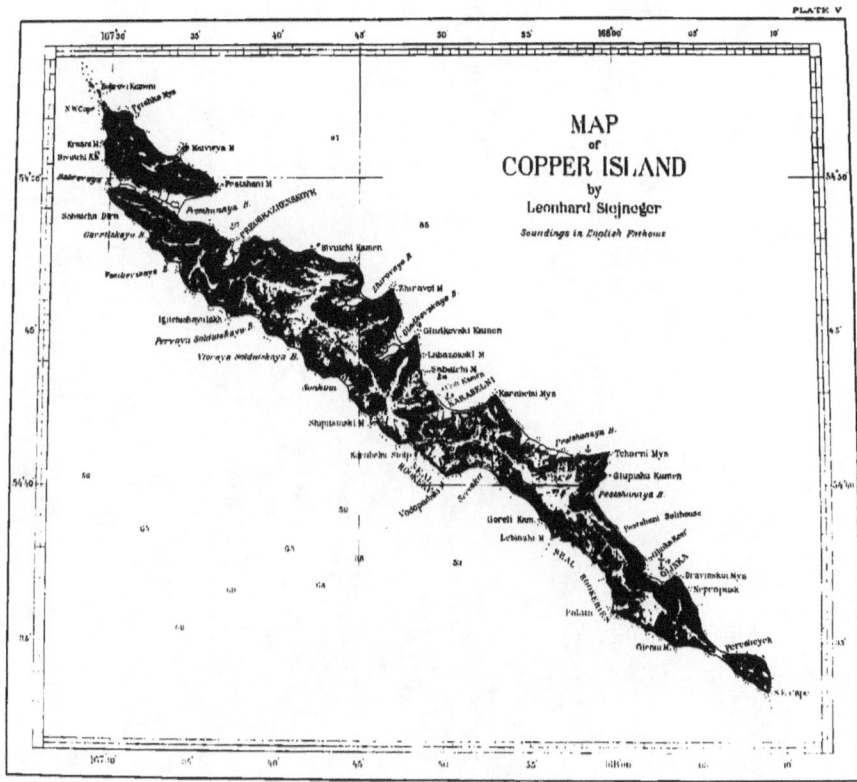

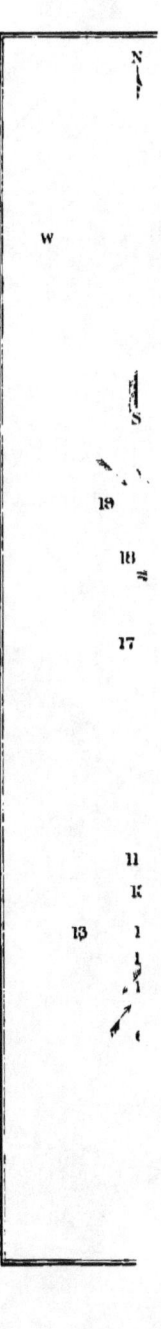

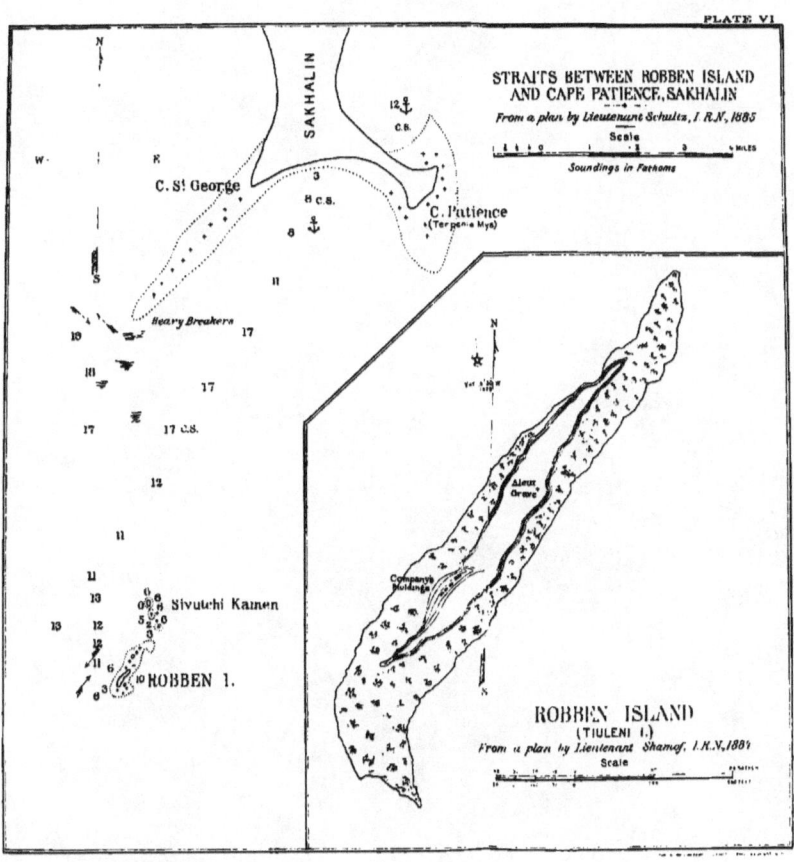

Kisiko

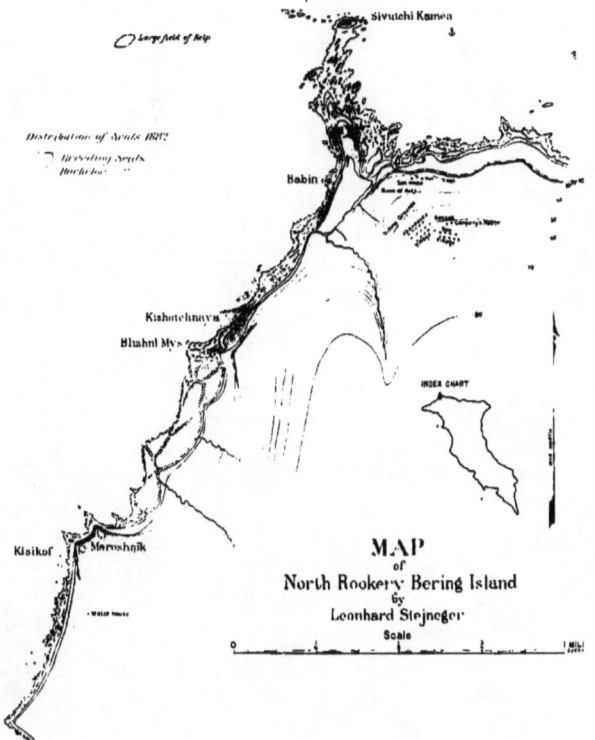

8

Kisikof

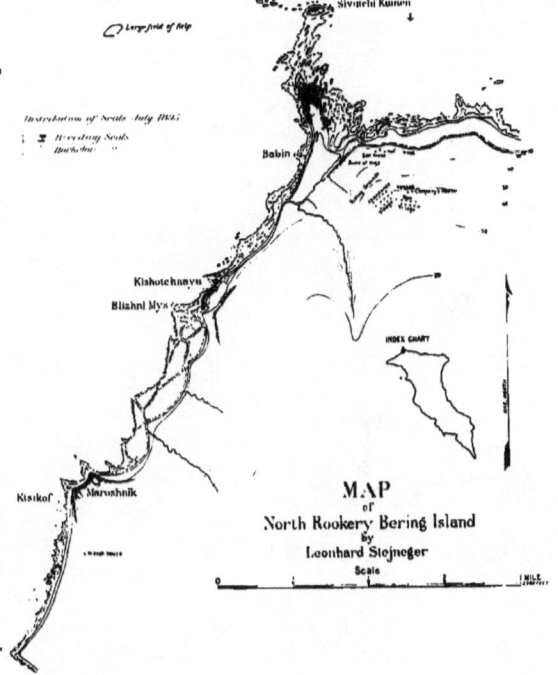

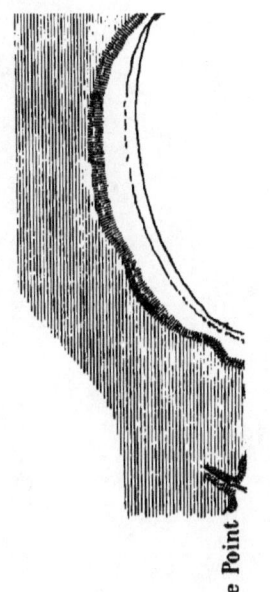

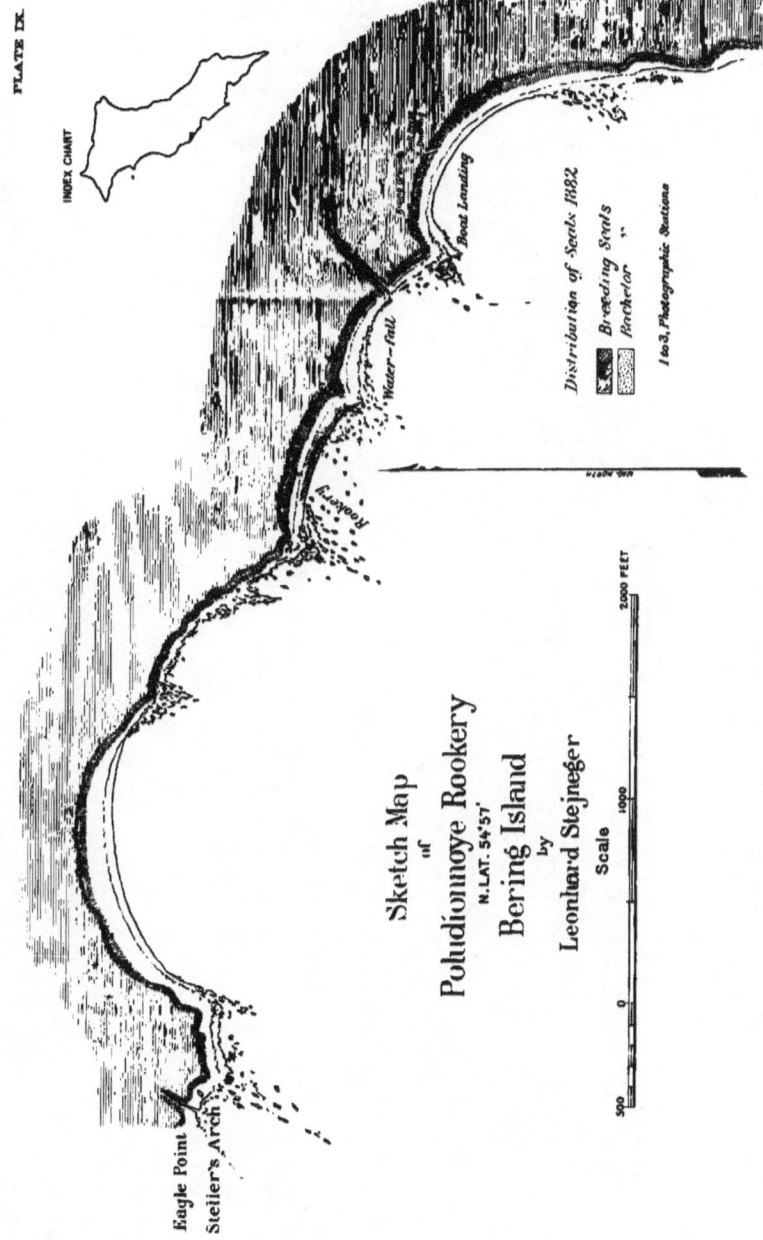

10

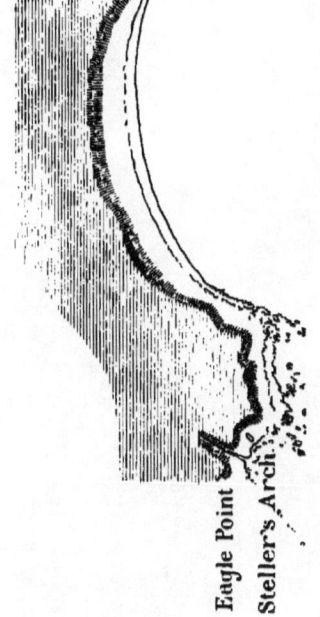

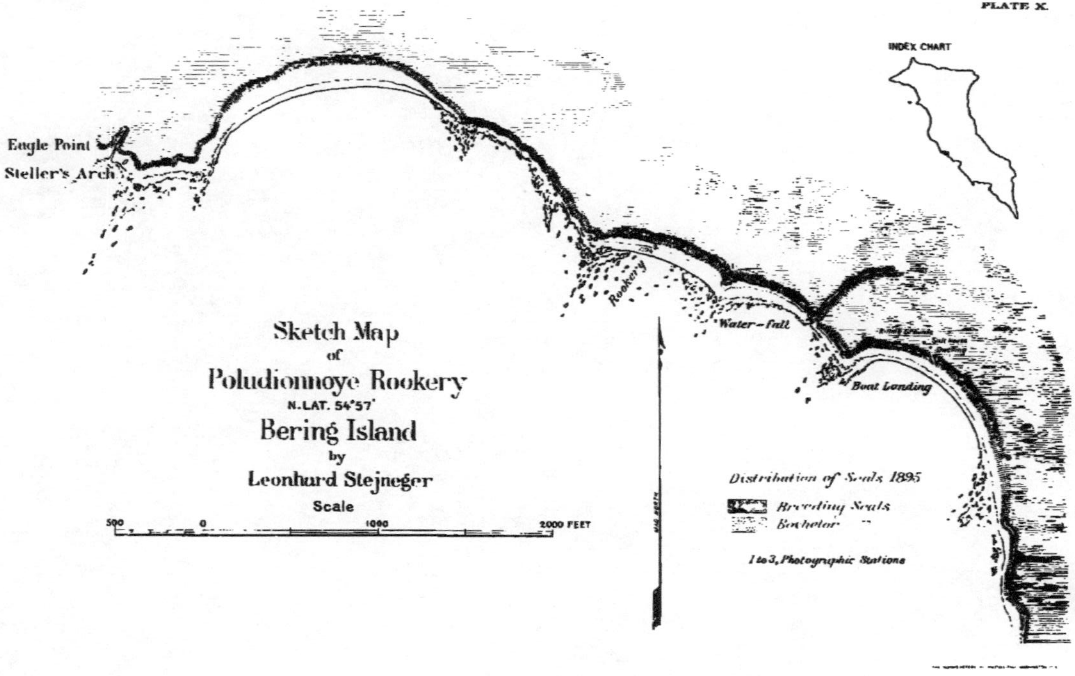

PLATE X.

INDEX CHART

Sketch Map
of
Poludionnoye Rookery
N. LAT. 54°57′
Bering Island
by
Leonhard Stejneger

Scale
500   0   1000   2000 FEET

Distribution of Seals 1895
Breeding Seals
Bachelor
1 to 3, Photographic Stations

Eagle Point
Steller's Arch
Rookery
Water-fall
Boat Landing

11

INDEX CHART

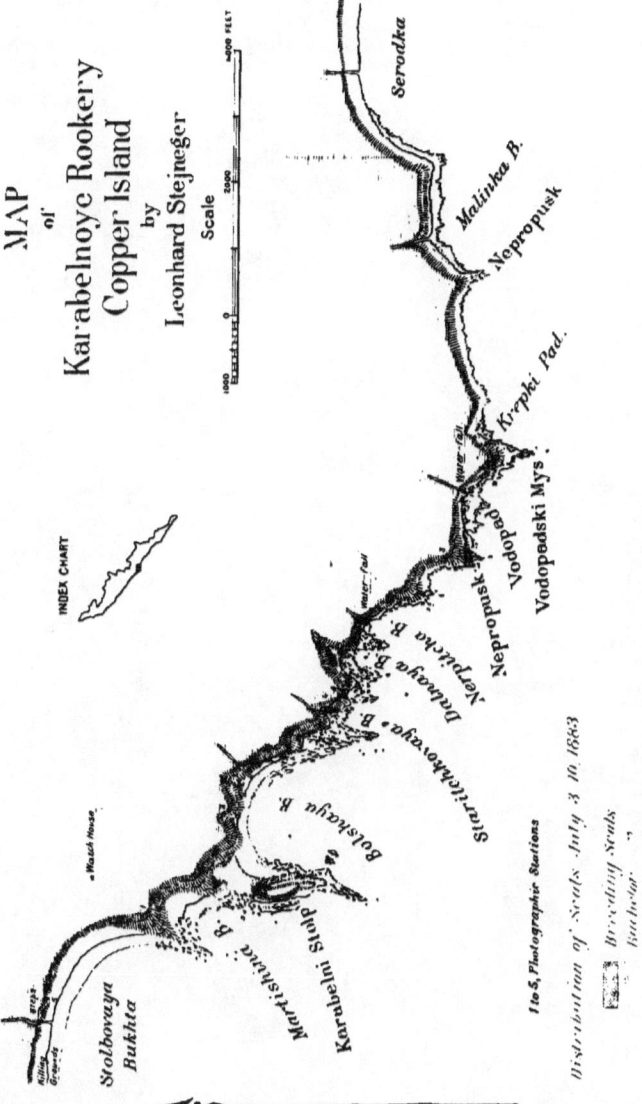

INDEX CHART

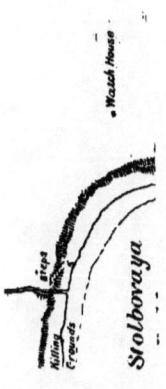
Stolbovaya

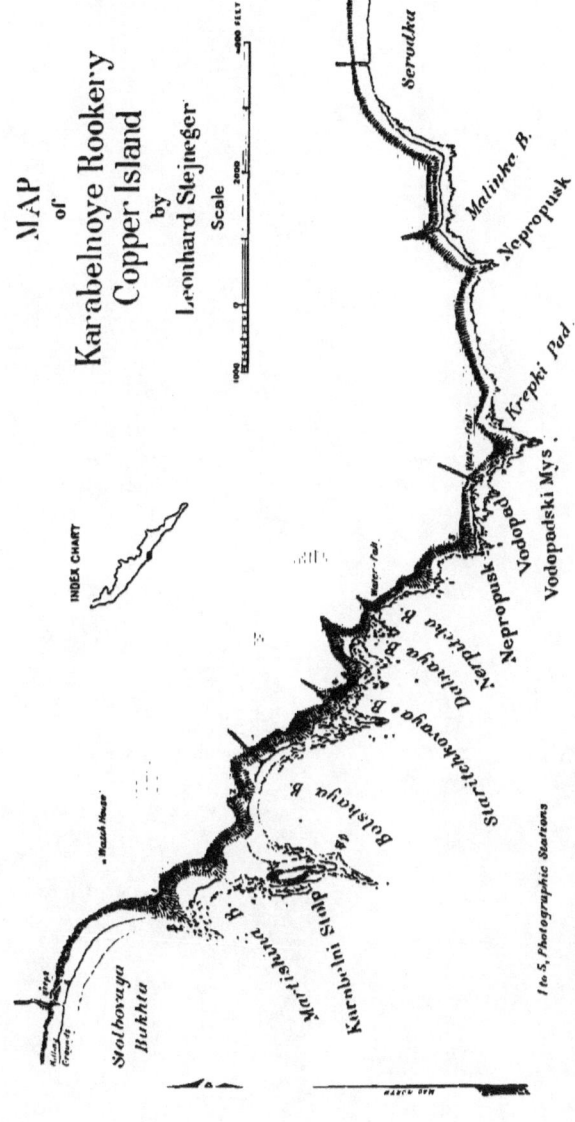

13

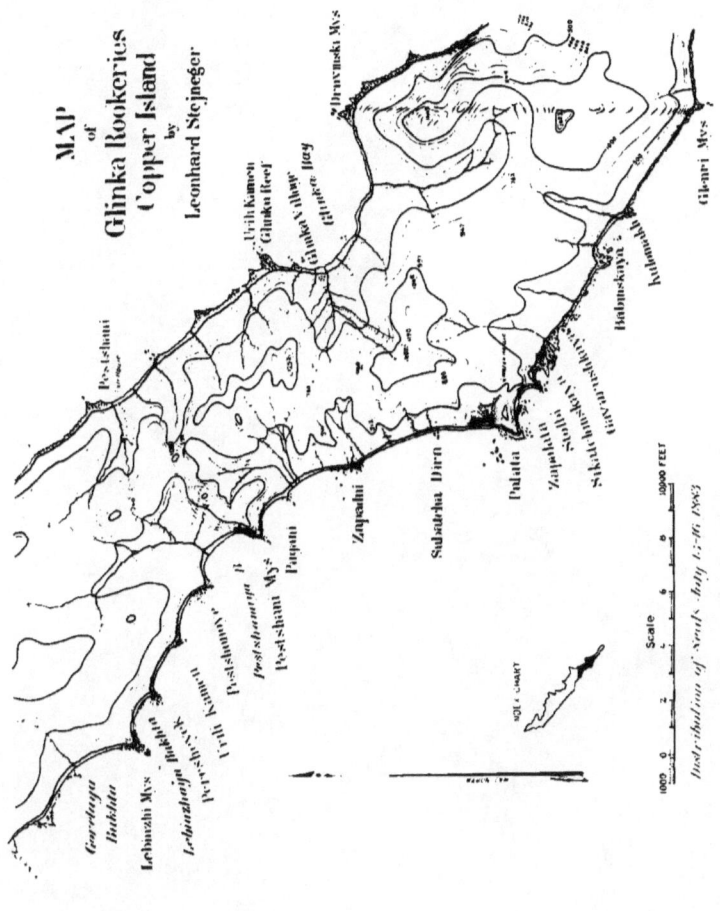

14

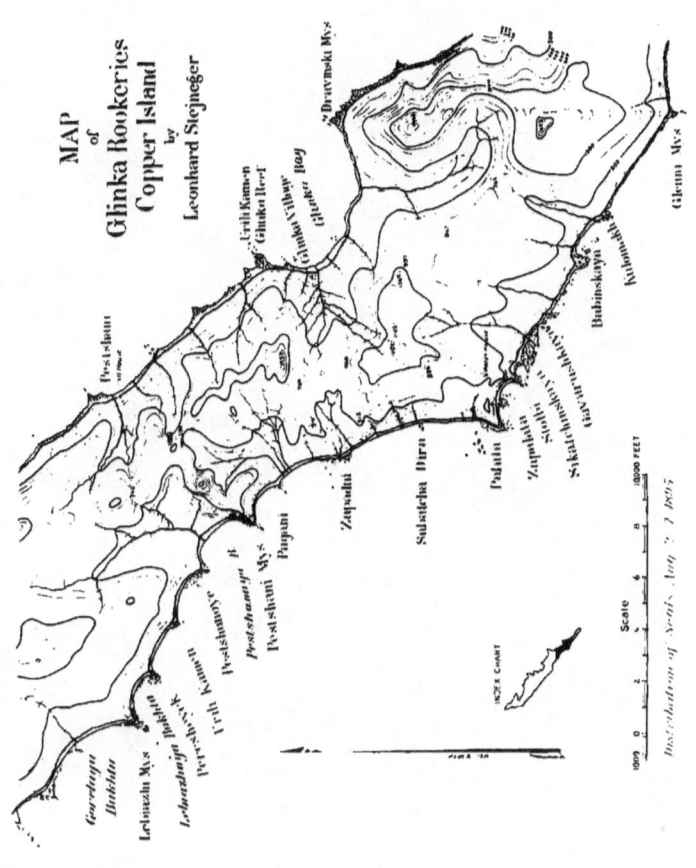

a.— *Bradeless hauling*, NORTH ROOKERY, BERING ISLAND

b.— YURT, OR SOD HUT, NIKOLSK, BERING ISLAND

PLATE 16.

a. —WOODEN FRAME OF YURT, NORTH ROOKERY VILLAGE, BERING ISLAND.

b. KAMCHATKAN CATTLE, BERING ISLAND.

a. NIKOLSKI VILLAGE, BERING ISLAND.

b. NEW SCHOOLHOUSE AND GOVERNOR'S OFFICE, NIKOLSKI, BERING ISLAND.

a. COMPANY'S HOUSE, NIKOLSKI, BERING ISLAND

b. COMPANY'S STORE, NIKOLSKI, BERING ISLAND

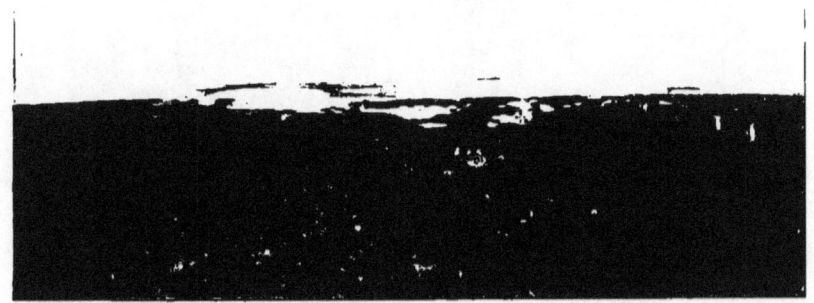

11.—REEF AND SIVUTCHI KAMEN, NORTH ROOKERY, BERING ISLAND, FROM SLEDGE ROAD.

b. SAME FROM DRIVEWAY AT LOWER END OF KILLING GROUNDS

REEF AND SIVUTCHI KAMEN, NORTH ROOKERY, BERING ISLAND.
Pencil sketch by the author, July 30, 1897, to show distribution of seals.

PLATE 21

a. West half.

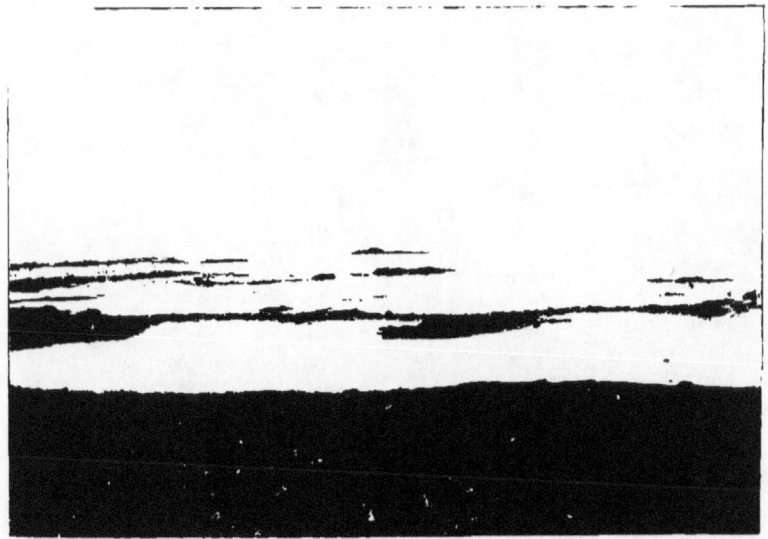

b. East half.

REEF AND SIVUTCHI KAMEN, NORTH ROOKERY, BERING ISLAND, JULY 15, ... TO SHOW DISTRIBUTION OF SEALS

a. Western half.

b. Eastern half.

REEF AND SIVUTCHI KAMEN NORTH ROOKERY, BERING ISLAND, JULY 15, 1895, FROM DRIVEWAY.

SALT HOUSE WITH SKIN CHUTE, NORTH ROOKERY, BERING ISLAND.

a.—BEACH, NORTH ROOKERY, BERING ISLAND. NATIVES READY TO LOAD SKINS INTO THE BOATS.

b.—VILLAGE AT NORTH ROOKERY, BERING ISLAND, FROM SALT HOUSE.

PLATE 26.

a.—REEF NORTH ROOKERY, BERING ISLAND, JULY 4, 1895. BREEDING SEALS IN THREE DISCONNECTED PATCHES TO THE LEFT.
Reduced from photographs by C. H. Townsend.

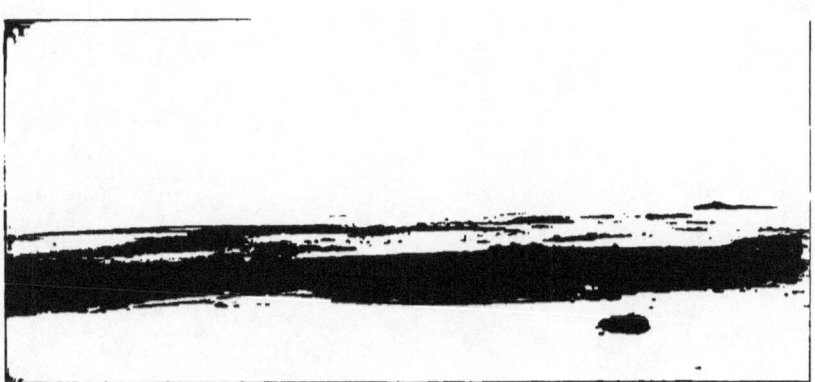

b.—SAME, JULY 7, 1895, SHOWING THE BREEDING SEALS OCCUPYING A CONTINUOUS AREA. ALSO THE BAND ACROSS THE SANDS.
Photograph by N. Grebnitski.

PLATE 27.

a. REEF AND SYUTCHI KAMEN, NORTH ROOKERY, BERING ISLAND.
Photograph by Colonel Volushinof, 1885. From nearly same standpoint as plate 22.

b. STELLER'S ARCH, NEAR SOUTH ROOKERY, BERING ISLAND.

SOUTH ROOKERY BERING ISLAND, FROM PHOTOGRAPHIC STATION No. 1 MAP PLATE

a.—Western half.

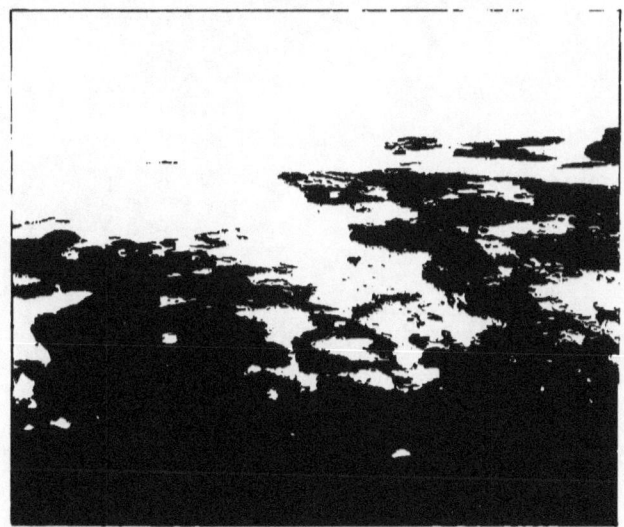

b.—Eastern half.

SOUTH ROOKERY, BERING ISLAND. REDUCED COPIES OF PHOTOGRAPHS BY COLONEL VOLOSHINOF, TO SHOW DISTRIBUTION OF SEALS IN 1895. NEARLY SAME STANDPOINT AS PLATE 30.

a. SALT-HOUSE, SOUTH ROOKERY BERING ISLAND.

b. WATERFALL AT SOUTH ROOKERY BERING ISLAND.

PREOBRAZHENSKOYE VILLAGE, COPPER ISLAND.

a. KARABELNI VILLAGE, COPPER ISLAND.

b. GLINKA VILLAGE, COPPER ISLAND, FROM HILL.

GLINKA VILLAGE COPPER ISLAND FROM THE BEACH

PLATE 36.

INTERIOR OF SALT-HOUSE, INNAA, COPPER ISLAND.

HAIDA COOPER ISLAND. NET YERS RETURNING TO THE YAN VILLAGE

PLATE 38.

KARABELNOYE ROOKERY, COPPER ISLAND, LOOKING WEST TOWARD KARABELNI STOLP, FROM PHOTOGRAPHIC STATION N 3 (MAP PLATE 12) AUGUST 1 1895.

KARABELNI STOLP COPPER ISLAND. FACSIMILE OF PENCIL SKETCH BY THE AUTHOR. JULY 3, 1883, FROM PHOTOGRAPHIC STATION No. 1 (PLATE 38*b*), TO SHOW DISTRIBUTION OF SEALS

KARABELNOYE ROOKERY, COPPER ISLAND. FACSIMILE OF PENCIL SKETCH BY THE AUTHOR, JULY 3, 1883, FROM PHOTOGRAPHIC STATION No. 3 (PLATE 39), TO SHOW DISTRIBUTION OF BREEDING SEALS.

KARABELNOYE ROOKERY COPPER ISLAND FACSIMILE OF PENCIL SKETCH BY THE AUTHOR JULY 3, 1883, FROM PHOTOGRAPHIC STATION No. 2 (PLATE 40), TO SHOW DISTRIBUTION OF BREEDING SEALS.

PLATE 44.

a.
From a photograph by N. Grebnitski, August 1, 1895.

b.

KARABEL NOYE ROOKERY, COPPER ISLAND.

VIEW OF STEPS AND WATERFALL AT GLINKA KRABELNOYE ROOKERY, COPPER ISLAND.

PLATE 46.

PALATA COPPER ISLAND, FROM ZAPADNI.
From a photograph by N. Grebnitski, August 5, 1895.

PALATA REEF, COPPER ISLAND.
Photograph by N. B. Miller, June 1, 1892.

PALATA ROOKERY, COPPER ISLAND, FROM A ROCK OFF THE ROOKERY, LOOKING UP THE GULLY. AUGUST 2, 1895.

PALATA ROOKERY, COPPER ISLAND. FROM SAME STANDPOINT AS PLATE 48. LOOKING TOWARD SABATCHA DIRA. AUGUST 2, 1895.

PALATA ROOKERY, COPPER ISLAND, FROM NEARLY SAME STANDPOINT AS PLATE 55, LOOKING DOWN THE GULLY. AUGUST 7, 1897.

PALATA ROOKERY, COPPER ISLAND, FROM HILL MARKED 826 FEET ON MAP, PLATE 41. AUGUST 7, 1-5.

PALATA ROOKERY, COPPER ISLAND. FROM A SKETCH BY THE AUTHOR, JULY 16, 1883, FROM SAME STANDPOINT AS PLATE 51, TO SHOW DISTRIBUTION OF SEALS.

COPIES OF PHOTOGRAPHS BY COLONEL VOLOSHINOF, TO SHOW DISTRIBUTION OF SEALS IN 1895.

a.—ZAPADNI ROOKERY, COPPER ISLAND, FROM SAME POINT AS PLATE ... AUGUST ...

b.—URIL KAMEN ROOKERY, COPPER ISLAND, FROM PERESHEYEK, AUGUST 3, 1895.

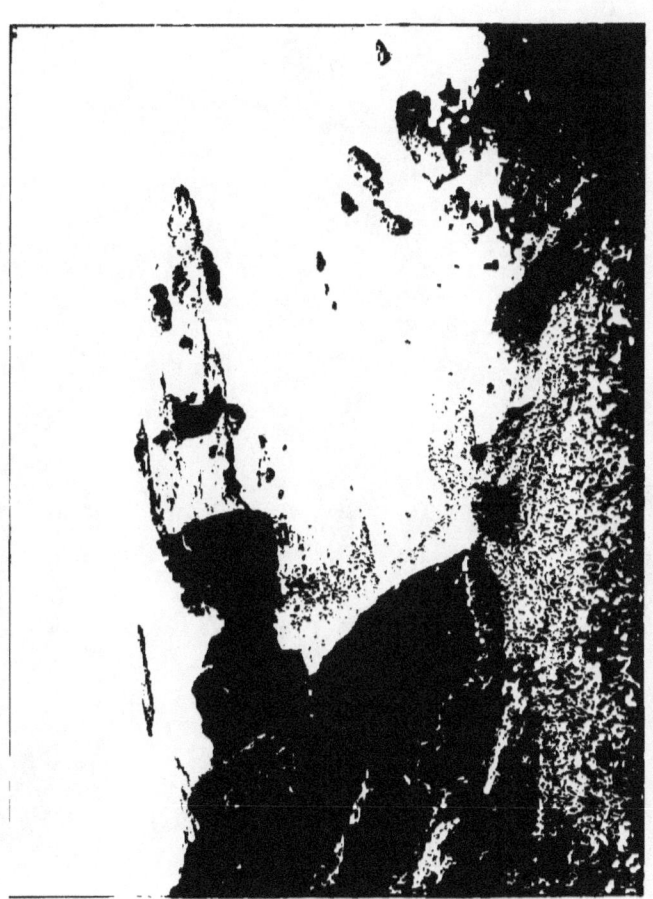

ZAPALATA ROOKERY, COPPER ISLAND, LOOKING EAST TOWARD STOLBI. AUGUST -, 1895.

ZAPALATA ROOKERY, COPPER ISLAND, LOOKING WEST TOWARD END OF PALATA, FROM SAME POINT AS PLATE 55. AUGUST 7, 1895.

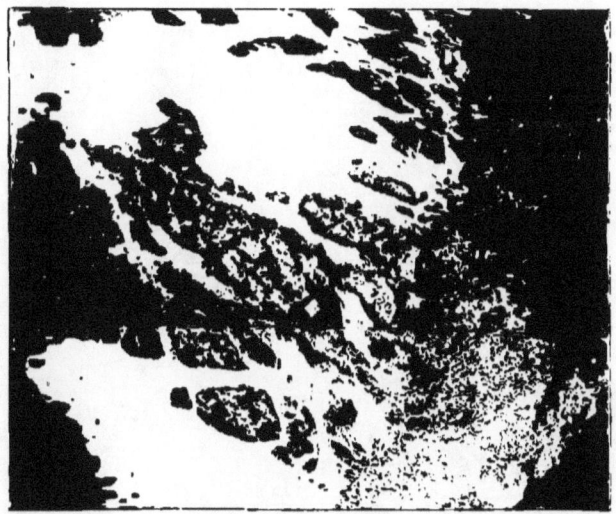

a.—ZAPALATA ROOKERY, COPPER ISLAND. FROM A PHOTOGRAPH BY COLONEL VOLOSHINOF TO SHOW DISTRIBUTION OF SEALS IN 1885. SAME STANDPOINT AS PLATE 56.

b.—SIKATCHINSKAYA BUKHTA ROOKERY, COPPER ISLAND. FROM A ROCK OFF THE ROOKERY.
Photograph by N. Grebnitski, August 2, 1895.

a. DRIVEWAY FROM ZAPADNI ROOKERY, COPPER ISLAND, LOOKING DOWN THE VALLEY. AUGUST 8.

b. DRIVEWAY FROM PESTSHANI HAULING GROUNDS, COPPER ISLAND.

c. PESTSHAN SALT HOUSE, NEAR GLINKA VILLAGE, COPPER ISLAND.

a. HUTCHINSON, KOHL, PHILIPPEUS & CO'S STEAMER ALEKSANDER II.

b. RUSSIAN SEAL SKIN COMPANY'S SCHOONER BOBRIK, CAPT. D. GROENBERG

c.—REDUCED COPY OF CHORIS'S PICTURE OF FUR SEALS VOY. PITT. AUT. MONDE PLATE XV (1822).

SALMON WEIR (ZAPORR), SARANNA RIVER, BERING ISLAND.

a.—Western half, with salmon weir.

b.—Eastern end, with driftwood for fuel, etc., in front.

SARANNA VILLAGE, BERING ISLAND.

PLATE 62.

DRIVE FROM ZAPAL 'PER ISLAND, AUGUST   EARLY MORNING DRIZZLING RAIN.

PLATE 63.

a. SALT-HOUSE AT POPOFSKI, NEAR KARABELNI VILLAGE, COPPER ISLAND.

b. SEALS SLIDING DOWN THE LAST EMBANKMENT, GLINKA VILLAGE, COPPER ISLAND. DRIVE AUGUST 8, 1895.

PLATE 6·1.

DEAD SEAL PUPS IN WINDROWS, REEF NORTH ROOKERY, BERING ISLAND, SEPTEMBER 1975.

a.—From hill behind the town.

b.—From Russian Seal Skin Company's wharf.

PETROPAULSKI, KAMCHATKA.

a.—From hill behind the town.

b.—From Russian Seal Skin Company's wharf.

PETROPAULSKI, KAMCHATKA.

a.—Russian Seal Skin Company's wharf, magazines, and steamer Kotik. Capt. C. E. Lindquist.

b.—Headquarters of Russian Seal Skin Company.

PETROPAULSKI, KAMCHATKA.

www.ingramcontent.com/pod-product-compliance
Lightning Source LLC
Chambersburg PA
CBHW031904220426
43663CB00006B/762